VB COM

A Visual Basic Programmer's
Introduction to COM

Thomas Lewis

Wrox Press Ltd. ®

VB COM

Reprinted   November 2000

Published by Wrox Press Ltd. Arden House, 1102 Warwick Road, Acocks Green, Birmingham, B27 6BH. United Kingdom.
Printed in USA
ISBN 1-861002-13-0

Trademark Acknowledgements

Credits

Author
Thomas Lewis

Additional Material
Richard Anderson

Managing Editor
Dominic Shakeshaft

Editors
Craig A. Berry
Kate Hall
Jon Hill

Technical Reviewers
William Andreas
Chris Blexrud
Matt Bortniker
Gerard Frantz
Darren Gill
Richard Grimes
Hope Hatfield

Technical Reviewers
Richard Lindauer
Richard Pilcher
Craig Randall
Mike Richardson
Frederick T. Rossmark Jr.
Marc Simpkin
Rob Vieira
Donald Xie

Design/Layout
Noel Donnelly

Cover
Andrew Guillaume
Concept by Third Wave
Photo by McCoy's Photography

Index
Catherine Alexander
Andrew Criddle

Acknowlegements

I want to take the time to thank a few people on the technical end. First, I want to thank all the technical reviewers for the book. Believe me, they do not pull punches and were of great help to make the book what it is. Second, I want to thank Kate and Craig. I probably made your lives much harder than they should have been and I appreciate your hard work and effort. Finally, a very special thanks to Dominic Shakeshaft, who believes in the VB COM vision and must be the best editor on the face of the earth. I also thank all of those at Wrox Press for the opportunity and for all your hard work.

I would also like to single out Richard Anderson for providing invaluable assistance when the going got tough. I really appreciate the time and effort he put into ensuring that this book successfully fulfilled its objectives.

I want to thank my wife Sally. For all the time you gave up doing things so that I could focus on the book, for motivating me when I was at a standstill, and for opening my eyes to new things, and helping me be the best I can. I love you.

I want to dedicate this book to my parents, Bill & Sue Lewis. For through their wisdom, strength, and love, they always believed in me. I will always admire them and be proud that I am their son.

The VB COM Series

The VB COM Series from Wrox Press is dedicated to teaching VB COM across all levels of the Visual Basic programming community - from learners to professional enterprise programmers. This series intentionally introduces VB COM to an audience that has hitherto been told that it doesn't need to know about VB COM. Our long-term aim is to ensure a mature and well-informed community of programmers who use Visual Basic.

VB COM

Table of Contents

VB COM

Introduction

Why Do We Need To Learn About COM?

Microsoft's COM (Component Object Model) and its associated technologies provide one the largest technological advances for programmers of recent years. When you program in Visual Basic you are surrounded by COM objects; you're immersed in them! So it follows that every time you program in VB, COM decisions are being made behind the scenes; decisions that could have a profound effect on your Visual Basic programs.

This is serious stuff: VB is making COM decisions without telling you. That's all very nice in your first days of learning to program in Visual Basic, as the "you don't need to know" slogan protects you from some of the complexities of what's really going on. But there comes a point in every VB programmer's career where COM knowledge becomes essential: you have to know what's going on behind the scenes so you can engage with and exploit the power of VB and COM. The VB programmer who understands COM can begin to make accurate, COM-aware decisions when in their VB applications. Without COM knowledge, VB programmers are simply walking in the dark.

The point of this book is that most VB programmers need to understand more about VB COM. Professional VB programmers and intermediate programmers alike, all need to learn more about COM if they are to engage with today's exciting programming technologies. Hopefully, I've also managed to show, in this book, that VB COM is an extremely interesting aspect of programming in Visual Basic today. But still, you might ask - how has it come to be that VB programmers know so little about VB COM? We need to consider a small history of VB to answer this...

The first edition of Visual Basic was released in the early 1990s. There was an expectation amongst those who created it that Visual Basic would be used rather neatly to mock-up an application quickly. This was the RAD (Rapid Application Development) theory of what was so great about Visual Basic. The programmer, having explored a programming problem in Visual Basic, could then go away and write the 'real' application in another language, probably C++.

Visual Basic has, however, evolved over the years. It's grown up. These days we can do serious development in Visual Basic itself; there's no need for us to go and use C++ when we can create the same application in half the time using Visual Basic.

So it all looks easy - VB is a nice language, and we can write real applications with it. End of story? Not quite, I'm afraid, for here is a great truth: to write great programs in Visual Basic, you need to understand COM. Unfortunately, the original marketing drives for VB have persisted: "you don't need to worry about stuff" when you program in VB. So many programmers have remained cosseted in their IDEs where Visual Basic hides all the nitty-gritty from them, believing that what they cannot see they do not need to learn about. This is a mistake.

This book, the first in the Wrox *VB COM Series*, aims to set things right in the VB community. This is not another Enterprise COM book aimed exclusively for professional programmers. Instead, I have presented an introduction to COM for any VB programmer who knows how to do a little programming in VB, has explored the IDE, feels a little curious about what's happening behind the scenes, and is ready to become VB COM literate. I have started at the beginning, so we can build a right understanding of Visual Basic and COM.

The VB COM Series

The Wrox Press *VB COM Series* of books is dedicated to teaching VB COM across all levels of the Visual Basic programming community - from learners to professional enterprise programmers. This book is the first in the series, and it starts from the beginning so that the community can build upon firm COM foundations. This series intentionally introduces VB COM to an audience that has hitherto been told that it doesn't need to know about VB COM. Our long-term aim is to ensure a mature and well-informed community of programmers who use Visual Basic.

An array of more advanced COM issues will be addressed logically and soundly throughout later titles in the Wrox *VB COM Series*.

What You Need to Use this Book

This book was written with the Professional Edition (or higher) of Visual Basic 6 in mind. However, much of this book can be used with Visual Basic 5 Professional or Enterprise Edition, and the COM tutorial within is just as applicable to VB5 as it is to VB6.

For the Automation examples in Chapter 3, you'll need Excel 97 or Excel for Windows 95.

To complete Chapter 6, Distributed COM, you would ideally have Windows NT 4, Windows 98, and/or Visual Studio 6.0. Those of you with Windows 95 can download Distributed COM from Microsoft's web site, http://www.microsoft.com/.

In Chapter 7, Microsoft Transaction Server, you'll need to have Microsoft Transaction Server running on your machine. Microsoft Transaction Server comes with NT 4 and Visual Studio. If you're running Windows 95 or 98, you can get Microsoft Transaction Server by downloading Personal Web Server from the Microsoft web site.

What's Covered in This Book

In Chapter 1, we'll take our first look at COM. I will explain what COM is and why COM components can be so beneficial to our programming lives.

We begin Chapter 2 by discussing objects and object-oriented programming. With a good knowledge of objects in general under our belts, we can then move onto COM objects. The remainder of the chapter is devoted to COM interfaces and specifically introducing you to the `IUnknown` interface.

In Chapter 3, we'll take a look at Automation, a COM-based technology that allows you to manipulate one application from within another. We'll look at a new interface, `IDispatch`, which is fundamental to Automation. We will learn how to bind our objects to an object variable and discover that the way we choose to do this effects the way we access the `IDispatch` interface, and hence the performance of our COM objects.

Chapter 4 discusses the COM components that we can create in Visual Basic, namely ActiveX code components. Class modules allow the Visual Basic developer to define COM interfaces, so we begin this chapter by taking an in-depth look at classes. We then move on to discussing the two types of COM components that we can create, ActiveX DLLs and ActiveX EXEs. We round off this chapter with a short introduction to the Visual Component Manager, which allows us to view all the components on our machine.

In Chapter 5 we look at how we can create our own custom controls, called ActiveX controls. We'll see how we can define the COM interfaces of our control with the ActiveX Control Interface Wizard. Finally, we'll discuss how we distribute ActiveX controls to other developers and we will see how to use the Package & Deployment Wizard.

Chapter 6 covers Distributed COM (DCOM), which allows our components to interact remotely across a network. We will discuss how COM objects do not always make good DCOM objects and that components need to be written with consideration to DCOM issues from day one if they are to be efficient and scaleable. We will discuss security, an important issue when working with networks. At the end of the chapter, I've included a section outlining potential errors and how to avoid them.

In Chapter 7, we discuss Microsoft Transaction Server (MTS). We'll see how we can use MTS to write more scalable, robust and secure applications that could be used by potentially 1000s of users.

In Chapter 8, the final chapter, we'll talk about what the future may hold for COM. We'll discuss Microsoft's Windows DNA, a guideline on building applications for the Microsoft Windows platform using Microsoft technologies such as COM. We will then move onto discussing COM+; the next evolutionary step for COM. Finally, we will discuss the Digital Nervous System, which can be thought of as what your network is or should be.

Conventions Used

I've used a number of different styles of text and layout in the book to help differentiate between different kinds of information. Here are some of the styles I've used and an explanation of what they mean:

> **These boxes hold important, not-to-be forgotten, mission-critical details which are directly relevant to the surrounding text.**

Background information, asides and references appear in text like this.

- ❏ **Important Words** are in a bold font
- ❏ Words that appear on the screen, such as menu options, are in a similar font to the one used on screen, for example, the File menu
- ❏ Keys that you press on the keyboard, like *Ctrl* and *Enter*, are in italics
- ❏ All filenames, function names and other code snippets are in this style: DblTxtBx

Code that is new or important is presented like this:

```
Private Sub Customer_OnAdd()

  MsgBox "The AddToDatabase method has been invoked."

End Sub
```

Whereas code that we've seen before or has little to do with the matter being discussed, looks like this:

```
Private Sub Customer_OnAdd()

  MsgBox "The AddToDatabase method has been invoked."

End Sub
```

Source Code

All the projects that are given in this book can be downloaded from Wrox's web sites at:

```
http://www.wrox.com/
http://www.wrox.co.uk/
```

Tell Us What You Think

This is my first book and I hope that you'll find it useful and enjoyable. You are the one that counts and I would really appreciate your views and comments on this book. You can contact me either by email (feedback@wrox.com) or via the Wrox web site.

VB COM

Introduction to COM

The Microsoft **Component Object Model**, lovingly referred to as **COM**, is probably the most mysterious acronym yet to come from our friends in Redmond. Speak with any Visual Basic programmer and ask them a very simple question: What is COM?

- ❑ "It is the glue for Microsoft applications."
- ❑ "It lets you create components."
- ❑ "It allows software objects to talk to other software objects."
- ❑ "It is a standard for components."
- ❑ "I don't know, I just work here."

You will find that almost everyone you speak to will have a different view of what COM is, but it would be unfair to lay the blame for this confusion at the door of the programmer. The standard marketing definitions are not well known because COM is not a product you can go down to the store and purchase. In addition, Microsoft has not made things any easier, since it seems to change the definition each time a new set of PowerPoint slides are shown to the public.

When I decided that I wanted to know what this "COM" thing was and what it meant to me as a Visual Basic programmer, I knew I was on a journey. You can think of this book as the field notes I made on that trip. Luckily, I found that with Visual Basic as my guide, I was able to take quite a few shortcuts, so put your hiking boots on and let's hit the trail!

> **From this point forward, I will refer to the Component Object Model as COM.**

Defining COM

In this section, I'm going to attempt to define COM in a piece-by-piece fashion. Let's start with the basics and cover what the letters *C-O-M* stand for.

Components and Objects

Components and objects are key concepts in COM, but like "COM" itself, the words are often misused and can mean different things to different people. This is because the terms are tricky first to define and then to distinguish, and for that reason I intend to leave doing so until a more rigorous discussion in the next chapter. I want to keep this introduction at a higher level, and so I shall begin by explaining some of the concepts of **component-oriented design** without going too deeply into what actually makes a component.

Traditionally, applications were distributed in single, large executable files, which are now known as monolithic applications. These had many inherent problems, paramount of which was that if one line of code needed to be changed, then the entire application needed to be rebuilt. This made the development and maintenance of such applications problematic at best.

Component-oriented design circumvents these problems by breaking applications down into components that can be distributed in separate binary files - either dynamic-link libraries (DLLs) or executables (EXEs). In this context, components are pre-compiled, interacting pieces of software that can act as 'building blocks' for creating applications. In some ways, these components can be thought of as raw elements: in the same way that chemical elements can be combined in a multitude of ways to create different compounds, components can be combined to create different applications. Although COM is not *essential* for component-oriented design, it does make the entire process considerably easier to implement.

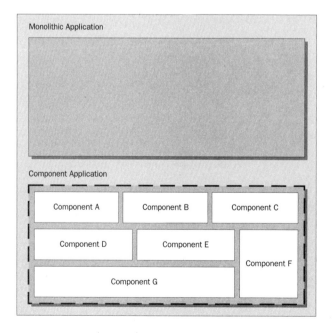

The idea is that a given component can be re-used in different applications that require similar functionality. So, for example, you could construct an invoicing component for one application that could then be reused in other applications that also require an invoicing tool.

Another advantage of this mode of design is that it allows the individual components of an application to be updated easily. Only one of the comparatively small binary files needs to be replaced, unlike in the old monolithic case where the entire application had to be recompiled in order to reflect changes in the source code.

Interfaces

Interfaces are really what COM is all about. I shall cover them in far greater detail in the next chapter (and indeed throughout the rest of the book). Basically, the interfaces of a component are the mechanism by which its functionality can be used by another component. The precise structure of an interface is defined by COM, but in essence it's just a list of functions implemented by the component that can be called by other pieces of code.

At this point, a brief discussion of clients and servers would probably be beneficial, as we'll be talking about them a lot throughout the book.

Clients and Servers

The term 'client/server' encapsulates two separate, discrete entities. These entities could simply be two components, two applications or even two computers. The client requires some service, and requests a server to perform this service on its behalf. The server performs the service and, if required, returns a result to the client.

For example, a client may need some data from a database. In this case, the server could simply be the database, or there could be some additional objects between client and database. In the latter case, these objects would be the 'server' from the client's point of view. From the database's angle, however, the objects form the client and the database is the server. In other words, the client/server distinction merely refers to a request for a service or services. The client does the requesting, and the server performs the request.

In terms of COM components, each component can act as both **client** and **server**. A server is a component that exposes interfaces and therefore a list of functions that a client can call. It follows that the client is a component that uses that interface:

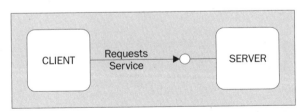

COM enforces a strict separation of the client and server such that they only know of each other's presence by the existence of their interfaces. To a COM client, the server is really just a set of interfaces, and I'll have more to say on this subject in the next chapter.

Throughout the rest of the book, I'll be developing this definition of a component and its interfaces.

A Quick Aside

The diagram of the server you can see above might look a bit peculiar, but it is the standard way of drawing a COM component, and you'll be seeing a lot more of it throughout the rest of the book:

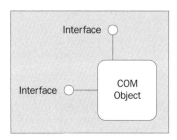

Again, don't worry about the definitions of components and interfaces; for now I just want to draw your attention to how they are drawn in these COM diagrams. The large box represents a component or an object, while the "blobs on sticks" represent the interfaces exposed by that object. For obvious reasons, COM diagrams like this one are sometimes called **lollipop diagrams**.

The Model

If we follow the COM model we will create components described in such a way that they can interact with one another at runtime. The COM model specifies what the interfaces of a component must look like at the binary level, which means that provided your programming language can produce code that obeys the specification, it doesn't actually matter which one you use. This is how COM's much-vaunted **language independence** is achieved.

Defining COM in a few words is not the easiest thing to do because it comprises several things. Let's expand on the explanations I've given so far by examining exactly what it is that COM provides.

COM is a framework for creating and using components

Because COM is a language-independent standard, it's possible to build and subsequently use components with different languages such as Visual Basic, Visual C++, Delphi or Visual J++. A COM client (sometimes also called a **container**) is an application whose architecture supports the use of these software components.

COM provides a mechanism for components to communicate with each other

COM achieves the communication promised by the title of this section by the combination of two things. First, there is the **binary standard** it imposes, which means that your components not only provide a mechanism to communicate, but also know how to speak to other COM-enabled components or applications.

Second, there is the set of services provided by the **COM runtime** (also called the **COM library**) that is required to be present on a computer before communication between the components can occur. These services, which are available to all components, come in the form of a set of API functions.

COM promotes the use of component-based development

Before the advent of component-based development, the predominant technique was procedure-based development. This style is linear in nature, and programs written using it start at the first line of code, and finish either when the last line is executed, or an `Exit` statement is reached. Applications written in this fashion tended not to be very adaptive to what was happening around them.

In Visual Basic today, it is quite easy to reference (that is, to plug in) a library of functionality. Where we used to have to write complex API calls to talk to a database, we now simply have to set a reference to the appropriate library of functionality (as in the following figure) to be able to use it in our own programs. In this particular instance, we're creating a reference in our Visual Basic project to a COM-based library that will allow us to communicate with a database:

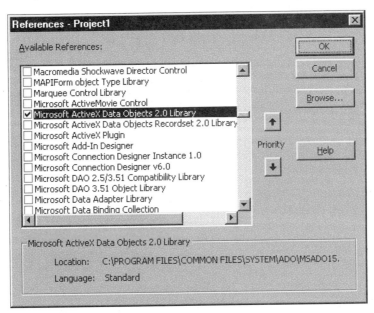

Component-based development also allows the programmer to take advantage of using pre-packaged components or tools. An example would be if you were writing a communications program that dealt with receiving and sending information over a modem. You could go out and buy (fairly inexpensively) a package that would handle the communications functionality for you, ridding yourself of the need to write large amounts of code to see if a port was open. You would just have to reference the library, and write a small amount of your own code. These libraries may be thought of as black boxes: you don't need to concern yourself with *how* they work; you just know that they *do* work.

COM promotes object-oriented programming

COM (and component-oriented design in general) was created with **object-oriented programming** in mind. This is a methodology that promotes thinking about software 'objects' and the way those objects interact with each other, rather than their implementation. Although this isn't a book on OOP, it is very difficult to discuss COM programming without covering many aspects of object-oriented programming. Therefore, from time to time we will be discussing further some of the aspects of object-oriented programming.

The History of COM

In order better to understand what COM is useful for, and why it works the way it does, it's revealing to delve into the genesis of COM and trace how it has evolved into its present form. There are two technologies that we can identify as the springboard for COM: **OLE** and **DDE**. OLE (later called OLE 1.0) is short for **Object Linking and Embedding**, which in its original form was a technology that tried to solve the problem of **compound documents**.

A compound document contains data of several different formats. To help you picture what I mean, think about a word processing document such as a status report. It's probable that you would want to include some calculations from a spreadsheet in a document like this, and maybe a pie chart as well. Before OLE, even if you *were* somehow able to put the information into the document, there was no standard technique for automatically updating the document when figures in the spreadsheet changed, or for changing the pie chart to a bar chart, for example.

OLE 1.0 provided a solution for this problem by enabling you to take your spreadsheet and place it directly into a word processor document, as in the figure below. Changes to the spreadsheet are automatically and immediately reflected in the document, edits to the embedded spreadsheet can be made *through the document* simply by double clicking on it, and *all* the data in the document can be stored together in a single file.

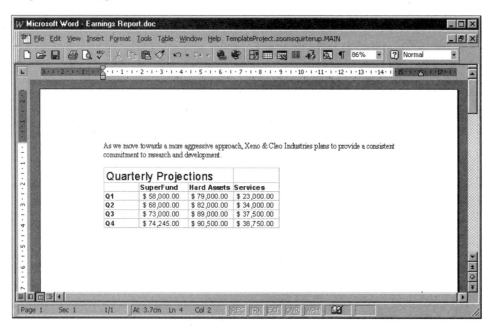

This was a great piece of technology, but it was rather ahead of its time in terms of the hardware that was available to support it. Working with OLE 1.0 required quite a bit of memory and CPU time, but it *did* get the minds at Microsoft thinking about the best way of getting software components to interact with one another, and in as efficient a manner as possible.

Before even OLE 1.0, a little gremlin called **Dynamic Data Exchange** (DDE) was being used to allow pieces of software to interact with each other. It allowed data to be transferred between two applications, and also made it possible for one application to be notified when data in another changed. However, DDE didn't catch on - not only did it suffer from poor performance, but also it was difficult to use, and quite easy for the link between the two applications to break. Even today though, you can still find information about DDE in the Visual Basic help files.

The Second Generation

Microsoft decided to make a second stab at component interaction in the early part of 1993, at which time OLE 2.0 came into existence. COM was a core component of OLE 2.0, and so the latter can be used as a way of explaining the features we know COM to have today. By providing COM as a means for components to communicate with one another, OLE 2.0 went well beyond the linking and embedding used to create compound documents. In response, Microsoft's marketing department came to the decision to drop the name "Object Linking and Embedding" and simple call it "OLE" (most people pronounce it "oh-lay"). OLE was the rubber stamp applied to anything that dealt with COM technologies.

One of the products of this expansion was **OLE Automation**. Put simply, OLE Automation (which today is just called **Automation**) allows a client to call the services exposed by a suitably endowed server, which is usually a major application. For example, it's possible using this technology to create an instance of Microsoft Excel, put numbers into a new workbook, crunch the numbers and then close the application again all from a Visual Basic program, without a single line of Microsoft Excel VBA code! Indeed, many software companies make their living from programming Automation clients that work with the Microsoft Office suite of applications.

If you've come across **VBXs** in your Visual Basic career, you're probably thinking that they must fit in to the story at around this point - aren't they reusable software components that you can use in Visual Basic? Well, you're on the right road, but you're headed in the wrong direction! VBXs were pre-packaged components written to tie into Visual Basic *specifically*, providing services such as list boxes or communication controls. These VBXs were great at the time because they provided support for the development methodology called **Rapid Application Development** (RAD). Just like the example in the last section, if you needed to have communication functionality in your program, it was as simple as dragging a control from the toolbox onto a Visual Basic form.

Although VBXs had the achievement of spawning a third-party industry that provided pre-packaged developer tools for the Visual Basic programmer, they also had three significant problems. First, they were not COM-based and were therefore a proprietary technology for Visual Basic - there was no way to use them from other programming languages. Second, you couldn't actually *build* a VBX using Visual Basic - instead you had to use something like C++, and even then they were difficult to write. Third, VBXs were limited to a 16-bit architecture.

According to Microsoft's web site, "COM supports the only currently viable component marketplace. The market for third-party components based on COM has been estimated at US$670 million in 1998, with a projected 65 percent compound annual growth rate, growing to approximately US$3 billion by 2001. (Source: Giga Information Group)"

It's great to know there are thousands of companies out there right now building components to make our lives easier!

Here Comes the Internet

In response to the Internet storming the beaches of computing, Microsoft marketing went into an elevated state of naming in the early part 1996 and decided that their Internet technologies would fall under the name **ActiveX**. At the same time, Microsoft came out with a new specification for **OLE controls**, otherwise known as OCXs (because the files containing them have the extension `.ocx`). These replaced VBXs: they *were* based upon COM technology, and they were easier to create, too. In fact, creating them was made even easier when Microsoft allowed Visual Basic developers to create their own controls with Visual Basic 5. A final name change gave OLE controls the title by which we know them today: **ActiveX controls**.

The reason for "ActiveX" being added to the name harks back to the first part of the previous paragraph. Microsoft enabled Internet surfers who were using their Internet Explorer browser to view web pages that had OLE controls embedded in them, but because OLE controls had suddenly become a part of the Internet strategy, their name had to change! ActiveX controls were designed to be very functional and fast, as well as lightweight in terms of size compared to their VBX precursors, since (as now) bandwidth was at a premium.

With Visual Basic, it's now possible to create ActiveX controls, ActiveX DLLs and ActiveX EXEs. ActiveX DLLs and ActiveX EXEs are similar to ActiveX controls, but they do not have the user interface attached to them that one would normally associate with ActiveX controls. In fact, the DLLs and EXEs are more typical of the COM-enabled software components that we will be writing in this book, and we will of course be discussing them further in forthcoming chapters.

Why COM?

COM technologies allow developers to deal with a myriad of problems that traditional software development simply could not handle. In this section, we'll address these issues and talk about the real-world problems that can be solved with COM-enabled technologies.

The Problem with Software

Software reuse is the goal that everyone's trying to reach, but no one ever seems quite able to get to. Much software development, especially that of a few years ago, does not support effective code reuse. You may have your routines sitting around in `.bas` files or text files somewhere on the hard drive or the network, but even finding them can be difficult if you don't have a centralized location for them, and they usually contain code that is specific to the last project you worked on. In response to this, most developers resign themselves to the cut-and-paste method of development: find the pieces you want, paste them into the program, and debug them.

Another software development problem pertains to dynamic-link libraries. These are usually files with a `.dll` extension that hold pieces of code that can be accessed by another program dynamically, at runtime. Unfortunately, it's not always easy to make calls to the library, and plenty of time can be wasted just in debugging your application's connection to it. (What? It wanted a string instead of an integer? Oh, that's why I'm getting the blue screen of death!) Also, if and when the library is updated, it's all too easy to break the compatibility between the new library and applications written to use the old version. If it turns out that you need two versions of the library on the same system, this can cause significant problems for your applications.

Software components written for one language do not always work within another language. Could I take my `.cls` files, stick them into a Visual C++ project and expect them to work? Of course not - a `.cls` file would just look like a bunch of text. What's needed is a solution that will allow you to create software components in one language that can be used in multiple languages. Wouldn't it be great to be able to create a component in Visual Basic that could be used in Visual C++, Visual InterDev, Delphi, *and* Internet Explorer?

In general, legacy applications do not expose a way to allow developers to use their resources programmatically from another application. For example, let us say that we have an application that is good at presenting data and another that is good at creating graphs. It would be nice for the presentation application developer to be able to use the resources of the graph application for their own application rather than have to develop their own graph engine.

Lastly, traditional applications are unable to exploit components that are located on another networked machine. You may have a component that is good at crunching numbers or can provide database services better on a separate machine than putting all the libraries onto the client machine. If only there were a way of creating applications whose separate pieces run on different machines, so that the most appropriate set of resources could be chosen for each part. How good would that be?

COM to the Rescue

It's about time we began to consider how COM solves these issues and provides this kind of functionality for us. The beauty of using Visual Basic and COM together is the combination of the two makes it quite easy to address the problems without too much effort on the part of the developer - Visual Basic does most of the hard work for you!

COM-based components promote software reuse. COM components are usually written to be generic, which allows them to be used in a multitude of ways by different pieces of software. A graphing component, for example, could be COM-enabled so that you could use it in whatever container you choose. You may want to put a graph in your Microsoft Word document, or you might want to put it on a Microsoft Access form. The great thing is that you can use it in *either* application, and it will work the same way in one as it does in the other.

Looking at the pair of screenshots below, you can see that the Microsoft Chart Component looks and acts the same in both applications. This is very productive because if a developer knows how the chart control works for one application, they are likely to know how to make it work in another application.

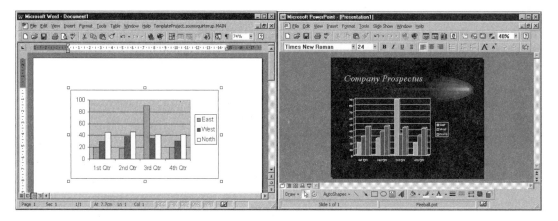

As to the problem of being able to find your components after you've written them, COM has a solution that deals with this and more. Every time that you create a COM component with Visual Basic, an entry is placed in the **system registry** that indicates exactly where on the computer is the file containing your component. In fact, COM goes further than this: it *requires* that in order for a component to be used, an entry for it must exist in the registry. Without such an entry, the COM runtime will be unable to find the component when it is asked to do so.

> *This theme will be developed in the next chapter, along with a more complete description of how the registry works.*

COM components are language independent. COM components can not only be *used* in Visual Basic, but also *written* in Visual Basic. More importantly, you can take a COM component you created in Visual Basic and integrate it into your Visual C++ or Visual J++ project. Although you can't create COM components in Visual InterDev, you can certainly use them by calling them from Active Server Pages. At the moment, language independence is typically limited to the programming languages Microsoft supports, but this is changing as the momentum for COM continues to grow.

COM objects have object-oriented features: obeying the strictures of **encapsulation**, they are accessed using only public methods and properties, so that any data they contain is hidden from public consumption. However, object-oriented programming is a tool of this book rather than its subject matter, so I'll limit any further discussion of it until it is relevant to the matter at hand. I suggest reading *Beginning Visual Basic 6 Objects* by Peter Wright (Wrox Press) as a good primer in creating and using software objects.

Time for me to get on my soapbox. If you haven't been to a Usenet newsgroup with "OOP" (short for Object-Oriented Programming) in its name, you may not know that there seems to be something of a Jihad over OOP. The purists will tell you that all the software you write must adhere to the concepts of object-oriented programming.

For my part, I like to invoke the old saying, "When your only tool is a hammer, everything looks like a nail." I am not against OOP; indeed, I am quite happy that Visual Basic uses classes and encapsulation - it has made it simpler to develop applications, and it makes debugging much easier. I do think, though, that Microsoft is beginning to push the envelope (yet again) and reappraise the argument that says you should use object-oriented development just because you are supposed to. I am sure to get flame mail on this one, but I think it is better for the developer to decide how they want to design their programs based on what their users require, rather than on an ideological point.

Another great feature of COM is called **DCOM**, or **Distributed COM**. This was first shipped with Windows NT4, and was released as an add-on for Windows 95 in late 1996. It also ships as standard with Windows 98. DCOM allows your applications to call upon components that may not even be on the same machine as they are. DCOM takes the notion of **location independence** that's supported by COM's use of the registry to store the locations of components (provided that there's an entry, it doesn't matter exactly where the component is) and extends it to the network. Furthermore, it provides security for components that are distributed in this way. I will go into more detail on this subject in the DCOM chapter.

You should be able to see from this discussion that there are a number of advantages to using COM and DCOM as platforms for building and using components. COM goes out of its way to provide a robust and powerful environment for your software development needs.

A Sample Problem

To reinforce the point, let's take a look at a problem for which COM could provide a viable solution. Phil is the project leader of a new application for his company *Frogs & Turtles*, a retail chain that sells garden plants and accessories. Currently, they are using proprietary software that runs at each retail chain and on each order taker's system at the catalog telephone center. This application batches all orders into a text file and uses a modem to transfer the orders for the next day overnight, where they are then updated to the main database. If there are orders for something that's not in stock, a fax is sent to the representative that took the order the next morning. Unfortunately, there are some problems with the current system.

The first problem is that the software is proprietary, so Phil and his group of developers are unable to add any features to it or debug any of the problems they have found without having the code base. Second, customer satisfaction is low due to inventory control problems. Because they have grown so quickly, their technology has not kept up with their demand: they cannot tell what their inventory levels are until the nightly batches are through. In addition, when a customer puts in an order late in the day, they will not know until the representative calls the next morning that their order is on backorder. Third, when orders are filled out wrongly and entered into the system, it can mess up reporting, wreck the order, or even crash the system the order took place on.

Phil's bosses asked him to develop a system that would solve their growing problems. As always, they gave him two months to complete a project that needed six. (Bosses putting ambiguous, over-ambitious deadlines on a developer? Never heard of that!) In addition, his bosses asked if the Internet could be used as the means of communication between the retail stores and the telephone center. In response, Phil decided to research COM and see how it could be used with Visual Basic (since most of his developers were Visual Basic programmers). He concluded that he would implement COM-based techniques to solve their problems. Throughout the rest of the book, I will demonstrate some of the techniques Phil used to develop his solutions.

COM and Visual Basic

By now, you should have an idea of what COM is and what it can do for you, so it's time to wheel out the big guns. Microsoft Visual Basic can make a developer very productive when it comes to creating and using COM components. In fact, Visual Basic itself relies very heavily on COM technologies.

One of the advantages of using Visual Basic to create COM components is the ease with which it can be done. Visual Basic hides a lot of the plumbing needed to implement COM components and lets you focus on developing what your components will do, or what business functionality they will address.

The Visual Basic COM Players

Microsoft Visual Basic allows you to create a number of different COM-enabled projects, three of which we will be concentrating on in this book. First, there are ActiveX controls, which have a user interface associated with them. As a Visual Basic developer, you are probably most familiar with the ActiveX controls that are available as tools in your toolbox:

Also, if you go to Visual Basic's Project menu and select Components... (or just use *Ctrl-T*), you can see all the ActiveX controls that are **registered** on your local machine (that is, those that have entries in the system registry):

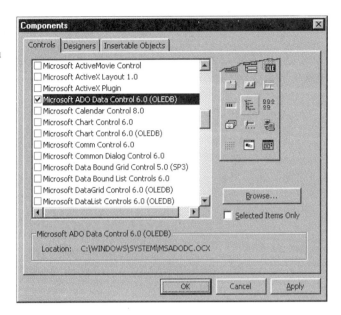

ActiveX controls generally have a `.ocx` file extension, as you can see if you look at the Location field in the previous screenshot.

The second kind of project we'll be looking at is the ActiveX DLL. These are COM-enabled files with a `.dll` extension, and they contain the COM components that you will find yourself using most often. Unlike their ActiveX control counterparts, components in ActiveX DLLs typically do not have user interfaces. Generally, they are made up of a class or a set of classes that are blueprints for the COM objects that you will create.

Thirdly, ActiveX EXEs are very similar to the ActiveX DLLs, except they are **out-of-process servers**, which means that they don't run in the same memory space as the application that calls them. By the same reasoning, ActiveX DLLs are often called **in-process servers**, because they *do* run in the same memory space as the application that calls them. Don't worry if some of these terms are unfamiliar to you at the moment; just understand that there *is* a difference, and I will have plenty to say about the advantages and disadvantages of in- and out-of-process servers later in the book.

Individually and collectively, these three different project types allow us to easily create reusable components with Visual Basic. Moreover, because these ActiveX components are built on COM we can use them with COM components irrelevant of language or container.

In Chapter 5, we'll create a simple ActiveX control consisting of two text boxes that our developer, Phil, might want use in his application. In Chapter 6, we'll look at how he can distribute COM objects across a network and we'll see the importance of ActiveX EXEs in achieving this. Finally, in Chapter 7 we'll see how Phil can easily provide multi-user support for his ActiveX DLLs.

Summary

You will notice that this chapter is short relative to the rest of the chapters in the book. This is because I wanted to provide you a quick primer of what COM is. If you stopped reading this book right now (which you shouldn't), you would at least know what COM is and what it can do for your development.

Specifically, we discussed the concepts behind COM and how we could define it. There are many parts to COM, and it provides us with many services and considerable functionality to solve software problems.

Next, we delved into the history of COM, from its humble roots in OLE 1.0 to its role in Microsoft's Internet strategy. This history helps us to establish how COM came into being and developed into what it is today.

Lastly, we discussed the problems with typical software development and how COM actually helps us to solve these problems. Also, I explained a real-world programming scenario in which the use of COM might be helpful, and we will spend some time in future chapters using COM technologies to solve the not-so-unique problems we uncovered.

At the beginning of the chapter, I mentioned that we were on a journey. At this point, we have made a few steps down the path. Strap your boots on, because we are now heading up the mountain!

VB COM

2

COM Architecture

In this chapter, we'll take a comprehensive look at the some of the underlying architecture of COM. First and foremost, you'll discover *how* COM allows components to interact. As a Visual Basic programmer, you'll find that you won't have to concern yourself with implementing most of the details described in this chapter. However, having a solid grounding in how COM works will help you to exploit both COM and Visual Basic to their greatest advantage. This discussion will also give you a good understanding of how and why things work in the chapters to come.

Visual Basic itself has been carefully created to work well with COM, so in this chapter you will also attain some insights into why Visual Basic works the way it does. In particular, you will learn:

- ❑ Objects and how they apply to Visual Basic and COM
- ❑ How COM applies object-oriented principles
- ❑ What interfaces are and how we use them in COM
- ❑ How Visual Basic makes it easy to use COM

COM and Objects

COM is object-oriented, so in order to understand it properly, you need to grasp at least a few basic object-oriented principles. We'll start by spending a short time defining how objects and object theory fit with COM.

Peter Wright's Beginning Visual Basic 6 Objects, *also published by Wrox Press, provides a good introduction to object-oriented programming and principles.*

The Concept of Objects

Let's start at the very beginning and first define what we mean by an object.

> **A software object is often an abstraction of a real-world entity. An object has state, behavior and identity.**

Software objects often represent and are modeled upon real-word concepts or relationships. For example, if we were designing a farm simulator, we might have a cow object, a sheep object and a pig object. Similarly, if were writing a freeway simulator, we might have a car object, a truck object and an on-ramp object. These objects are close representations of their real-world counterparts.

Object-oriented programming (OOP) helps to provide a frame of reference for the programming models we are trying to create. Thinking about problems in terms of objects instead of abstract code routines can help use to produce more efficient, intuitive programs. Let's start, though, by taking a look at the three basic characteristics of an object that I introduced in the above definition.

State

All objects have state (in other words, data) that essentially comprises the values of their properties. For example, a cow object in our farm simulator might have two properties: a `Weight` of 700 and an `Age` of 6. These properties combined make the object's **state**.

Behavior

Behavior is the name given to the things that can be done with an object. In Visual Basic terms, we're talking about the subroutines or functions that can be called to make our object perform some action. A sheep object, for example, may have a method called `Eat`, which when called increases the values of the sheep's `Weight` property. The combined semantics of all the methods of an object represent its **behavior**.

Identity

Identity is the way in which a particular object is uniquely identified. If we had two pig objects in our farm simulator, we would use **identity** to refer to a specific pig. In the real world, we would commonly refer to our animals by their names, as we're unlikely to give two animals the same name.

Classes

In simple terms, a **class** is a collection of related properties and methods that are common to one or more objects. When we start running our farm simulator program, we might have hundreds of pig objects in the system, and each of those objects would have the same properties and methods. The differences between the objects would be found in their states (that is, the *values* of their properties) and their identities. We can say that each object is an **instance** of a class.

> **A class is the blueprint from which an object is instantiated. An object always knows its own class.**

Consider the following Visual Basic code for creating and interacting with two pig objects:

```
Dim Tom As CPig
Dim Bert As CPig

Set Tom = New CPig
Set Bert = New CPig

Tom.Sleep
Bert.Eat
```

The names used in this and the other code samples in this chapter have been changed to protect the innocent.

In this code, we create a couple of objects of a class called CPig (it's common in Visual Basic to give classes names that begin with a C), each with a unique identity of Tom and Bert respectively. We then define some **behavior** for these pigs: we tell one to go to Sleep, and we tell the other to Eat. As both pigs are instances of the same class, we know exactly what behavior (that is, methods or properties) we can use, and that anything we can do with Tom, we can do just as well with Bert.

Notice that in the above code, we first have to Dim *our objects, and then* Set *them. With the* Dim *commands, we are simply declaring that* Tom *and* Bert *are of the type 'class of* CPig*'. It is only with the* Set *command that we actually create the two objects called* Tom *and* Bert*. The difference is subtle, but it's critical in Visual Basic, and you will see why later.*

The state of our objects is contained in the properties Name and Age, which are defined in the CPig class, while their behavior is implemented by the methods Eat and Sleep. Each pig's identity is the object instance defined and contained by the Dim and Set statements. The Visual Basic class CPig, which we use to define our pig objects in the code above, would thus be defined as follows:

```
' Local variable(s) to hold property value(s) - STATE
Private mvarAge As Integer    ' Local copy
Private mvarName As String    ' Local copy

Public Sub Sleep()    ' Behavior
End Sub

Public Sub Eat()       ' Behavior
End Sub

' Property routines to provide access to the object's state
Public Property Let Name(ByVal vData As String)
   mvarName = vData
End Property
```

```
Public Property Get Name() As String
   Name = mvarName
End Property

Public Property Let Age(ByVal vData As Integer)
   mvarAge = vData
End Property

Public Property Get Age() As Integer
   Age = mvarAge
End Property
```

Looking at this code, you'll see that we keep local copies of the `Age` and `Name` properties of pigs in two `Private` variables called `mvarAge` and `mvarName` respectively. After that, we define two `Public` methods, `Sleep` and `Eat`, to define the behavior of our `CPig` class. The two pairs of `Property Let` and `Property Get` statements that follow these lines allow the `CPig` class to accept new values for the `Age` and `Name` properties; this is, of course, a way to change the state of any object based on the `CPig` class.

> You'll see these `Property` statements that allow us to change the state of objects throughout the book. We'll be discussing their use in a lot more detail later on, but in a nutshell we use `Property Let` to assign new values to object properties, and `Property Get` to read object properties.

The Black Box Concept (Encapsulation)

In programming, an object should be thought of as a black box that can process and generate messages without revealing its internal workings. You can ask it to perform a certain operation by sending it a message, and you may get some tangible output – in which case the object sends a message back to you. In object-oriented (OO) terms, sending a message is equivalent to calling a function or a subroutine in Visual Basic.

Here's a nice rule of thumb: when you call one of its methods, you should never need to know how an object implements an operation internally. Let's consider a simple analogy with a real world object: a car. The following sequence diagram shows the order in which we would expect the interaction between a car owner and a car door to happen:

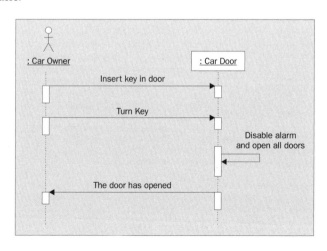

When you open your car before driving to work in the morning, you probably put the key into the car door and turn it. The expected result of this action is that the door will open, but you don't need to concern yourself with the inner workings of the lock. This is a basic example of **encapsulation**.

Unless you're the one creating it, you should never need to know about the inner implementation details of an object, in the same way that only people who make car doors really need to know how they work. You just need to know how to interact with an object using the interface it exposes to the world. In our car analogy, the interface is the keyhole, into which you insert and turn a key. As long as it continues to support this familiar interface, the internal implementation of the mechanism can change or be different on an object by object basis, without affecting the people that use it.

> **Never depend upon the implementation details of an object, because it is quite possible that they will change. It is the interface that's all-important when you're programming COM.**

Polymorphism

In our analogy above, with the car, the owner doesn't know the internal actions performed by the door locking mechanism when the key is turned. This means the owner could buy a new car, whose locking mechanism is completely different, and yet still know how to open the door. That may sound simplistic, but this is the power of **polymorphism**. You can use the *same interface* to perform an operation on an object, but the implementation may be different depending upon the class of which the object is an instance.

With my BMW, turning the key unlocks all the doors and deactivates the alarm. On my wife's Ford, it just opens the driver's door. Do we care that the locking mechanisms are different? No. As long as I can get in the car and drive, I'm happy. Should my BMW be out of commission, I don't need my wife to teach me how to open the door of her car – they both use the same interface. In fact, to demonstrate the power of polymorphism, the key-lock interface is used in doors, deposit boxes and numerous other objects, yet once we know how to open one, we can open them all!

Let's use our farmyard example to demonstrate polymorphism in action. Take a look at this code:

```
Dim Sharon As CSheep
Dim Andrea As CPig
Dim Caroline As CCow

Set Sharon = New CSheep
Set Andrea = New CPig
Set Caroline  = New CCow

Sub GoToSleep(Animal As Object)
  Animal.Sleep
End Sub

GoToSleep Sharon
GoToSleep Andrea
GoToSleep Caroline
```

In this code, we declare objects of three different classes: CSheep, CPig and CCow. We then call the GoToSleep method (our Visual Basic subroutine) three times, passing each object in turn as a parameter. Now here's the clever bit: the GoToSleep subroutine calls the Sleep method of the object passed to it, regardless of its class! We can therefore say that the GoToSleep method is polymorphic.

Allow me to spell that out once more, very carefully. When the Animal parameter is Sharon, the Animal.Sleep method called is the one that belongs to the CSheep class. When the Animal parameter is Andrea, the Animal.Sleep method that's actually called is the one defined in the CPig class. Exactly the same goes for Caroline and the CCow class of course.

Programming with an OOP Hat On

Object-oriented programming is vitally important to COM, so let's consider how we would go about implementing some of the object-oriented principles we have discussed for our pig objects. In the code for the CPig class you saw earlier, all of the member variables were defined as Private:

```
Private mvarAge As Integer   ' Local copy
Private mvarName As String   ' Local copy
```

By making them private to the class (and thus preventing direct access), nobody can violate the object and perform any invalid actions that would leave the object in an illegal state. For example, if I decided that in my farm simulator, no pig is allowed to be older than ten, I could enforce that rule by making a simple change to the appropriate Property Let routine:

```
Public Property Let Age(ByVal vData As Integer)

    If vData > 10 Then
        MsgBox "Invalid Age"
        Exit Property
    End If

    mvarAge = vData

End Property
```

If we had made the member variables public, anybody could set the Age to any value they wanted, like this:

```
Pig.mvarAge = 1000
```

Does it really make sense to have a pig that is 1000 years old? Is it even possible? By **encapsulating** our variable in this fashion, we are protecting the state of our object.

In a later version of the farm simulator, we may decide that any pig older than ten should be sold. If we've taken the OOP approach in our code, the change is fairly simple: we just revisit the relevant Property Let routine and add a few more lines of code. If it's greater than or equal to ten, we sell the pig by invoking the PutPigUpForSale method. The new code looks like this:

```
Public Property Let Age(ByVal vData As Integer)

    If vData > 10 Then
        PutPigUpForSale Me
        Exit Property
    End If

    mvarAge = vData

End Property
```

If we hadn't taken the OOP approach, we would have had to search the whole project for every reference to the Age property, and then decide whether we needed to add the code to sell the pig. The single line of our earlier example would probably have to be followed by another line like this:

```
Pig.mvarAge = 1000
PutPigUpForSale Pig
```

Now this code is even worse than before: we have hard-coded a rule of the simulator into the normal program logic. If we decide to change the rules again, we'd have to revisit all the code once more. By using encapsulation, we can enforce and protect 'business rules' for our objects in a straightforward and logical way.

The Concept of COM Objects

Now that we have looked at the basic principles of objects and object-oriented programming, let's examine how these concepts are realized in COM. You may not have known it at the time, but the above code is an almost perfect implementation of a COM component in Visual Basic. Wasn't that lucky?

Defining COM Objects and Visual Basic Objects

COM objects and Visual Basic objects are not quite the same things. Before we can consider how they differ, let's first establish exactly what we mean by the two terms.

❑ *Visual Basic Objects*. A Visual Basic object is an instance of a Visual Basic class that is usually defined and used within a single application. It's possible to share and use a class across multiple applications, but generally that involves having to use unfriendly techniques like duplicating the source file or sharing it using a source control system. It certainly isn't possible to use a Visual Basic object from another programming language, such as C++. You have to tell Visual Basic specifically that your objects are COM objects that you want to be exposed by the server you're creating. If you don't do this (by selecting an appropriate project type), Visual Basic won't know that you want to create a COM server, and it won't provide the necessary support for COM.

❑ *COM Objects*. A COM object is an instance of a COM component, which (as we covered in Chapter 1) should be thought of as a compiled piece of code that can provide a service to the system, not just to a single application. There are generally hundreds of components in the system that can potentially be used in thousands of different applications. A different software house could write each component, and each software house could use a different programming language. The possibilities are limitless.

The phrases "COM object" and "COM component" are frequently used interchangeably, and while this is not always correct, it is unlikely that you will be misunderstood if you find yourself making this mistake. Strictly, though, they are different things: the former is an instance of the latter.

Contrasting COM Objects and Visual Basic Objects

Now we've considered what COM objects and Visual Basic objects are, it's time to consider some of the profound ways in which they are different from one another.

When we interact with a Visual Basic object, we use its **class interface**. This is made up of the public properties and methods that are defined in the object's Visual Basic class. What's more, the Visual Basic class interface contains actual *implementation* details for all its methods and properties, as we saw earlier when we interacted with our pig object:

```
Tom.Sleep
```

In this case, we had already declared Tom to be an object of our CPig class:

```
Dim Tom As CPig

...

Set Tom = New CPig
```

Because the Sleep method was defined as a public routine in the CPig class, it's automatically a part of the CPig class interface. The important issue here is in the way you regard this interaction, and it should be like this: we can say that we're interacting with Tom the pig through the CPig class interface.

The precise implementation of the Sleep method is contained in the Visual Basic class interface for CPig. Ours, for example, could be like this one:

```
Public Sub Sleep()

  MsgBox "zzzzzzz"

End Sub
```

In contrast, when we interact with a COM object, we do it through a **COM interface**. COM interfaces are really what COM is all about, so we're going to spend some time discussing interfaces – not just in this chapter, but throughout the rest of the book as well. As you're about to see, COM interfaces differ significantly from Visual Basic class interfaces in that there is *no* procedural definition within a COM interface.

The COM Interface

The COM interface is the mechanism by which a consumer or client interacts with a component. An interface is actually a very simple concept to understand:

> An interface is a contract between a consumer and a component that describes the component's *functionality* to the consumer without describing the *implementation* at all.

If we consider our pig object from earlier in the chapter, we would define the interface as being the two methods Eat and Sleep, plus the two properties Age and Name. If we gave this interface a name, let's say IFarmYardAnimal, we could then use this name to describe the contract between our farm simulator and *any* animal – not just the pigs!

We'll be considering many more of the issues surrounding COM interfaces throughout the book, so there'll be plenty of practical examples giving you the chance to see this idea in action. Right now, let's take stock for a moment and consider how these COM interfaces differ from our Visual Basic classes.

Visual Basic Classes and COM Interfaces

When we were discussing classes earlier in this chapter, I described a Visual Basic class as being a collection of related properties and methods, and in truth the same description is fitting for a COM interface. What then is the difference between a Visual Basic class and a COM interface?

You can think of an interface as a class that has no implementation. In other words, an interface is simply a list of properties and methods that a COM component supports. When we define an interface, we just outline a set of properties and methods, without providing any programmatic details of how they should work.

> *We'll see how to implement COM interfaces in Visual Basic later on in this chapter.*

So: we've found out that the most essential difference between a class in Visual Basic and a COM interface is the clear and distinct separation of interface from the implementation. In object-oriented terms, a class without any implementation is known as an **abstract class**.

Consumer Diagrams

A kind of diagram that I call a **consumer diagram** is useful when you want to see a complete picture of the contract between a consumer and one or more components. Using the notation I introduced in the previous chapter, these diagrams depict what interfaces a component must support to be usable by its consumers:

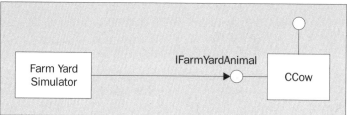

This picture shows our farmyard simulator as the consumer that uses the `IFarmYardAnimal` interface of a component called `CCow`. If we consider all of the animals we have discussed so far, we could draw another diagram that shows them too:

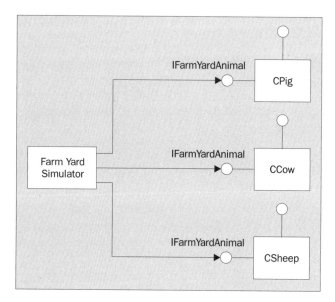

Visual Basic Classes and Coclasses

Now you can begin to see how things fit together. The **components** you see represented in the above diagram are often referred to as **coclasses** (**c**omponent **o**bject **class**es), and they are directly equivalent to Visual Basic classes. For each of our Visual Basic classes that supports COM there exists a coclass, and this is what COM uses to create a new COM object. When we tell COM that we want our Visual Basic objects to be COM-enabled by compiling our project, a new "COM-ified" version of our class is created. Our consumer diagram could therefore look like this:

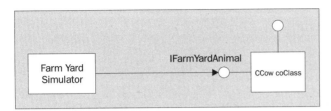

You'll remember that I explained in the last chapter how the COM runtime is able to locate coclasses on your computer by looking them up in the registry. The way it does this is by associating an identifier called a **class ID** or **CLSID** with the coclass. By looking up the CLSID, it can discover the path to the component.

The question that should be forming in your mind now is, "All right, but how does the COM runtime find out the CLSID of the coclass it's looking for?" The answer to this puzzle will be revealed shortly, when we discuss **type libraries**.

The COM Interface Contract

Several times, I have described an interface as a **contract** between a consumer and a component, and this really harks back to the earlier point I made about encapsulation. Provided that we never change the interfaces that we create (that is, as long as we do not break the contract), the consumer does not have to worry about the implementation of our components.

If you think back to the car door example that I gave earlier in the chapter, the implementation of the locking mechanism was immaterial to us as consumers, because the *interface* of the lock was the same across different cars. Provided that this lock interface remains consistent, I can quite happily buy new cars in the future, safe in the knowledge that I'll always understand how to unlock the doors!

But, what if the engineers at BMW have a brainwave and come up with a radical, new voice-activated mechanism for unlocking car doors? You can picture the scene: I go to the garage, excited at the prospect of trying out a new model. I can't wait to give it a test drive, but when I attempt to get into the car, key at the ready, I find that there's no longer a key-lock interface. Imagine my disappointment: I need a whole new interface simply to get into the car!

This is probably stretching the example a little, but in fact this is exactly the problem you face when designing and updating your own components. Once you've published an interface, it's vitally important that you don't change it. It's possible to expand the functionality of your components with new, additional interfaces, but you should always continue to support the old ones. To avoid me having to learn a new way of opening car doors, the engineers at BMW could still incorporate their voice-activated door lock, provided that they keep the key lock as well.

Of course, as a sentient being, I could learn how to use the new interface. In the world of computing, however, we haven't quite got that far: a new *consumer could be provided with the knowledge to use the new interface, but* old *consumers wouldn't even know it existed. They rely on the presence of the old interface in order to keep working.*

This aspect of COM programming is called **interface versioning**, and we'll look at some code examples later in the chapter that use our farmyard example. For now though, make sure you take away the idea that interface is an immutable contract between consumer and component.

To help explain for fully just how immutable interfaces must be, we're going to go on and consider the binary implementation of an interface.

Interface Internals

We've discussed what an interface is and what it provides, so let's take a closer look at how it works behind the scenes, deep inside the COM runtime that I introduced in the previous chapter. COM is a binary specification, so it shouldn't be a surprise that we are going to have to look at some fairly low-level and potentially confusing details. If you find that you're still uncertain after reading it the first time, don't worry: try it again – maybe try it a few times – and eventually things will become clear. The examples along the way should help.

Pointers

A **pointer** does exactly what its name suggests – it points to something. More specifically, it points to a piece of memory in your computer that contains an interesting value. Now, Visual Basic doesn't let you use pointers in your programs like some languages do (C and C++ come to mind), and this is generally a good thing because pointers can be the cause of many headaches and random crashes in your applications. However, to understand the binary implementation of interfaces clearly, it's essential that you understand how pointers work.

Pointers to Objects

When you declare an object in Visual Basic, you are implicitly defining a pointer. This code, for example, defines a pointer to an object of type `Rabbit`:

```
Dim George As Rabbit
```

Although strictly speaking rabbits are not farmyard animals, they are creatures that one would normally find running around on the fields of a farm. Besides which, they are the only animals for which I had any clip art.

A pointer doesn't point to anything until you assign it a value; a pointer that has not been assigned a value is known as a **null pointer**. Think of a null pointer like this:

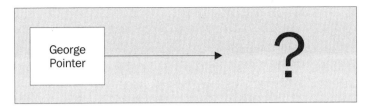

If you were to try to use `George` in your code at this stage, Visual Basic would raise a runtime exception because you would be trying to access something that does not exist – an unknown quantity. In C++, a program that does this generally crashes. However, if we assign an object to our `George` pointer, like this:

```
Set George = New Rabbit
```

We will now be able to invoke the methods and access the properties of this new object. We can redraw our picture to show that our pointer now points to a valid object:

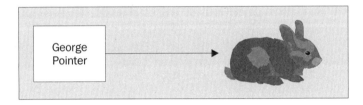

Aliasing

Pointers are useful because they allow us to **alias** an object – or more specifically, a memory location. This means that we can use two pointers to point to the same thing twice. In Visual Basic, you alias an object when you write code like this:

```
Dim George As Rabbit
Dim Barney As Rabbit

Set George = New Rabbit
Set Barney = George
```

We now have two pointers that both point to the same rabbit:

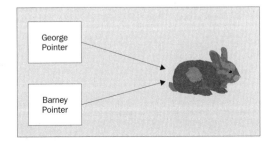

In our farmyard simulator, we might have an individual pig object that's being used by several parts of the simulator. If any part of the simulator causes the state of the object to change, all the other parts of the application that have a pointer to the object will see the changes that have been made. This happens because the pointer is an alias that refers each part of the application to the *same* memory location, even though each part of the application might be using a different name for the pointer.

Pointers to Functions

Pointers can point to just about anything, including functions. You can obtain a pointer to a function in Visual Basic by using the `AddressOf` operator, but you can't actually call a function using that pointer. The operator is provided so that you can pass a function pointer as a parameter to a Win32 API function like `EnumWindows`.

> *See* Visual Basic 6 Win32 API Tutorial *by Jason Bock, also published by Wrox Press, if you would like to learn more about using the* `AddressOf` *operator.*

Interface Architecture

Now we come to the crux of the matter. Essentially, a COM interface is a binary description of the layout of a block of memory containing an array of function pointers. The array has a fixed structure, and is known as a virtual method table (**vtable**). The pointers in the array point to the functions of a COM object that can be called by a consumer of the interface.

When a consumer wants to use the services of a COM object, it obtains the vtable for the appropriate interface, and 'looks up' the method it wants to call. It then uses the function pointer to invoke the method. Each interface has its own vtable layout, and a COM object can expose any number of interfaces:

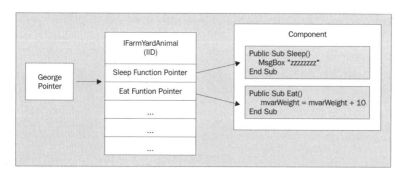

A Binary Contract

The order of the functions in the vtable, the parameters for each function, the name of the interface, and the amount of memory needed physically to store the pointers is known as the **interface signature**. Once a COM interface has been published, this signature must not change: it is *absolutely immutable*. If you alter any aspect of an interface signature once you've published it, you run the very real risk of breaking all the applications that are using it.

When a program is compiled, the binary layout of each interface signature it uses is compiled into it. If a program using our IFarmYardAnimal interface calls the Sleep function, it will do it by using the first function pointer in the vtable. Similarly, if it calls the Eat function, it will use the second function pointer. These positions or indexes into the vtable are effectively hard-coded into the program when it is compiled.

To illustrate why this arrangement requires absolute immutability, consider the following two cases. First, imagine that we update a well-known interface by removing an obsolete method, or even just change the parameter types of an existing method. A client written for the old version of the interface will try to call a method that doesn't exist, or pass the wrong kind of argument to one that does. Either will result in failure. Second, think what would happen if a client written to use the new version of the interface came across a component that was still implementing the old one. It would either find that the vtable contained an extra entry it knew nothing about, or else once again a method would be called with the wrong arguments.

> **Through this reasoning, you can see how an interface is a lifetime binary contract with its consumers. Changing an interface is practically guaranteed to cause the failure of both old and new clients.**

Class Property Routines

By now, the fact that a vtable can only contain function pointers may have you wondering how COM deals with the implementation of properties. Well, when your class is compiled, each Property Let and Get statement is compiled into a function, so the interface just contains an additional pointer for each Property Let and Get.

Into the Great IUnknown

You have now seen the basics of how a COM interface allows a client to access a component's resources, but how can a client discover what interfaces the component supports in the first place? The answer lies in a special interface called IUnknown.

If you remember back to the lollipop diagram I first introduced in Chapter 1, there was a line extruding from the top of the box that I didn't really explain at the time. In fact, this line represents the IUnknown interface:

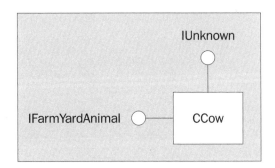

Every COM object must implement the `IUnknown` interface. In Visual Basic, you can use a pointer to the `IUnknown` interface to hold *any* interface pointer:

```
Dim Unk As IUnknown
Set Unk = <Any interface>
```

This code should look familiar to you. This is because when you set a pointer to an object you are really setting a pointer to its interface.

`IUnknown` is aptly named because it enables interfaces to be used without actually knowing anything else about them. It contains three functions:

- ❑ `QueryInterface`
- ❑ `AddRef`
- ❑ `Release`

QueryInterface

`QueryInterface` is the mechanism that a client uses to discover and navigate the interfaces of a component dynamically, and its implementation is really quite simple. You see: coclasses are not the only things in COM that have identifiers – interfaces have them too. To use `QueryInterface`, the client passes in an **interface identifier** (**IID**), and if the associated interface is supported by the component, it gets an interface pointer in return.

`QueryInterface` is probably *the* most significant method of all COM interfaces, as it allows run-time inspection of all the interfaces that a component supports. We've already seen that COM objects can implement many interfaces; without the `QueryInterface` method it would be difficult for a client to navigate around them, and impossible to provide true 'dynamic' discovery of a component's capabilities.

Identifers: GUIDs, UUIDs, IIDs and CLSIDs

You've now come across interface identifiers (IIDs) and class identifiers (CLSIDs). Both of these are types of **GUID**, which stands for **Globally Unique Identifier**. This acronym is also synonymous with **UUID**, or **Universally Unique Identifier**. A GUID is a 128-bit number (16 bytes) that can be expressed in string format. For example, the identifier for the `IUnknown` interface is:

{00000000-0000-0000-C000-000000000046}

Visual Basic generates GUIDs for your COM classes and interfaces when you compile your component. It generates these numbers using the services of the COM runtime – more specifically, a COM API call to `CoCreateGuid`.

A GUID is created with a complex algorithm that uses the system clock and the network card's MAC address. (If you don't have a network card in your machine, other variables such as hard disk space and time since last reboot are used, but then the ID generated is only *guaranteed* to be unique on your computer.) The algorithm for generating GUIDs could generate 10 million a second until the year 5770 AD, and each one would be unique. *(Source: Professional DCOM Programming by Dr Richard Grimes)*

Basically, as I explained in the specific case of coclasses, COM uses a GUID as a key for accessing information in the system registry, in much the same way that you would use a primary key for accessing a specific row in a database. After all, in the final analysis the registry is little more than a database, albeit a very important one.

AddRef and Release

So far, you've seen that we can cause the creation of COM objects by using Visual Basic's `New` operator. However, it can't have escaped your attention that there must be some way of causing objects to be destroyed as well – if there weren't, your computer's memory would quickly be filled with objects that had long since stopped being of any use to the programs that created them. The trouble is, as you have also seen, it's quite possible for one program to have several references to a single object (and indeed for several programs to have references to a single object). We can't have a situation in which finishing with a particular reference causes the object to be destroyed – that would run the risk of all the other references becoming invalid – and so there must be another way to manage the **lifetime** of a COM object. What actually happens is that COM objects are responsible for their own lifetimes, using a mechanism called **reference counting**.

In case you haven't guessed by now, it is the `AddRef` and `Release` methods of the `IUnknown` interface that manage an object's lifetime, and they do it like this. When a component is first created by the COM runtime, its 'life' begins, and `AddRef` is implicitly called by the component itself. `AddRef` is a simple function that increases the reference count of the component by one. The count starts at zero, and so after a component has been created, its reference count will be equal to one.

Every time the `QueryInterface` function hands out an interface pointer to a consumer, it calls `AddRef` to increase the reference count by one. Conversely, when a consumer has finished using the interface, the `Release` method is called, decrementing the count by one. If this count reaches zero, the object knows that no more consumers are using it, and so it destroys itself.

Thankfully, in Visual Basic we don't really have to worry too much about reference counting. The Visual Basic runtime will automatically call `AddRef` and `Release` if we don't do it explicitly, and we'll see how it performs this trick later in the chapter.

> *The way to call the* `Release` *method of* `IUnknown` *explicitly in Visual Basic is to set an interface equal to* `Nothing`*. It's a good idea to do this whenever you have finished with an object, to release any resources it's holding. However, Visual Basic will do this for you automatically when it determines that the object is no longer required – that is, when it goes out of scope.*

Implementing Interfaces in Visual Basic

In this section, we'll use a cow object from our farmyard example to demonstrate the two basic types of COM interface that Visual Basic produces on our behalf:

- ❑ The user-defined or custom interface
- ❑ The default interface

You've actually seen some of the code we'll need already, but let's go through it again in more formal style, this time relating it directly to a coded project.

The IFarmYardAnimal User-Defined Interface

As we saw from our consumer diagrams, `IFarmYardAnimal` is an interface that all of our animal objects will implement. It contains the basic `Eat` and `Sleep` methods, plus the `Name` and `Age` properties. Let's fire up Visual Basic and get coding!

1. Start by creating a new ActiveX DLL project. When you do this, you'll notice that Visual Basic automatically adds a class to the project; this is because a COM server (a DLL or EXE that contains COM components) that doesn't contain any COM components wouldn't be much use!

2. Open the Project Properties dialog and enter a Project Name and a Project Description like this:

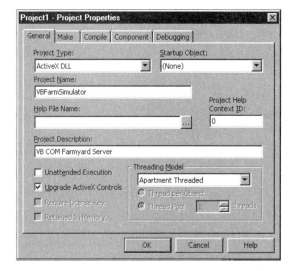

> The name of the project is very important because not only is it used to identify the server, but also it will show up in the **References** dialog, based on the name you give the project. I'll have more to say on the subject of this dialog before the end of the chapter.

3. Change the name of the default class to `IFarmYardAnimal`, as this is what we'll be using to define our custom interface. The Project window should now look like this:

4. Next, we need to tell Visual Basic that the `IFarmYardAnimal` class is actually an interface that will be implemented by other classes. Visual Basic does not differentiate between the definitions of classes and interfaces. Both are defined as classes, but interfaces do not have any implementation code – they are abstract classes, as I explained earlier. To indicate that the class is being used to define an interface, change the Instancing property to PublicNotCreatable. This will prevent anybody from using the New keyword against our class – after all, it doesn't make much sense to allow people to create an instance of it when there's no implementation.

5. The next step is to define the properties and methods of our interface. You've seen most of this code before, so add the following to the class's code window:

```
Option Explicit

Public Sub Sleep()
End Sub

Public Sub Eat()
End Sub

Public Property Let Name(ByVal vData As String)
End Property

Public Property Get Name() As String
End Property

Public Property Let Age(ByVal vData As Integer)
End Property

Public Property Get Age() As Integer
End Property
```

Believe it or not, that's it! We've created a COM interface; what we need now is a component to implement it.

Creating a Component to Use the Interface

Now that we have defined our interface, let's create a coclass (component) that will implement it. Here are the steps you need to go through.

1. Add a new class module and change its Name property to CCow.

2. Bring up the code window for the new class and add the following line:

```
Implements IFarmYardAnimal
```

3. This informs Visual Basic that our component implements the IFarmYardAnimal interface. If you try to compile the project using the File | Make VBFarmSimulator.dll option at this stage, you will be prompted with the following message box:

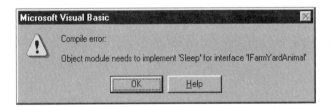

Visual Basic is complaining because we've said that the class implements the IFarmYardAnimal interface, and yet we haven't provided an implementation for it. Notice, though, how Visual Basic is using the word 'interface' in the message. It knows exactly what we're up to!

4. Go back into Visual Basic and click on the left combo box within the source window for the CCow class. You will see that there is an entry for our interface:

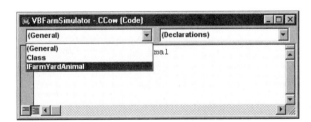

5. Select IFarmYardAnimal, and then click on the right combo box. Visual Basic will show all the methods and properties of the selected interface that we have to implement in our CCow class:

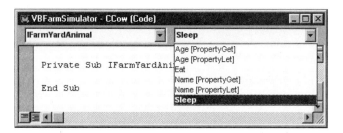

6. Click on each entry in the right combo box in turn, and Visual Basic will create the prototypes for the methods and properties necessary to implement the interface. The Visual Basic code for our class will now look like this:

```
Option Explicit

Implements IFarmYardAnimal

Private Property Let IFarmYardAnimal_Age(ByVal RHS As Integer)
End Property

Private Property Get IFarmYardAnimal_Age() As Integer
End Property

Private Sub IFarmYardAnimal_Eat()
End Sub

Private Property Let IFarmYardAnimal_Name(ByVal RHS As String)
End Property

Private Property Get IFarmYardAnimal_Name() As String
End Property

Private Sub IFarmYardAnimal_Sleep()
End Sub
```

7. The only real point worth making about this code is that Visual Basic has declared all of the methods and properties as `Private`. This is done to enforce usage of the `IFarmYardAnimal` interface to access them. If the methods were not private then it would be possible to break the defined semantics of our coclass from within Visual Basic by writing code like this:

```
Dim Betty as New CCow
Betty.Sleep
```

This is very bad practice, and you should avoid doing it in your own programs. This code breaks the defined semantics of our object, because it implies that the `Sleep` method is a part of the `CCow` class interface. We will see how to access the `Sleep` method properly shortly.

8. Now that we've implemented the methods for the interface, we could compile the project without any errors. We've written a complete COM component that supports the IFarmYardAnimal interface and any other programming language or application that supports COM can now use it. Obviously, the component we have created is not much use as it stands because there is no implementation, but it does demonstrate the most important principles of COM: components and interfaces.

Let's finish our CCow class by adding some implementation for the Sleep method, and a method that's particular to this class, Moo. Change the code like so:

```
Private Sub IFarmYardAnimal_Sleep()
    MsgBox "The Cow Sleeps..."
End Sub

Public Sub Moo
    MsgBox "Moo!"
End Sub
```

When either of these methods are called, they simply display a message box. Although not particularly useful, they will give us a visual indication when our methods are being called successfully.

9. Finally, compile the DLL. This causes Visual Basic to create and register the COM server that contains our coclass and its interfaces.

Default Interfaces

It's not obvious from the code written so far, but we've actually implemented *two* interfaces on our component, not counting the interfaces that a class inherits by default through Visual Basic (see the next section). A lollipop diagram for our CCow coclass would look something like this:

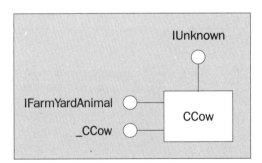

The _CCow interface is called the **default interface** of the coclass. Whenever you declare a class in Visual Basic, you're *actually* declaring a COM interface and providing the implementation in one go. This interface is constructed from the public members of the class; in our case this is just the Moo method. As usual, Visual Basic is hiding awkward details and making the process easier for you. This implicitly defined interface has the same name as the class itself, prefixed with an underscore.

Visual Basic is a little bit sneaky in situations like this. Whenever the name of an interface begins with an underscore, you don't actually need to type it, so when you declare a variable like this:

```
Dim Cow As CCow
```

You're *really* declaring it like this:

```
Dim Cow As _CCow
```

> **All** interfaces in Visual Basic are implicitly prefixed with an underscore. If you hadn't already guessed, most interfaces (excluding the default interface) also start with an 'I' for interface.

If you've ever accessed a component in Visual Basic using the `Object` variable type, what you're doing is accessing the methods and properties of its default interface. So, when you write code like this, Visual Basic assumes that the `Moo` method is a part of the default interface for the component `CCow`:

```
Dim Cow As Object
Set Cow = New CCow
Cow.Moo
```

To be more precise, the methods are accessed using the `IDispatch` *interface. This interface provides a dynamic mechanism for accessing the methods and properties of an interface. This type of access is known as 'late binding'. It is slower than using the interface directly, which is known as 'early binding'. We will discuss this in more detail in the next chapter.*

Other Interfaces Added by Visual Basic

When you create a component using Visual Basic, there are a number of interfaces that are added on your behalf. You can use the OLEView tool that Microsoft provides with Visual Studio to create an instance of our component and look at all the interfaces it supports:

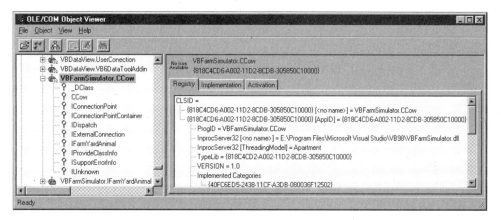

OLEView will only show interfaces that are listed under the registry key
HKEY_CLASSES_ROOT/Interface. *You can find details on obtaining and using OLEView in Appendix A.*

As you can see, our component actually supports *ten* interfaces! Where did the other eight come from? Well, Visual Basic is designed to allow developers to focus on application development and business problems. It shields you from these low level implementation details, unlike other languages such as C++, where they are exposed. The COM support in Visual Basic adds a myriad of **standard interfaces** for you behind the scenes, and a couple of **custom interfaces** depending upon the type of the component. If we were to compile an ActiveX control and look at its interfaces, we'd find that Visual Basic had implemented 25 interfaces for us!

> **A standard interface is one that's defined by Microsoft. A custom interface is an interface that's defined by a third party – and that includes you.**

Because Visual Basic takes care of their implementation for us, you'll be pleased to know that in order to use them you don't actually have to know what all these interfaces do. We will, however, come across some of them again later in the book, and I shall go further into their purpose when we do so.

Do We Need So Many Interfaces?

Although Visual Basic has implemented eight additional interfaces, they are not all actually necessary for our COM component. If we were writing it in C++, we could get away with just having IUnknown, IDispatch, IFarmYardAnimal and CCow. Visual Basic adds all the extra interfaces because it doesn't know exactly what you're going to need – it makes its best guess.

Visual Basic does exhibit *some* intelligence over the interfaces it adds to your component, and you can have some influence as well. If you were to go back to the Properties window for the CCow class and set the Persistable property to 1 – Persistable, you would find that Visual Basic adds the interfaces IPersist, IPersistPropertyBag, IPersistStream and IPersistInitStream. You would also find that the _DClass interface is replaced by _DPersistableClass. Once again, we don't actually *need* all of these interfaces to **persist** our component (that is, save its state to some kind of permanent storage), but because Visual Basic doesn't know what applications (containers) your component is going to be used in, it supports all the most common interfaces.

Fortunately, having support for so many interfaces doesn't effect the overall size of your component. Our compiled farm simulator DLL is 24k. Creating an identical project using C++ would result in a similarly sized DLL. So where's the catch? Why would anybody use C++, which takes longer to develop with? The answer is outright performance and a library called MSVBVM60.DLL.

Every project that is compiled with Visual Basic needs this DLL. If your components were to be downloaded over the Internet, you would have to place this DLL in the .cab file to ensure that your component would run. That sounds reasonable, but MSVBVM60.DLL is 1.34 megabytes in size! With a C++ component, we can get away with no dependencies at all, although in doing so the size does increase to 34k. The moral of the story is that as usual, C++ provides a finer granularity of control at the cost of more complexity, while Visual Basic makes it easier at the cost of size and some performance.

Creating a Consumer for the Component

It's about time we built some client code so that we can see our farmyard components in action. I've chosen an EXE project to test our component from another Visual Basic application because it's good for demonstration purposes, but you could equally well use any of the other project types supported by Visual Basic.

1. Start a new Standard EXE project. Using the Project | References... menu item, bring up the References dialog and locate the entry for our farmyard simulator:

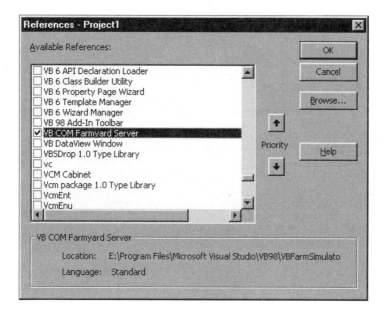

Notice how the entry in the dialog is described using the project description, and not simply the project name.

2. Add a command button to the form and implement the Click event handler like this:

```
Private Sub Command1_Click()

    Dim Cow1 As CCow
    Dim FarmAnimal As IFarmYardAnimal

    Set Cow1 = New CCow
    Cow1.Moo

    Set FarmAnimal = Cow1
    FarmAnimal.Sleep

    Set Cow1 = Nothing
    Set FarmAnimal = Nothing

End Sub
```

3. Run the project and click the button you've added. You should see two message boxes, indicating that the component has been successfully created and our methods called:

The code here is quite simplistic, and we'll discuss the COM actions that we can't see happening in the next section. But before we do, we should cover exactly what was happening with the References dialog.

Type Libraries

When we used the References dialog to add a reference so that our client could use our CCow component, we were not referencing the coclass, or even the object, but something I mentioned earlier in the chapter: the **type library**. A type library is the mechanism by which components within a COM server are described to the consumers of that server. It is a simple database that contains a list of what components, interfaces, enumerations and structures are available inside a COM server, and it's generated for you by Visual Basic when a COM project is compiled.

Type libraries are themselves recorded in the registry, under HKEY_CLASSES_ROOT/ TypeLib.

By referencing the type library, we are also enabling Visual Basic's IntelliSense, allowing us to browse the server's objects and methods using the Object Browser:

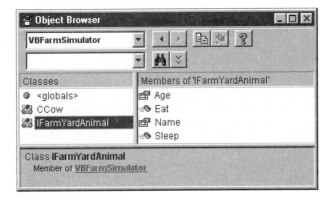

Strictly speaking, we are actually looking at class and interface definitions, so the name of the Object Browser is a little misleading. Also, you won't see the default interfaces as the leading underscore marks them as being hidden.

Behind the Scenes of our Component

Now that we have completed a working component, let's discuss the code we've just written in order to understand the COM that's involved.

Step 1 - Declaring Variables

The first two lines declare two variables for holding references to the two interfaces that our component supports:

```
Dim Cow1 As CCow
Dim FarmAnimal As IFarmYardAnimal
```

These lines read IIDs for the `CCow` and `IFarmYardAnimal` interfaces from the type library.

Step 2 - Instantiating a Component

The next line of code creates an instance of your component, and assigns the default interface to the `Cow1` variable:

```
Set Cow1 = New CCow
```

This one line of code actually requires a lot of work from COM. It uses two major services of the **COM runtime** that I mentioned in the previous chapter: **location** (finding an instance of the `CCow` component to work with) and **creation** (creating an instance of it to use).

Location

The COM runtime locates servers using the system registry, which includes amid the vast quantity of information it contains a list of all COM components within the system. You can view this data store by running a utility called RegEdit from the Run dialog of the Start menu:

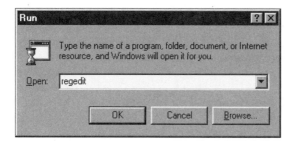

> You should always be very careful when running this utility; always make sure you know exactly what you're doing. Make a mistake, and you can render your whole system inoperable.

The mechanism used for locating a component works like an address book. The location of a component can be found by looking up the component under the HKEY_CLASSES_ROOT\CLSID key; this then provides information about the location of the DLL, etc.

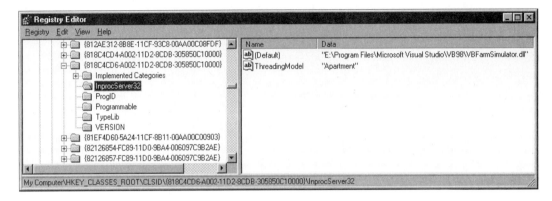

In fact, when you create an object in Visual Basic by using the New keyword, Visual Basic implicitly knows the CLSID for the component from the coclass defined in the type library. The line of code:

```
Set Cow1 = New CCow
```

Would actually be converted and implemented by the Visual Basic runtime as something like:

```
Set Cow1 = New {818C4CD6-A002-11D2-8CDB-305850C10000}
```

You can find more information about COM and the registry in Appendix A.

Creation

Once the COM runtime has located a server, it will ensure that it is running (loading it if necessary) before creating an instance of the requested component. The process is quite complex, and really beyond the scope of this book. For now, all you need to know is that the process of locating the server is handled by the **Service Control Manager (SCM)** of the COM runtime.

As part of the component creation process, we have to specify which of the component's interfaces we are interested in using first. In the line of code above, assigning the result of the New operation to our Cow1 variable results in Visual Basic asking for the default interface, _CCow.

The final piece of COM activity going on is that the reference count of the server is increased by one thanks to an implicit call to the AddRef function of IUnknown.

The process of calling the Moo method (which is the next line of code) is the same as calling the Sleep method, so we'll leave the discussion on calling methods until we reach that line.

Step 3 - Assigning a Variable

Once we have created the `Cow1` object, we assign the variable that references it to a second variable, `FarmAnimal`. This causes Visual Basic to ask the object for its `IFarmYardAnimal` interface by passing in the IID of that interface. In fact, as you may have realized, under the covers a call is being made to the `QueryInterface` function of the object's `IUnknown` interface. As our object supports `IFarmYardAnimal`, `QueryInterface` passes back a reference to it, and this returned reference is then assigned to our variable:

```
Set FarmAnimal = Cow1
```

If we tried to assign our `Cow1` variable to another variable that was defined as an interface that our component *doesn't* support – say, `IPig` – Visual Basic would raise an error and (assuming we have not implemented any error handling) show this dialog:

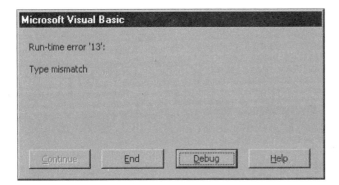

This dialog is not as friendly or descriptive as it could be, but we can hope for better things in the future. In the meantime, if you see a dialog like this one while you're developing your own programs, at least you now know what it means.

Once again, the single line of Visual Basic code we're considering here also implies a call to `AddRef` to increase the reference count, because we have handed out another interface pointer that needs to be kept track of.

Step 4 - Calling a Method

Now that our `FarmAnimal` variable holds a reference to the `IFarmYardAnimal` interface, or rather, a pointer to the `IFarmYardAnimal` vtable, we can call the methods defined by the function pointers in the vtable. In this case, we want to call the `Sleep` method:

```
FarmAnimal.Sleep
```

What's really going on here is that we are using the `IFarmYardAnimal` vtable to look up the location in memory of the method on our object. Once the location has been discovered, we can then call the method and the message box will be displayed.

Step 5 - Releasing an Object

Finally in this example, we are explicitly releasing the object by setting the references to `Nothing`:

```
Set Cow1 = Nothing
Set FarmAnimal = Nothing
```

With these lines, the `Release` function of the object's `IUnknown` interface is being called twice. Because each call reduces the reference count by one, the count will be reduced to zero and the object will destroy itself.

In fact, it is not strictly necessary to code these lines because Visual Basic will handle the destruction of our object when it goes out of scope – that is, when the `Click` event handler finishes. However, it's good programming practice to destroy our objects when we have finished with them, especially when their scope is potentially much greater than it is here.

Interface Versioning

Before we conclude our discussion on the underlying COM architecture, let's consider one more important aspect of interface-based programming. Earlier in the chapter, I stated that an interface is the contract between a consumer and a component. Once the interface has been published, it should be considered immutable – its methods and properties should never change. What then do you do if you need to add functionality to your interface once it has been released? The answer is that you write a *new* interface that incorporates this additional functionality, assign it a new IID (actually, Visual Basic does this bit for you), and add support for this new interface to future versions of your component.

If we consider our earlier consumer diagram, you could imagine a situation in which version 1.0 of our farm simulator has been released, but when we release version 2.0 we want to add a new method to our component. Without breaking our 1.0 installations, we could add another interface:

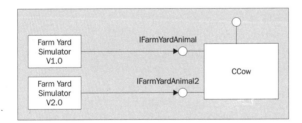

Adding the new interface is simply a matter of duplicating the steps we performed earlier in the chapter. To keep our example simple, `IFarmYardAnimal2` will have just one method called `Sing`.

1. Reopen the `VBFarmSimulator` project, add a new class module called `IFarmYardAnimal2`, and set its **Instancing** property to **PublicNotCreatable**:

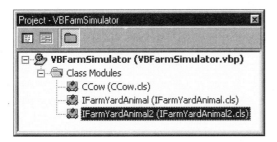

2. As before, this class contains no implementation, so simply define the method like so:

```
Option Explicit

Public Sub Sing()
End Sub
```

A more suitable name for the new interface would probably be `ISingingAnimal`. *The name of an interface should generally reflect the functionality of the methods it exposes.*

3. Next, open the `CCow` class and add our new interface to it by using the `Implements` keyword:

```
Option Explicit

Implements IFarmYardAnimal
Implements IFarmYardAnimal2
```

4. Pull down the list box on the left and select **IFarmYardAnimal2**. This will create the definition for the `Sing` method. Add the following implementation and recompile the DLL. This will also add our new interface into the type library.

```
Private Sub IFarmYardAnimal2_Sing()
    MsgBox "lah lah lah"
End Sub
```

We can now modify our version 2.0 farm simulator client to use both interfaces, and make our cow "sleep" using `IFarmYardAnimal`, and "sing" using `IFarmYardAnimal2`.

1. Open the client project and add the following lines of code:

```
Private Sub Command1_Click()

    Dim Cow1 As CCow
    Dim FarmAnimal As IFarmYardAnimal
    Dim FarmAnimal2 As IFarmYardAnimal2

    Set Cow1 = New CCow
    Cow1.Moo

    Set FarmAnimal = Cow1
    FarmAnimal.Sleep

    Set FarmAnimal2 = Cow1
    FarmAnimal2.Sing

    Set Cow1 = Nothing
    Set FarmAnimal = Nothing
    Set FarmAnimal2 = Nothing

End Sub
```

We don't need to change the project's references, because the type library we're using is the same as the one in the previous example. It has simply been updated with information about the new interface.

2. If you run the project now, after the message box about the cow sleeping, you will see the following message box:

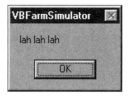

All that's going on here is that `QueryInterface` is passing out a reference to the `IFarmYardAnimal2` vtable, which we're then using to find the location in memory of the `Sing` method, and to call it. Finally, we're being good and releasing the reference.

Summary

Phew! We've come a long way in this short chapter, and the knowledge you have learned here should stand you in good stead for the rest of your programming career.

We began with a quick recap of objects and object-oriented theory, and then progressed to see how these principles are incorporated into COM. After that, we started a long dark journey into the underbelly of COM, and in particular the interface, which is really what COM is all about. Once we'd explored the murky depths of COM interfaces, we then looked at how they apply to Visual Basic and the components we create.

Through the use of the farmyard simulator, I hope you got an idea of the simplicity of using COM and its interfaces in Visual Basic. At the same time, however, I hope you were able to appreciate just how much is really going on beneath the smooth surface that Visual Basic provides.

Throughout the rest of the book we will be discussing the COM implications of the programming decisions that we make. However, to truly understand these ramifications we need to have some idea of how COM is behaving transparently behind our VB code. This chapter may have seemed complex and even a little scary, which is not really surprising, as we introduced a lot of new concepts. We will be coming back to some of these concepts again and again throughout the following chapters so a clear understanding will be vital.

Now that we have a grasp of the underlying COM architecture and mechanisms we can begin to build to explore how to utilize this knowledge in the Visual Basic applications that we write.

Looking ahead, the next chapters will discuss the tools that we can use to create and enhance our Visual Basic COM components. Also, we will be helping poor Phil with his difficulties, and trying to create some components that address the business issues he faces.

VB COM

3

Automation

Overview

We now turn our attention to **Automation**. Automation is a COM-based technology within Microsoft products such as Visual Basic and Excel. This means that Automation objects are COM objects; they have all the features that we have discussed in Chapter 2. The definition of Automation according to the Visual Basic 6.0 Help File is: A technology that enables applications to provide objects in a consistent way to other applications, development tools, and macro languages. A better definition is:

> **Automation allows an application to programmatically manipulate another, through a set of well-defined interfaces.**

That's easy to remember, isn't it? There is a lot more involved in Automation and we will be covering it in this chapter. We will discuss:

- ❑ Calling upon Automation objects using Visual Basic
- ❑ The concept of early and late binding and how it effects Automation
- ❑ Using events of an Automation component to provide feedback
- ❑ Describing and defining an object model
- ❑ Using Visual Basic to control Microsoft Excel

In this chapter we will see how Phil, our overworked project manager, will use Visual Basic to create a Microsoft Excel report. Not only will Phil be able to create a report in Microsoft Excel using Visual Basic, but he will also be able to use the features included in Microsoft Excel such as the Chart Wizard.

So after reading this chapter you will be able to see exactly how to use Visual Basic to call upon the rich features that other applications expose for your use through the "magic" of COM.

Microsoft Excel and Visual Basic

One of the most widely used applications is Microsoft Excel. Microsoft Excel, a spreadsheet program, allows users to not only easily display data in a columnar or row format, but also allows a user to perform calculations and graphs with built-in wizards.

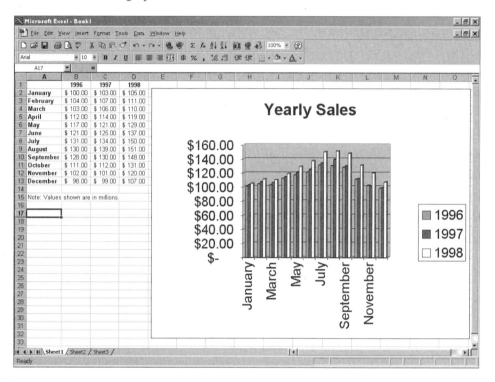

Millions of users of Microsoft Excel spend as much time using the application as you do programming in Visual Basic. Microsoft Excel has surpassed Lotus 1-2-3 as the most widely used spreadsheet application on the market. It is a very productive tool that can provide investment bankers with financial information or help grandma keep track of the dues gathered for her bridge club. Its uses are endless.

So what does Microsoft Excel have to do with Visual Basic?

There are two answers to that question. The first is that Microsoft Excel has **Visual Basic for Applications**, commonly referred to as **VBA**, built right into the product. VBA *is* the Visual Basic language. The difference between them being that the Integrated Development Environment (IDE) in Visual Basic allows programmers to create stand-alone applications and other features. In fact, all the applications in Office 97 have VBA built into them. You can think of Office applications as VBA + program-specific macros. VBA allows the Microsoft Excel developer to create applications within Microsoft Excel. The following screen shot shows the VBA development environment. To see this from within Microsoft Excel, go to the Tools menu and select Macro and Visual Basic Editor.

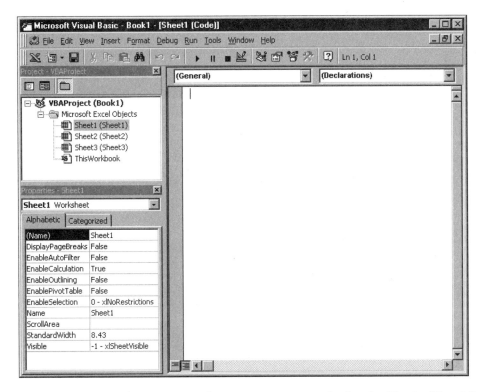

As you can see, the Visual Basic for Applications environment looks a lot like the Visual Basic environment. If you are familiar with Visual Basic it will be quite easy for you to create Microsoft Office applications. In addition, you get all the great features that Visual Basic is known for, such as:

❑   Easy form generation
❑   IntelliSense technology
❑   Event-driven programming
❑   Debugging tools

Visual Basic for Applications has been implemented in more than a hundred applications on the market today. Companies such as Micrografx, Visio, and Cognos have licensed Visual Basic for Applications into their products. This allows developers to create their own custom applications based upon the rich features that these package applications expose to the development environment.

The second answer to the question asked previously is that we can use Visual Basic to call upon the functionality of Microsoft Excel and manipulate Excel objects from our own Visual Basic code. Why would we want to do this? More than once I have been approached by someone with a Microsoft Excel spreadsheet in hand asking if there is any way to automate the process of getting data into Microsoft Excel spreadsheets without having to manually input the data. This data might come from a database such as customer information or financial information, which can be very time-consuming to have to put in by hand. Why not create a Visual Basic application that will take the data out of the database and put it into a spreadsheet for the managers to look at instead of doing it manually?

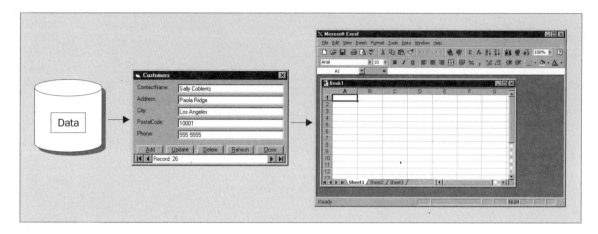

Think about it. Microsoft has spent a lot of money, research, development and testing on Microsoft Excel. With Visual Basic, you can use all the functions that have been exposed to you in Microsoft Excel. We can add data, calculate percentages or averages, create charts and graphs, and do just about anything else we desire that Microsoft Excel can do.

A Quick Example

Is using all the functionality of Microsoft Excel easy to do from Visual Basic or does it require complicated API calls and hooks into the Windows Messaging system? No, it is quite simple. Let's create a very simple application that will take input from a Visual Basic application and store it in Microsoft Excel.

Simple Automation Application

1. With all instances of Microsoft Excel closed, start up Visual Basic and choose the Standard EXE option.

2. Draw three text boxes and a command button on `Form1`. Set the `Name` and `Caption/Text` properties according to the following table:

Object	Name	Text/Caption
Text1	`txtName`	Leave blank.
Text2	`txtDepartment`	Leave blank.
Text3	`txtID`	Leave blank.
Command1	`cmdExcelSend`	&Put into Excel.

Your form should look like this:

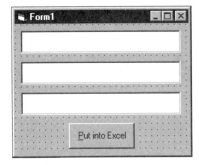

3. Since we want to use Microsoft Excel, we need to set a reference to it within Visual Basic. Select Project from the Visual Basic menu and choose References… Choose the Microsoft Excel 8.0 Object Library, this is the object library used by Microsoft Excel 97.

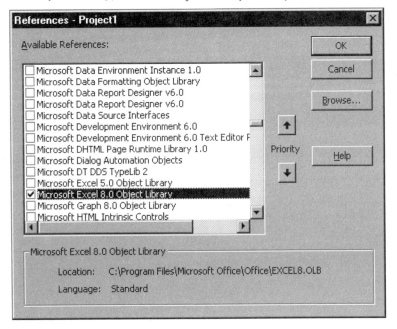

4. Double-click the command button on the form we created and enter the following code:

```
Private Sub cmdExcelSend_Click()

' Declare the object variables.
  Dim objExcel As Excel.Application
  Dim objWorkbook As Excel.Workbook
  Dim objSheet As Excel.Worksheet

  Set objExcel = CreateObject("Excel.Application")

' So we can see our Excel instance.
  objExcel.Visible = True
```

```
Set objWorkbook = objExcel.Workbooks.Add
Set objSheet = objWorkbook.Worksheets.Add
objSheet.Cells(1, 1) = "Witness the power of COM Automation!"
objSheet.Cells(2, 1) = txtName
objSheet.Cells(2, 2) = txtDepartment
objSheet.Cells(2, 3) = txtID

End Sub
```

5. Save your form as `Employee.frm` and your project as `ExcelExample.vbp`.

6. Now run the application. Put a name in the first text box, a department in the second, and an ID in the third and click the <u>P</u>ut into Excel button:

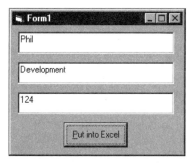

7. The Excel spreadsheet should look like this:

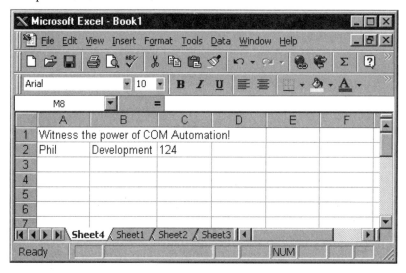

Although this is a simplistic example and in no way complete (no developer would ever think about omitting error handling in their code, would they?) it shows how easy it is to use Visual Basic to talk to Microsoft Excel.

Automation

As we discussed at the beginning of this chapter, Automation allows one application to manipulate another. We can do this with Automation because it is a COM-based technology.

A COM component that makes Automation objects available to other applications is known as an **Automation server**. The application or programming tool (such as Visual Basic) that accesses the Automation objects provided by the Automation server is known as the **Automation controller**. An **Automation object** is just an application's object that is exposed for access by other applications.

Calling an Automation Server

In our quick example earlier, we used just one method of calling upon the services of our Microsoft Excel Automation server. In the example, the assumption was that Microsoft Excel was not running. What would have happened if it had been? In this section, I will show you the different methods that we can use to handle these sorts of issues.

Setting a Reference to the Type Library

The first thing that should be done is to set a reference to the type library that we are going to use. In our quick example, we were able to set this using our References dialog within Visual Basic. This helps our application to find the type library that we specify. It is important that we specify this because when we try to declare an object variable based on a class such as `Excel.Application` without setting the reference we get a compiler error when we run the code.

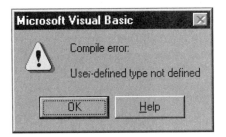

The References dialog lists **type libraries**. The possible filename extensions of which include `.dll`, `.exe`, `.ocx`, `.olb` and `.tlb`. Any type libraries that you have created yourself using Visual Basic will be either `.exe` or `.dll`. Type libraries are files that describe an object in a standardized format so that COM clients can find which properties and methods of an object are supported. An obvious benefit of this to us as Visual Basic programmers is that when we choose a type library from the References dialog, we can now use the IntelliSense and QuickInfo technology built into Visual Basic. These tools enable the developer to get a drop-down list of properties and methods of an object that is being used while coding:

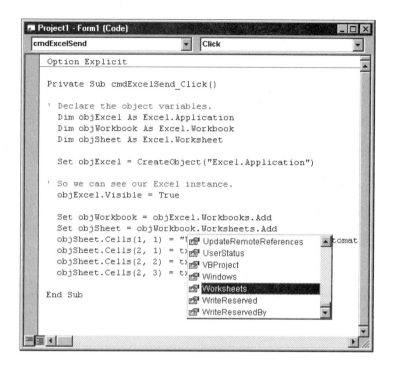

```
Project1 - Form1 (Code)
cmdExcelSend                              Click

   Option Explicit

   Private Sub cmdExcelSend_Click()

   ' Declare the object variables.
      Dim objExcel As Excel.Application
      Dim objWorkbook As Excel.Workbook
      Dim objSheet As Excel.Worksheet

      Set objExcel = CreateObject("Excel.Application")

   ' So we can see our Excel instance.
      objExcel.Visible = True

      Set objWorkbook = objExcel.Workbooks.Add
      Set objSheet = objWorkbook.Worksheets.Add
      objSheet.Cells(1, 1) = "     UpdateRemoteReferences        tomat
      objSheet.Cells(2, 1) = t     UserStatus
      objSheet.Cells(2, 2) = t     VBProject
      objSheet.Cells(2, 3) = t     Windows
                                   Worksheets
   End Sub                         WriteReserved
                                   WriteReservedBy
```

Priority

What happens when two or more type libraries are using the same class name that you have chosen in the References dialog? The Priority buttons on the References dialog are a solution. When you create an object in your Visual Basic code, Visual Basic goes to the references that are chosen and looks at them in the order they are in the list from top to bottom. Therefore, if two type libraries have the same class name, Visual Basic will choose the first one it finds in the list with that class name.

To avoid having to use the priority buttons to specify rank, it is best to just explicitly declare which type library to use. Look at this code:

```
' Declare an object variable.
Dim objExcel as Application
```

```
' Declare an object variable explicitly.
Dim objExcel as Excel.Application
```

In the first line of code, we do not specify the library (in this case Excel), just the class we are trying to access (Application). In the second line we are declaring an object variable using both the library and the class name. By declaring it this way, there is no confusion as to which type library we are asking to get a pointer to the Application class.

It is much preferable to explicitly declare which type library to use than to set up the priority in the References dialog. Not explicitly declaring the library can lead to problems if there are ambiguous references made to multiple type libraries.

Browsing Objects

Through the References dialog, we can specify type libraries, which provide access to COM components. Since Visual Basic uses these type libraries as a map to these COM objects, how can we look and see what these objects are made up of? The answer is the **Object Browser**. To use the Object Browser within Visual Basic, you can either choose it from the View menu or press the F2 key. The Object Browser allows the Visual Basic developer to view the properties, methods, constants, and events that are associated with the interfaces of the class.

Let's view the objects that are provided to us by Microsoft Excel. With your copy of `ExcelExample.vbp` loaded into the Visual Basic IDE, press F2. From the drop-down combo box in the left-hand corner of the Object Browser, select Excel:

On the left side of the explorer-style Object Browser is a listing of the global constants, enumerations, structures, interfaces and the classes in our Automation server. Select Application and a list of the properties, methods, and events of the `Application` class is shown in the right-hand pane. The pane at the bottom shows the library (in this case Excel) that the selected item belongs to. If you have a function or subroutine selected, it would show the parameters of the routine and their type and may also include a description if the designer of the object added one.

This is a great way to find out what makes up an object. I have been able to figure out how to control other COM-enabled applications just by creating a reference to the application's library and using the Object Browser to find what properties, events, and methods are available to me. There is one caveat about the Object Browser in that it does not display object models in a hierarchical manner. We will touch on this later in the chapter.

Declaring an Object Variable

In our quick example, we had to declare a variable to hold a reference to our object.

```
' Declare the object variables.
Dim objExcel As Excel.Application
```

Here we have our variable `objExcel` and we are giving it the type `Excel.Application`. `Excel.Application` consists of two parts, the library name and the class name. `Excel` is the library name and `Application` is the class we are going to use. We are explicitly typing what object we are going to use.

Do we have to do it this way? No. We could declare our object variable as a generic `Object` type.

```
' Declare the object variable as a generic Object.
Dim objExcel as Object
```

Now we could assign this object variable to any object we like. Shouldn't we do this always? Doesn't this give us a lot of flexibility? The answer is that it depends.

When an object is declared using the `Object` type, it is considered to be **late binding**. When we explicitly give Visual Basic the type it needs as we did previously, this is referred to as **early binding**. Early binding is a lot quicker than late binding. We will discuss these concepts more, later in the chapter.

Assigning a Reference to a Variable

So now we have two things: A reference to the type library we want to use and an object variable that will contain our object. We have not yet assigned an object reference to our variable. To do this we can either use the `CreateObject` or `GetObject` command or use the `New` keyword command.

CreateObject

The `CreateObject` function allows you to create an instance of the server you are calling. In our quick example, we used the `CreateObject` function to create our object and assign a reference to the object variable that was declared:

```
Set objExcel = CreateObject("Excel.Application")
```

The `Set` statement is responsible for assigning an object reference to a variable or property. `objExcel` is our object variable and the `CreateObject` function creates the instance of the Microsoft Excel `Application` class. The syntax of the `Set` statement is as follows:

```
Set objectvariable = CreateObject("progID",["servername"])
```

The **progID** (**programmatic identifier**) is the fully qualified class name that we are trying to use. Fully qualified means we are specifying not only the class but the type library too.

The servername is optional and specifies the name of network server where the object will be created. If it is on the same machine as the client, then we can just leave it blank. If we wanted our object to be created on another server in the network named Hatcher, we would specify `"Hatcher"` as the servername. If the server is unavailable, be sure to include error handling since the client will receive a runtime error.

GetObject

`GetObject` is used to assign a reference to a new or existing object in a `Set` statement. In our quick example, we assumed that Microsoft Excel was not running. But what would we do if it was running? We would want to use `GetObject` so that we could use the already running instance of Microsoft Excel. The syntax for the `GetObject` is very similar to `CreateObject`:

```
Set objectvariable = GetObject([pathname][,progID])
```

The **pathname** parameter specifies a file path to an existing file. If the pathname is not specified, `GetObject` acts like `CreateObject`, creating a new instance of the class. If the pathname is omitted, then a **progID** is mandatory and will be used to make the connection. It's worth noting here that creating the instance by simply using a pathname requires that the file being opened has been properly associated with the progID in the registry. If not, the `GetObject` will fail.

Therefore, we can access our Microsoft Excel application programmatically in three ways:

- ❑ If the component is running, when we specify just a pathname, it will open up the file. If the component is not running, Automation will determine the application to start and the object to activate based on the pathname specified. In the case of Excel, the instance of the parent application and the actual object (a workbook by default, although you can specify a different object by giving a progID) would both have a `Visible` property of `False`.

```
' GetObject using pathname.
Set objExcel = GetObject("C:\book1.xls")
```

- ❑ If we specify a progID with no pathname and the component is running, our object variable will reference the object. If the component is not running, a runtime error occurs.

```
' GetObject using progID with no pathname.
Set objExcel = GetObject(, "Excel.Application")
```

- ❑ If `GetObject` uses an empty string as its pathname parameter then it will return a new object if the component is running. If the component is not running, then the component is instantiated and will create a new object for us.

```
' GetObject using an empty string for pathname.
Set objExcel = GetObject("", "Excel.Application")
```

For future use, keep in mind that GetObject cannot be used to obtain a reference to a class created with Visual Basic.

New Keyword

We can also assign a reference to an object variable using the New keyword. With the New keyword, Visual Basic will create a new instance of our object the first time you use the object variable.

> **Using the New keyword creates some overhead in your application. Each time Visual Basic comes across a variable that has been declared using New it checks to see if an object reference has been assigned to it.**

Here's how we can create our Microsoft Excel object using the New keyword:

```
' Declare an object variable for Microsoft Excel.
Dim objExcel As Excel.Application
```

```
' Use the New keyword to create a new instance.
Set objExcel = New Excel.Application
```

Working with Properties

In our quick example, we had to insert the following line of code:

```
' So we can see our Excel instance.
objExcel.Visible = True
```

This code tells our instance of Microsoft Excel to become visible. If we did not include this line, our Visual Basic client application would have been fine but we would not see Microsoft Excel even though it is loaded and our application was able to run. Visible is a property of the Application object in Microsoft Excel. We are able to access properties of applications just like we explained in Chapter 2. objExcel is the object (or rather an instance of the Microsoft Excel Application class), Visible is the property and it can be passed a Boolean value which is either true or false.

Working with Methods

The syntax for methods is much like that for properties. For example, to quit the instance of our Microsoft Excel server, we could have written the following line of code:

```
' Quit Excel.
objExcel.Quit
```

Again, objExcel is our object and Quit is the method. With this method called from our Visual Basic application, the Quit method in the Application class would have been executed from Microsoft Excel.

Working with Events

Events allow the Visual Basic programmer to know when something has occurred. The `Click` event of a button is an example. When the `Click` event occurs, we can write code behind that event. This simply translates into: if something happens, do this. We can also use events that our Automation server generates. To do this, we first need to redo our declarations. In our quick example, instead of having our declarations within a subroutine, move them in the General Declarations section of the form as shown:

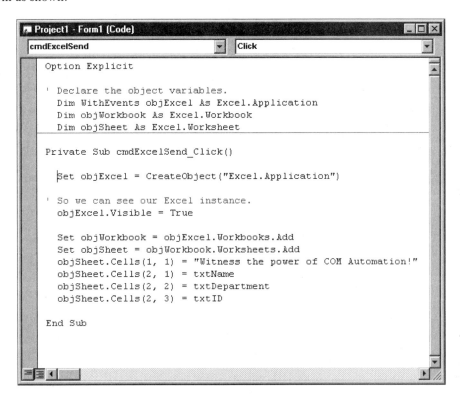

```
Option Explicit

' Declare the object variables.
    Dim WithEvents objExcel As Excel.Application
    Dim objWorkbook As Excel.Workbook
    Dim objSheet As Excel.Worksheet


Private Sub cmdExcelSend_Click()

    Set objExcel = CreateObject("Excel.Application")

' So we can see our Excel instance.
    objExcel.Visible = True

    Set objWorkbook = objExcel.Workbooks.Add
    Set objSheet = objWorkbook.Worksheets.Add
    objSheet.Cells(1, 1) = "Witness the power of COM Automation!"
    objSheet.Cells(2, 1) = txtName
    objSheet.Cells(2, 2) = txtDepartment
    objSheet.Cells(2, 3) = txtID


End Sub
```

Second, we need to declare our `objExcel` variable with the `WithEvents` keyword. `WithEvents` tells Visual Basic that the object variable will be used to respond to events triggered by our Automation object. Without this keyword, it is not possible to respond to events.

Once `WithEvents` is used with an object variable, you can click on the **Object** drop-down and see it listed there. The events that can be generated from the object you select are displayed in the right-side combo box:

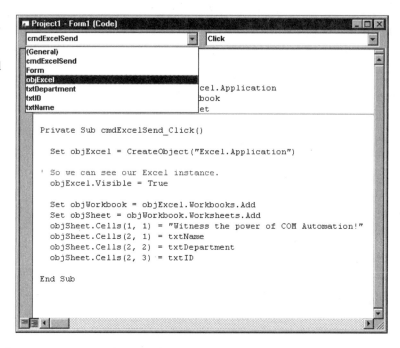

```
Private Sub cmdExcelSend_Click()

    Set objExcel = CreateObject("Excel.Application")

    ' So we can see our Excel instance.
    objExcel.Visible = True

    Set objWorkbook = objExcel.Workbooks.Add
    Set objSheet = objWorkbook.Worksheets.Add
    objSheet.Cells(1, 1) = "Witness the power of COM Automation!"
    objSheet.Cells(2, 1) = txtName
    objSheet.Cells(2, 2) = txtDepartment
    objSheet.Cells(2, 3) = txtID

End Sub
```

Now we can write code so that events generated in our Automation server create responses in our Automation client. Such as:

```
Private Sub objExcel_SheetCalculate(ByVal Sh As Object)

    MsgBox "Excel spreadsheet being calculated at this time."

End Sub
```

So when a sheet is being calculated in our Microsoft Excel Automation server, our Visual Basic application will display our message box.

You need to be aware though of two things when using the `WithEvents` statement. First, you cannot create arrays using `WithEvents`. Second, you cannot use the `New` keyword with `WithEvents` on the `Dim` line. Of course, you can still `Set` the variable `As New` if you wish.

Removing References

When we are done with our Microsoft Excel Automation server, can we simply call the `Excel.Quit` command and be done with it? No, we still have an object reference in our program in memory. To clear this is not very difficult. We simply set our object variable, `objExcel` equal to `Nothing`:

```
' Remove our object from memory.
Set objExcel = Nothing
```

It is a good idea to make sure that you set your object variable to `Nothing`. My first foray into Automation programming was with Microsoft Excel. I found that after I kept running my application over and over to test it that it got slower each time until finally my machine would crash. It wasn't soon after that I realized I was creating all these instances of Microsoft Excel behind the scenes and it was bogging down my machine. Take it from someone who has been there, get friendly with `Nothing`.

Now what if there is another client that is using the same Automation server? Will `Nothing` unallocate their reference to the Automation server? No, like we discussed in Chapter 2, the `QueryInterface` takes care of the reference counting and knows how to handle the `Nothing` keyword. Setting an object variable equal to `Nothing` calls the `Release` method of `IUnknown`. That is the beauty of COM; you can concern yourself with how to *do* something rather than how something is *done*.

Early vs. Late Binding

When we declared our object references, remember that there were two ways we could do it:

```
' Declare the object variables.
Dim objExcel As Excel.Application


' Declare the object variable as a generic Object.
Dim objExcel as Object
```

We then briefly touched upon the concept of binding. Binding is the way in which we set up our object references. We are binding an object variable to an object. We can actually enhance the performance of binding depending on which type we choose.

The code,

```
' Declare the object variables.
Dim objExcel As Excel.Application
```

is an example of early binding. Object variables that are dimmed as a qualified class of an object are called early bound object variables. What this means is that Visual Basic is able to detect the object's properties, methods, and events before our application is compiled. Since Visual Basic already knows where the object is based on the GUID and the registry and is aware of the interfaces of the object, it takes much less time for Visual Basic to bind to our Automation server.

When we declare object variable of type `Object`, this is considered late binding. Because we are using a generic `Object` type, Visual Basic does not know what we intend to use the object variable for. In our code we could write:

```
' Declare the object variable as a generic Object.
Dim objExcel as Object

Set objExcel = CreateObject("Excel.Application")
```

```
     objExcel.NotARealProperty = True      ' Can you say error?

     objExcel.Quit ·
     Set objExcel = Nothing
```

Notice the `objExcel.NotARealProperty` line. It will go ahead and compile, but once it gets to this line, we will receive a runtime error:

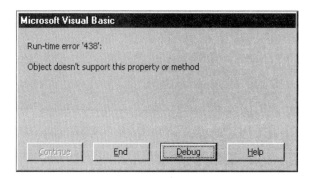

Late binding also keeps you from using the IntelliSense built into Visual Basic since it has no clue as to how you will use the object. In addition, late binding is slower than early binding.

As late binding is the slowest method to invoke the properties and methods of an object, you should only use it when it's unavoidable. For instance, you might have an object variable that is required to act on any one of several different classes of objects and you will not know which one to use until run-time. In this case, you should declare your variable `As Object`.

To understand how binding works at the COM level, we now have to turn our attention to the `IDispatch` interface.

IDispatch

The `IDispatch` interface provides information about the methods that an object supports and can execute them if required. In this way, the `IDispatch` interface is a fundamental part of Automation - it is the channel through which our Automation server and Automation controller communicate.

The `IDispatch` interface has a number of methods, but we shall only concern ourselves with two, `GetIDsOfNames` and `Invoke`.

GetIDsOfNames

The `GetIDsOfNames` method reads the name of a method and returns its **dispatch identifier** (commonly known as **DISPID**). A DISPID is an identification value for each method that can be called by the `Invoke` method.

Invoke

The Invoke method provides access to the properties and methods exposed by an object. Our Automation controller can pass the DISPID returned by GetIDsOfNames to Invoke to execute the required method of our object.

Late Binding and COM

The way we bind to an object in our VB code decides what happens behind the scenes with COM. For example, when we declare an object as keyword Object, the following occurs:

- ❑ The client gets a pointer to the IDispatch interface
- ❑ The client calls GetIDsOfNames, which returns a **DISPID**
- ❑ Once the client has gotten a valid DISPID, it can invoke a method using the Invoke function

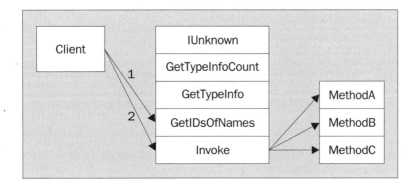

The reason why declaring an object using Object is slow is because for every method a call to GetIDsOfNames is required, since the client does not have access to a type library (even though you may have specified it in the **References** dialog in your Visual Basic project). Other languages such as C++ allow you to access the methods through a custom interface that supplies the methods for you, by directly calling the vtable that stores the methods.

Wouldn't it be nice if we could access those methods in whichever way we prefer?

Dual Interfaces

Dual Interfaces is the answer. Dual interfaces allow a server to expose an interface that exposes `IDispatch` and the methods in one interface. A dual interface as a combination of an `IDispatch` interface and a custom interface as shown below:

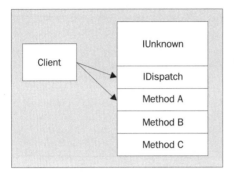

When Visual Basic creates ActiveX servers, it will always provide a dual interface for the object. Now clients that can call vtables directly such as C++ can use vtable calls and clients who prefer `IDispatch`, such as Visual Basic, can use `IDispatch` if they prefer.

Early Binding and COM

Let's go back to binding. Why is early binding faster than late binding? The reason is that when you create a client that uses early binding, you are packaging the DISPIDs within the executable you create. Therefore, there is no reason for the client to call `GetIDsOfNames` to gain the DISPIDs within the object. The client still has to use the `Invoke` method of the `IDispatch` interface to actually invoke the methods though.

Object Models

You have probably seen quite a few object model diagrams in the time you have been programming and may not have quite understood what you were looking at. Unfortunately, they are usually relegated to a page in the back of a programmer's guide in an Appendix. There are two types of object models: the logical models and the model diagrams. The logical object model is the hierarchical architecture of all the objects in an application and how they interact and depend on each other. Object model diagrams are visual representations of how an object model is implemented in an application.

Since applications can contain a many objects, these object models can be quite large. Just look at the object model diagram for Microsoft Excel:

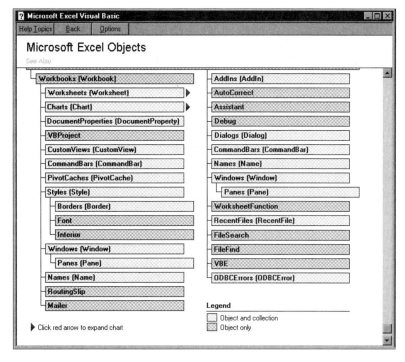

You can see that this is not all of it. The worksheets and charts objects can be expanded even further and the chart is larger than the one shown here. As you can see, Microsoft Excel has a very large object model.

Let's look at our quick example code to see how object models are implemented.

```
Private Sub cmdExcelSend_Click()

' Declare the object variables.
  Dim objExcel As Excel.Application
  Dim objWorkbook As Excel.Workbook
  Dim objSheet As Excel.Worksheet

  Set objExcel = CreateObject("Excel.Application")

' So we can see our Excel instance.
  objExcel.Visible = True

  Set objWorkbook = objExcel.Workbooks.Add
  Set objSheet = objWorkbook.Worksheets.Add
  objSheet.Cells(1, 1) = "Witness the power of COM Automation!"
  objSheet.Cells(2, 1) = txtName
  objSheet.Cells(2, 2) = txtDepartment
  objSheet.Cells(2, 3) = txtID

End Sub
```

After we have set our object variable to reference the `Excel.Application` class, we can look at the object model diagram for Microsoft Excel and see that we are currently at the top of the object model:

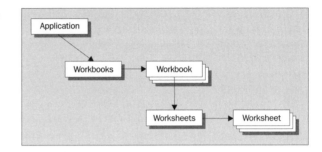

Now when we execute the line:

```
Set objWorkbook = objExcel.Workbooks.Add
```

We are at the `Workbooks` level where we now can create a `Workbook` by using the `Add` command. Then with the code:

```
Set objSheet = objWorkbook.Worksheets.Add
```

The `objSheet` variable now points to an Excel Worksheet where we can now work with the `Cells` objects. Could we have gone straight to our `Cells` objects instead of traversing through the hierarchy? No!

You may have noticed that there is a `Worksheets` object and a `Worksheet` object. The `Worksheets` object is an example of a **collection**. A collection is an object that holds a group of similar objects. Therefore, we can have multiple worksheets in our Microsoft Excel Automation server.

What if we want to go back up the hierarchy? There are two ways we can achieve this. First, there is the `Application` property. For example, let's say we are `Worksheets` level and we want to get back to the `Application`, we can do this by executing an `objSheet.Application` statement. If we want to just go up one level, we can use the parent property of the object. In this instance, `objSheet.Parent` would take us to the `Workbook` level.

Through object models and object model diagrams, we can see how the objects of an Automation server interact with each other. By understanding what object model diagrams represent and learning how to use them, you can quickly see how an Automation server is designed and what classes are available for you to implement.

Creating an Excel Spreadsheet with Visual Basic

Our industrious project manager Phil has been given a small task. A manager would like to take information entered for two years of data, have a chart that compares the two years of information and store it in a Microsoft Excel spreadsheet.

Phil mulls it over and realizes that he can use the benefits of COM Automation to provide a solution to the problem.

1. Start Visual Basic; making sure that Microsoft Excel is not loaded as before.

2. At the New Project dialog, select Standard EXE.

3. As before, set a reference to Microsoft Excel 8.0 Library and click OK.

4. Now we want to create the form to input the two years of data so let's begin by naming the form, `frmExcel`. On our `frmExcel` form, we need to create three control arrays. A **control array** is a group of controls that share the same name and type. In addition, control arrays do not take up as much resources as creating a distinct control for each instance. To create a control array, draw a text box on the form and change its `Name` property to `txt1997`. Now select the text box and copy it to the clipboard. Then click on the paste icon on the toolbar. When you do this, you will see the following message box:

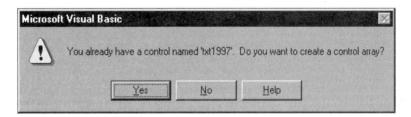

5. Select Yes. Now the original control is called `txt1997(0)` and the newly pasted one is called `txt1997(1)`. Create text boxes for each month of the year for 1997.

6. Now create another text box control array for the 1998 data. Name the first text box, `txt1998` and repeat the above procedure until you have twelve text boxes, `txt1998(0)` to `txt1998(11)`. Also, create a control array of twelve labels called `lblLabels` and change their `Caption` properties to the months of the year. Your form should now look like this:

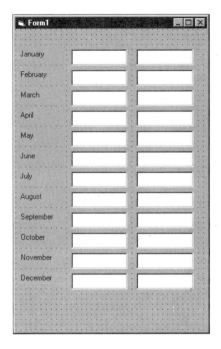

7. Next, create a command button on the form called `cmdExcel` and set the `Caption` property to `&Send to Excel`. Create two labels for our year headings and set their captions to 1997 and 1998. Your completed form should look like this:

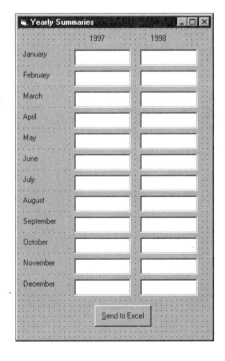

8. Make sure that you save the project. There's nothing more frustrating than getting the user interface just the way you want it and having to create it all over again because something happened.

9. Double-click on the <u>S</u>end to Excel button to bring up the code window for the `cmdExcel_Click` event and enter the following code:

```
Private Sub cmdExcel_Click()

   On Error GoTo ErrorHandler

   Screen.MousePointer = vbHourglass

' Object variable declarations.
   Dim objExcel As Excel.Application
   Dim objBook As Excel.Workbook
   Dim objSheet As Excel.Worksheet

   Dim intCount As Integer

' Create the object references.
   Set objExcel = New Excel.Application
   Set objBook = objExcel.Workbooks.Add
   Set objSheet = objExcel.Worksheets.Add

' Allow user to view spreadsheet.
   objExcel.Visible = True

' Set up titles.
   objSheet.Cells(1, 1) = "Months"
   objSheet.Cells(1, 2) = "1997"
   objSheet.Cells(1, 3) = "1998"

' Change the font attributes of the headers.
   objExcel.Range("A1: C1").Font.Bold = True
   objExcel.Range("A1: C1").Font.Size = 16
   objExcel.Range("A1: C1").Font.Shadow = True

' Seed data into Excel.
   For intCount = 1 To 12

      objSheet.Cells(intCount + 1, 1) = lblLabels(intCount - 1).Caption
      objSheet.Cells(intCount + 1, 2) = txt1997(intCount - 1).Text
      objSheet.Cells(intCount + 1, 3) = txt1998(intCount - 1).Text

   Next

   Screen.MousePointer = vbNormal

   Exit Sub

ErrorHandler:
   MsgBox CStr(Err.Number) & " - " & Err.Description
   Screen.MousePointer = vbNormal

End Sub
```

10. Save your project again and press the *F5* key to run it.

11. Type values into the text boxes for each year, then press the Send to Excel button. Once it is done, Microsoft Excel should be open and looking like this:

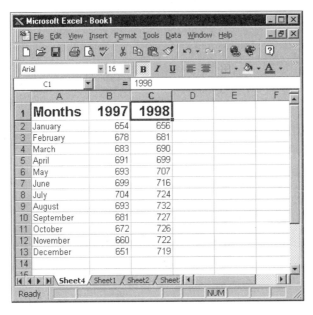

Notice that the data we got from Visual Basic is now in a new worksheet, Sheet4. This is because the value of Sheets in new workbook from the Options dialog was set to 3 on my machine. You can see this dialog box by going to Tools | Options:

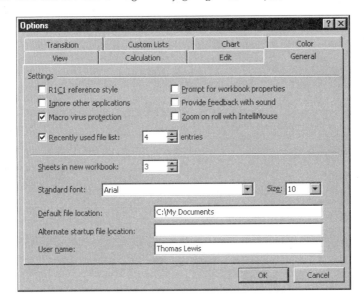

So What Did the Code Do?

We begin by declaring our object variables using the following code:

```
' Object variable declarations.
Dim objExcel As Excel.Application
Dim objBook As Excel.Workbook
Dim objSheet As Excel.Worksheet
```

We are early binding our variables because it is much faster that late binding. Is the Microsoft Excel instance running at this time? No, we have only declared our object variables. To start it up, we need to create a reference to the object with code like this:

```
' Create the object references.
Set objExcel = New Excel.Application
Set objBook = objExcel.Workbooks.Add
Set objSheet = objExcel.Worksheets.Add
```

We use the New keyword to tell our application to just go ahead and create a new instance of the Microsoft Excel server. Then we traverse the object model by creating a Workbook and a Worksheet object.

Now we must allow the user to actually see the instance of our Microsoft Excel server. If we did not include the following line, we would not be able to view our spreadsheet even though Microsoft Excel is loaded.

```
objExcel.Visible = True
```

Although I have set the Visible property early in the sample, it is suggested that you only set the Visible property to True after you have done all your processing. If you were going to display a thousand records in Microsoft Excel, you might find it lagging in performance while it tries to redraw the screen each time. I have seen this before and it is not pretty. Set it at the end when you are done with the processing.

Now we want to set up our titles for our columns:

```
' Set up titles.
objSheet.Cells(1, 1) = "Months"
objSheet.Cells(1, 2) = "1997"
objSheet.Cells(1, 3) = "1998"
```

We are now referencing the Cells collection of the Worksheet object. The first cell in the upper left-hand corner of a spreadsheet is called Cells(1, 1). Here we are telling it to put the "Months" string into the cell. We then add our 1997 and 1998 labels, placing them in the next two cells to the right.

We can also change how our data is displayed within our Microsoft Excel server. Here we use the Range object of our Application object. We can specify a range of cells and apply font formatting to them like this:

```
' Change the font attributes of the headers.
  objExcel.Range("A1: C1").Font.Bold = True
  objExcel.Range("A1: C1").Font.Size = 16
  objExcel.Range("A1: C1").Font.Shadow = True
```

Now we come to the workhorse code. This code takes not only the information we input into `frmExcel` but also our label captions for the month and places them into Microsoft Excel.

```
For intCount = 1 To 12

  objSheet.Cells(intCount + 1, 1) = lblLabels(intCount - 1).Caption
  objSheet.Cells(intCount + 1, 2) = txt1997(intCount - 1).Text
  objSheet.Cells(intCount + 1, 3) = txt1998(intCount - 1).Text

Next
```

Here we have created a `For…Next` loop which will create three columns within the Microsoft Excel spreadsheet. The first column is a list of month names, which we just pull from the label captions for our months. We can then create our 1997 and 1998 columns simply by looping through our control arrays using the subscript number to do this.

> *When I first began my foray into Visual Basic, I was king of the "100 labels and text boxes on one form". Then I found control arrays. This neat tool not only saves on resources, but also makes it easy to traverse through them. In those days, I would have had to write code such as:*
>
> *objSheet.Cells(intCount + 1, 2) = txt1997_Jan.Text*
>
> *objSheet.Cells(intCount + 1, 2) = txt1997_Feb.Text*
>
> *objSheet.Cells(intCount + 1, 2) = txt1997_Mar.Text*
>
> *…*
>
> *…*
>
> *objSheet.Cells(intCount + 1, 2) = txt1997_Dec.Text*
>
> *If I had 100 text boxes, I would end up writing 100 lines of code each time that I wanted to change them. Now with control arrays, I just create a loop. It makes life much easier.*

We also need to set up an error handler to handle any errors in our `Click` event. This returns an error number and its associated description as well as setting the mouse pointer back to normal:

```
On Error GoTo ErrorHandler
...
...
ErrorHandler:
    MsgBox CStr(Err.Number) & " - " & Err.Description
    Screen.Mousepointer = vbNormal
End Sub
```

This is a very, very, very basic error handler. In fact, it does not "handle" the error at all. I suggest always trying to anticipate errors that could occur and writing a handler that will deal with them gracefully. A user who receives an arcane error message will not quite know how to deal with it. It is better to incorporate functionality in your error handling that will lead the user in the correct direction instead of just telling the user they screwed up. Instead of giving a "File Missing" error message, you may want to say "Cannot find file, would you like to create a new one?"

So, with only three lines of code, we were able to transfer the data to the Microsoft Excel spreadsheet. Although our sample data was quite small, you can see how easy it would be to add a hundred or even a thousand more records to a Microsoft Excel spreadsheet.

We have one more thing to do. We need to create a chart that will compare each month's sales for both years. Now what if we had to do this in Visual Basic? We would probably have to use the graphics server control or some third-party tool to allow us to feed it data and it would be responsible for creating the visual representation. Then we would take that image and send it over to our Microsoft Excel instance.

Why not just let Microsoft Excel create the chart for us? We can use Microsoft Excel through COM Automation to help us create a chart. That is the benefit of COM Automation; it allows the developer to use components that are more suited for the task.

Using the Chart Object in Microsoft Excel from Visual Basic

1. Close Microsoft Excel and go back to the code window in Visual Basic for our `cmdExcel` click event. Enter the following code right after the `Next` statement:

```
' Create chart using the Excel Chart object.
With objExcel
   .Charts.Add
   .ActiveChart.ChartType = xlLineMarkers
   .ActiveChart.SetSourceData Source:=Sheets("Sheet4").Range("A2:C13"), _
     PlotBy:=xlColumns
   .ActiveChart.SeriesCollection(1).Name = "=""1997"""
   .ActiveChart.SeriesCollection(2).Name = "=""1998"""
   .ActiveChart.Location Where:=xlLocationAsObject, Name:="Sheet4"
   With ActiveChart
     .HasTitle = True
     .ChartTitle.Characters.Text = "Yearly Summaries"
     .Axes(xlCategory, xlPrimary).HasTitle = True
     .Axes(xlCategory, xlPrimary).AxisTitle.Characters.Text = "Months"
     .Axes(xlValue, xlPrimary).HasTitle = True
     .Axes(xlValue, xlPrimary).AxisTitle.Characters.Text = "Dollars in Thousands"
   End With
End With
```

2. Save your project again, then press the *F5* key. Our spreadsheet now contains a chart comparing the two years' data:

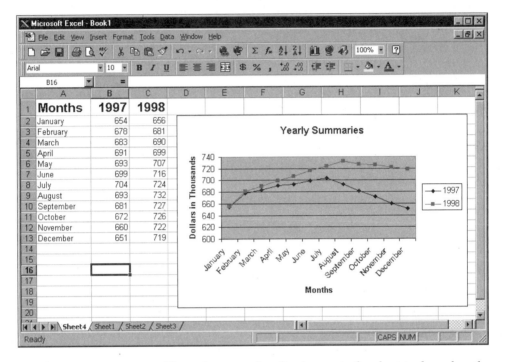

I am going to let you in on a secret. The code we used earlier to create the chart took me less than a minute to figure out. Did I have to pull out the object model diagram or try to figure out the complex parameters to be passed to the Chart object? No, I let Microsoft Excel do my dirty work. Let me tell you how.

In Microsoft Excel, there is a tool called the Macro recorder. What it does is it allows you to start recording what you do in a spreadsheet: clicking a cell, starting a wizard, applying formatting, etc. Then it takes what you have done and creates VBA code for you. Talk about a code generator! Then I took that VBA code, placed it in my application and set the appropriate object variable. Then I was done. Let me show you how.

Using Microsoft Excel as a Code Generator

1. Since we have Microsoft Excel open with our data and our chart, let's go ahead and use it. Select the chart and then delete it.

2. Select <u>T</u>ools | <u>M</u>acro | <u>R</u>ecord New Macro and set the <u>M</u>acro name to CreateChart:

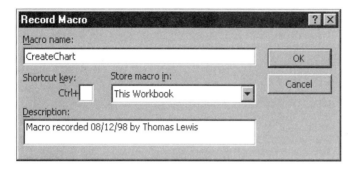

3. Click OK and we return to the active worksheet. A toolbar will appear which will allow us to stop recording our macro when we are finished:

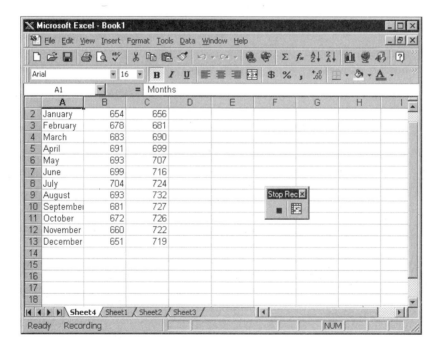

4. From the Insert menu, choose Chart.

5. Select Line as the Chart type and the sub-type as shown. Then click on the Next> button.

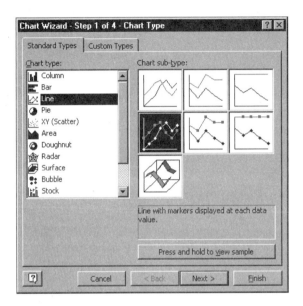

6. The Source Data dialog now appears. Select all the cells in the range A2 to C13 from our worksheet. The dialog should now look like this:

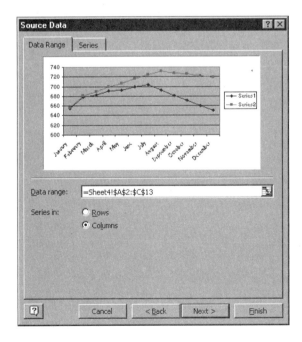

7. Click on the Series tab and change the series names to 1997 and 1998 respectively. Then click the Next> button.

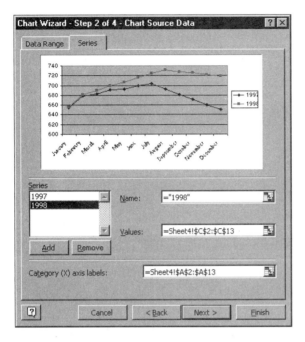

8. In Step 3, change Chart title to Yearly Summaries, Category (X) axis to Months and Value(Y) axis to Dollars in Thousands. The Chart Wizard supplies a visual of what the chart will look like. Click on the Next> button.

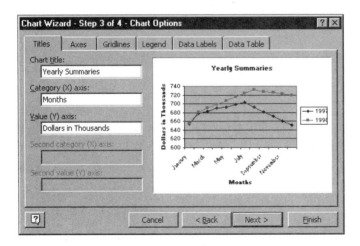

9. Finally, click on the Finish button on the last step of the chart wizard. Microsoft Excel will then go ahead and create the chart based on the information we gave it.

10. Now hit the Stop Recording button on the macro toolbar.

11. On the <u>T</u>ools menu, select <u>M</u>acro | <u>M</u>acros. The CreateChart macro should be listed. Select it and click the <u>E</u>dit button.

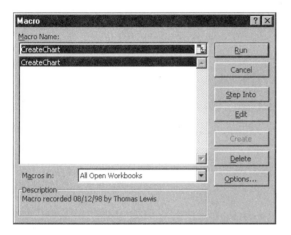

12. This will display the VBA editor in Microsoft Excel. You will also see the code generated by the macro recorder:

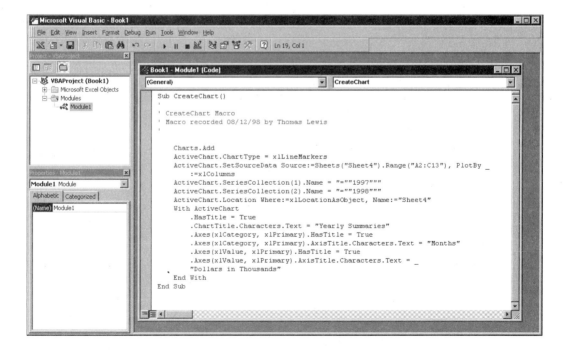

13. We can now take the code written here between the `Sub` commands and paste it into our Visual Basic code. Now the only thing we need to do is add the `With objExcel` block around our new code. Why do we need to do this? VBA in Microsoft Excel treats everything from the Application level of the object hierarchy. With Visual Basic, we must declare an object for the `Application` object and reference it to the object. Now we can create a chart using Visual Basic.

If you are trying to duplicate functionality within Microsoft Excel, just fire up the macro recorder, let it build the code and then you can figure out the best way to tweak it. Now, you can have Microsoft Excel (or any other Office application for that matter) build your code for you, and with the time saved from having to dig through the VBA programmer's manual or object model help file, you can go see a hockey game!

Things to Consider

When working with COM Automation, we are usually doing cross-process calls. A **process** is the correct term for an executing program. Our Automation server and our Automation controller are each running in their own processes. We have to call across processes to make a COM client call an Automation server and make it do something. It can slow things down considerably. If you can package your calls to the server, that would help performance such as sending an array of variant records to the Automation server instead of each record one-by-one.

Use error handling constantly. In our example, we used the `New` keyword to create our object but a better way would been to use the `GetObject` and `CreateObject` commands. However, you have to create error handlers for cases where you use `GetObject` but the object does not exist. Good error handling is like money; you can never have enough. I have yet to run into an application where there is too much, usually there is not enough, if any.

Another way to improve performance is to have Visual Basic actually run macro procedures from Microsoft Excel. For example, instead of having Visual Basic create the chart, we could have written code to run our `CreateChart` macro.

```
ObjExcel.Run("CreateChart")
```

To do this though, the macro must exist in the workbook.

Summary

Well that's it for our whistle-stop tour of Automation.

Automation is an extremely powerful tool - whether you're adding spreadsheets to Word documents, charts to PowerPoint presentations or creating Excel spreadsheets from data entered into a Visual Basic application. Don't overlook the fantastic capabilities available to you with this COM-based technology.

Let's now review what we've learnt in this chapter:

- ❑ How to use Automation
- ❑ The `CreateObject`, `GetObject` and `New` keywords
- ❑ Early and Late Binding and how they relate to COM
- ❑ Object models, in particular the Microsoft Excel Object Model
- ❑ How to use the Macro recorder

But what, I hear you ask, do I do when I want to create all those reusable components you've been talking about so much?

The answer can be found in the next chapter...

VB COM

4

ActiveX Code Components

Overview

So far, although we have covered a lot of what COM is about, we haven't yet really seen how to create our very own components in Visual Basic. This is where ActiveX enters the equation. ActiveX components allow us to easily create COM-enabled code. We've already seen some ActiveX components in action in Chapter 2 but now we are going to cover two particular types of Visual Basic ActiveX components in more detail, the **ActiveX DLL** and **ActiveX EXE**. These are not the only types of ActiveX components that we can create, but they are the most commonly used. We will be looking at a different type of ActiveX component, the ActiveX Control, in the next chapter.

ActiveX components are based on the concept of interfaces that we covered in considerable detail in Chapter 2. In Visual Basic, we use a **class module** to define an interface:

- ❑ What are classes and how we create them
- ❑ The elements that make up a class
- ❑ How to use the Class Builder Wizard to create class frameworks
- ❑ Creating an ActiveX DLL
- ❑ Creating an ActiveX EXE
- ❑ The differences between the two
- ❑ How to keep version compatibility
- ❑ How to store components in the Visual Component Manager

Let's get started.

Genesis of the ActiveX Code Component

Visual Basic 3.0 developers had a rapid GUI (Graphical User Interface), some fancy new custom controls (VBXs), event-driven programs and .bas files. However, developers were tormented by the programming elite with taunts of "Visual Basic is not a real language!" or "Visual Basic is for hobbyists only, you cannot create *real* programs with it." VB programmers worked with monolithic code where all of the code was in the form itself or dumped into .bas files. Code reuse? The best you could get was good old cut and paste. If you wanted to share components with someone else, good luck. Although Visual Basic 3.0 was off to a good start, it was not easy to share or write code components that you could use in your applications. VBXs were very interesting, unfortunately you could not write one in Visual Basic 3.0. You could write a VBX using C or C++, but those who tried found it not too easy a task.

A COM-based technology known as **OLE (Object Linking and Embedding**) already existed. It allowed users to link and embed 'objects' such as spreadsheets, sound clips and graphs into documents. You've probably already seen a Word document that had a spreadsheet embedded into it. And we've already seen OLE Automation in Chapter 3 as a means of driving Excel from a Visual Basic application.

Then came Visual Basic 4.0. There were several major differences between it and Visual Basic 3; not least, that Visual Basic 4 itself was based on COM. Visual Basic 4 does not support VBXs. Instead, Microsoft extended the already present OLE technology and created OLE controls, OCXs as the new custom controls for Visual Basic.

Then, shortly after the release of Visual Basic 4, the Internet hit the computer-programming world and in a renaming frenzy, OLE became ActiveX. ActiveX is a Microsoft technology that allows the implementation of COM interfaces by way of the class module.

Classes

In VB, classes are used to define the interfaces of COM components. That is why ActiveX EXEs and DLLs always contain at least one class module.

So why use a class module rather than the good old .bas file? One reason is that the .bas file is used throughout the life of the application. Once in use, it does not go away (released out of memory) until the application is done. With the class module, we can not only create our objects when we want to, but we can also release the objects from memory whenever we want to. .bas modules cannot provide services to another application by themselves. If I have a CalcPay function in a .bas file, I cannot call it from another application.

For another example, what if you create an investment component in Visual Basic that uses your proprietary copyrighted formulas to base forecasts on market indicators. You would not want to expose these formulas to the public, but you would like developers to be able to use these formulas in applications they create. If you put them in a .bas file, a developer would be able to look through your code. The code is left unprotected so other developers could alter your code if they wished. With a class module, you can actually compile it into a DLL (dynamic link library file) or an EXE (executable file), you would create the interface for them to call your functions, but they would not know the inner workings of the function. Sound familiar?

Let's now take a look at class modules in more detail. To begin with, we'll study class modules in the familiar Standard EXE project. When we can confidently use class modules, we'll progress to looking at ActiveX EXEs and DLLs.

Creating a Simple Class Module

1. Start up Visual Basic and select Standard EXE from the New Project dialog.

2. From the Project menu select Add Class Module.

3. In the Add Class Module dialog, select Class Module:

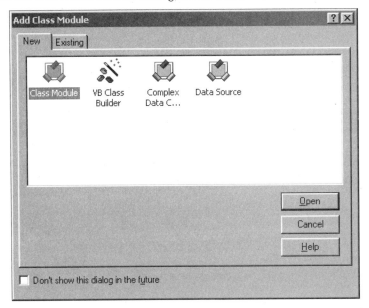

4. Name the class module CCustomer. Class modules do not have a visual interface to them; they're just code. That is why after we have added our class module, we are given a code window to work with. What we will do here is create a class that will be a blueprint for our Customer object. Our Customer object has 5 properties, 1 method, and 2 class module events. We will discuss why the variables are labeled Private soon. Place the following code in the class module:

```
Option Explicit

'local variables to hold property values
Private mvarFirstName As String
Private mvarLastName As String
Private mvarCustID As Integer
Private mvarTotalPurchases As Currency
Private mvarDateLastPurchased As Date
```

```
Public Sub Purchase(curAmount As Currency, dtmDate As Date)

  mvarTotalPurchases = mvarTotalPurchases + curAmount
  mvarDateLastPurchased = dtmDate

End Sub

Public Property Get DateLastPurchased() As Date

  DateLastPurchased = mvarDateLastPurchased

End Property

Public Property Get TotalPurchases() As Currency

  TotalPurchases = mvarTotalPurchases

End Property

Public Property Let CustID(ByVal vData As Integer)

  mvarCustID = vData

End Property

Public Property Get CustID() As Integer

  CustID = mvarCustID

End Property

Public Property Let LastName(ByVal vData As String)

  mvarLastName = vData

End Property

Public Property Get LastName() As String

  LastName = mvarLastName

End Property

Public Property Let FirstName(ByVal vData As String)

  mvarFirstName = vData

End Property

Public Property Get FirstName() As String

  FirstName = mvarFirstName

End Property

Private Sub Class_Initialize()

  Debug.Print "Class Initialized."

End Sub
```

```
Private Sub Class_Terminate()

  Debug.Print "Class Terminated."

End Sub
```

5. Now let's create an instance of our `CCustomer` class, `Customer`. Put a command button on a form and double-click on it to bring up the `Command1_Click` event. Place the following code in the code window:

```
Private Sub Command1_Click()

    Dim Customer As CCustomer
    Set Customer = New CCustomer

    Customer.CustID = 10
    Customer.FirstName = "Thomas"
    Customer.LastName = "Lewis"
    Customer.Purchase "150.00", Now

    MsgBox CStr(Customer.DateLastPurchased)
    MsgBox CStr(Customer.TotalPurchases)

    Set Customer = Nothing

End Sub
```

6. Save our project as `CustomerProject.vbp`, we'll be coming back to it several times during this chapter.

7. Now press *F8* to begin stepping through the code in debug mode.

By stepping through the code in debug mode, we can see what is happening when each line is executed. You will notice that after you press *F8* on the line:

```
Set Customer = New CCustomer
```

The debug line will go to our class module to the `Class_Initialize` event. The `Class_Initialize` event occurs when a new instance of a class is created. An instance is a copy of the class module that now resides in memory. This means we have now created our object. You would typically place initialization code that needed to be executed before the class is to be used in the `Class_Initialize` event. Here we have placed a `Debug.Print` statement which will place the string `"Class Initialized."` in the Immediate window.

If you do not have the Immediate window displayed when debugging your application, you can choose Immediate Window from the View menu or the *Ctrl + G* keyboard shortcut in Visual Basic to turn it on.

Once we have stepped through the `Class_Initialize` event, the debugger will bring us back to our form code and execute the statement:

```
Customer.CustID = 10
```

This line assigns the value 10 to the CustID property of our object. If you step through the code, the debugger will take you to the Property Let for CustID:

```
Public Property Let CustID(ByVal vData As Integer)

  mvarCustID = vData

End Property
```

What this procedure does is allow a client to assign a value to a property of the class. This is the public interface to the component. You see that we pass in vData, which is the integer (i.e. 10) that we passed it. Then we take the value of vData and assign it to mvarCustID, which is a private variable in our class.

Private Variables and Public Property Procedures

The private variables that we declared in our example are as follows:

```
'local variables to hold property value(s)
Private mvarFirstName As String
Private mvarLastName As String
Private mvarCustID As Integer
Private mvarTotalPurchases As Currency
Private mvarDateLastPurchased As Date
```

Now you might be asking, "Why do we send vData to the class to be placed in a Private variable within the class? Why not just make the variable (also known as a member variable - hence the mvar prefix) public and write to it directly?" The reason why is **encapsulation**. Encapsulation means that internal information is only accessed through public interfaces. These private variables hold information within the class. The user of our class does not even have to know what they are because they are using the Property Let and Get statements to get access to them. The public property procedures provide the interface.

We could go ahead and make them public by declaring the member variables as Public.

```
'public local variables to hold property values
Public mvarFirstName As String
Public mvarLastName As String
Public mvarCustID As Integer
Public mvarTotalPurchases As Currency
Public mvarDateLastPurchased As Date
```

But this is not a good idea. You are unable to restrict read/write access to public variables within a class module. You cannot validate the data placed into the member variable other than type validation. For example, what if you did not want the `mvarCustID` member variable to be an ID that has already been used. If you allow it to be public, anyone could come and set the value to whatever integer value they like. Also, you may want to create an event based upon a property of the object changing value. With public member variables, you cannot associate an event with the property change.

There are three types of property procedures: `Get`, `Let`, and `Set`. Let's explore these further.

Property Get

The `Property Get` procedure syntax looks like this:

```
[Public|Private|Friend] [Static] Property Get name [(arglist)][As type]
[statements]
[name = expression]
End Property
```

The `Property Get` statement allows us to retrieve the value of a property of an object. In the `Property Get` statement, the function will return a value that the class module developer dictates, this is known as **reading** the property value:

```
Public Property Get LastName() As String

  LastName = mvarLastName

End Property
```

Use `Public` when you want the procedure to be accessible to all other procedures in all other modules. A `Property Get` defined as `Private` can only be called within the class itself. The `Friend` option is allows the `Property Get` to be accessible throughout the project that is declared in, but it is not visible outside of that project.

Use `Static` if you want to preserve the value of a local variable between calls.

Use the `arglist` option if you want to pass arguments to the `Property Get` when it's called.

Property Let

The `Property Let` procedure syntax looks like this:

```
[Public|Private|Friend] [Static] Property Let name ([arglist,] value)
[statements]
End Property
```

The `Property Let` statement assigns a value to a property, this is known as **writing** a property value. As with the `Property Get` we can declare it as `Public`, `Private` or `Friend`. We can also include statements within the `Property Let` procedure. For example, if we created a `Property Let` statement that only allowed you to store a number that was not in use, it would look like:

```
Public Property Let CustID(ByVal vData As Integer)

  'Private function within the class that checks if vData has been used before
  IsValid = CheckID (vData)  'Returns True if it did not find existing ID.
  If IsValid Then
    mvarCustID = vData
  End If

End Property
```

In this procedure, if the ID has already been used we do not save it in the class. It would probably be a good idea to send an error to an error handler notifying the user that it was not saved because the value was invalid.

When we call the `Property Let` procedure from a client, the syntax would be:

`object.property = value`

That's it. We just assign our value to the property name and the class does all the work.

So now we know how to read and write a property value by using `Property Get` and `Let` accordingly. What if we wanted a read-only property? We could do this by specifying a `Property Get` procedure without its associated `Property Let` procedure. That way we can retrieve the value, we just could not assign a value to it. Alternatively, if we want to create a write-only property we just need to specify a `Property Let` without a `Property Get`. It's also possible to create a property that is **write-once**. All we have to do is add a little extra code into the `Property Let` to check that it is the first time that it has been called and prevent a new value from being written to it if this is not the case.

Property Set

The `Property Set` procedure syntax looks like this:

`[Public|Private|Friend][Static] Property Set name([arglist,]reference)`
`[statements]`
`End Property`

The `Property Set` is similar to `Property Let` but it allows you to set the value of an object property. That is, it allows you to set a value that contains a reference to an object. The last argument in the declaration, referred to as `reference` in the syntax above, must have an object data type (either `Object` or an instance of a class) or be a `Variant`.

Creating Methods

In our sample class, we created a method called `Purchase`:

```
Public Sub Purchase(curAmount As Currency, dtmDate As Date)

  mvarTotalPurchases = mvarTotalPurchases + curAmount
  mvarDateLastPurchased = dtmDate

End Sub
```

A method can be a subroutine (`Sub`) or function (`Function`) within our class. A method can be passed parameters, execute code and change the values of its parameters. A `Function` is also able to return a value to the procedure that called it, something a `Sub` can't do. In the code example, `Purchase` is a `Public Sub`. Methods are public by default unless made private. If a method is private, then it can only be called by code within the class, it could not be called by our test application (our client).

We passed it two parameters, `curAmount` and `dtmDate`. `curAmount` is added to the value stored in `mvarTotalPurchases` and the sum of these is assigned to `mvarTotalPurchases`, overwriting the old value. The date parameter value is assigned to the `mvarDateLastPurchased`. This is another way of assigning values to our member variables.

So why couldn't we just create a method to update all of our member variables? We can. We would just pass the values we wish to assign to the member variables through the parameter list. Then in the code for the method we can assign the values to our member variables. Is there a benefit to assigning values to member variables this way instead of through property procedures? Yes, we can cut down on the number of times we call the object. The more calls made to the object, the slower performance you may incur.

For these small sample apps we are talking about negligible performance penalties, but if we were trying to assign values to a 100 properties it would be much slower than breaking them up into methods to do this.

This penalty occurs because we are making multiple calls to our object. Let's see how this works:

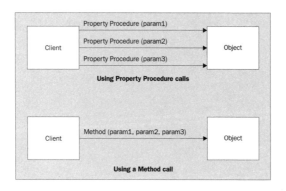

Enumerated Values

You have probably run across properties for a component where you have been provided with a list of constant values to choose from. We are able to create a list of values for clients to choose from for a property by using **enumerated values**. Look at the following screen shot:

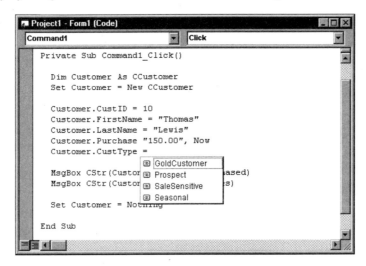

Creating an Enumerated Property

1. Let's add the enumerated values to our CCustomer class. Under the declared member variables put the following code:

```
Public Enum CustomerType
    Prospect = 1
    Seasonal = 2
    SaleSensitive = 3
    GoldCustomer = 4
End Enum
```

If we had left out the number values, the enumeration would have started with 0. So Prospect would have been 0 and GoldCustomer would have been 3.

2. Now let's create a property called CustType. First we need to declare the member variable. Place this declaration with our other member variable declarations:

```
Private mvarCustType As CustomerType
```

Notice that we declare it as being of type CustomerType, which is our enumerated type.

3. Now we need to create our `Property Let` procedure to allow the client to assign one of our enumerated values to the member variable within our class. We also need a `Property Get` procedure so that our clients can also retrieve the `CustType` value from our class. Add these two procedures to our `CCustomer` class module:

```
Public Property Let CustType(ByVal vData As CustomerType)

   mvarCustType = vData

End Property

Public Property Get CustType() As CustomerType

   CustType = mvarCustType

End Property
```

In our `Property Let` procedure the parameter `vData` is of `CustomerType`. If in the client a value not in our enumerated list of `CustomerType` is passed, Visual Basic will raise an error.

Remember that with an enumerated value, you are just passing around the long value (1-4) it is just that Visual Basic knows how to refer the constant `Seasonal` to a long value of 2.

Now in the code module of the test application when we type in:

```
Customer.CustType =
```

We get a list of values to choose from that make more sense than just some long value. So we could just store a value of 1 in a database if we liked instead of having to store the string `"Prospect"`.

Enumerated types make it easier for the users of your class to assign values based on recognizable text instead of an ambiguous number.

Handling Intrinsic Events

There are two types of events that can occur in a class. An **intrinsic** event and a **user-defined** event. You are already familiar with the first type of event. Intrinsic events our events built into each and every Visual Basic class you build. The two events are `Class_Initialize` and `Class_Terminate`. We can write code based on these events in every class.

The `Class_Initialize` event occurs when an instance of our class is created. We can place code in this event to do any preparation needed for the class such as initializing member variables. Shown earlier, it can also be used to debug your classes because you can write code that indicates when the object is instantiated.

The `Class_Terminate` event occurs when the object variable we used to create the instance of our object goes out of scope or we have set the object variable equal to the `Nothing` keyword. The `Nothing` keyword disassociates the object variable from the object. We can do this by using the following code:

```
Set Customer = Nothing
```

Our object can go out of **scope** also. Scope defines whether your variables retain their value in relation to where they are declared. You would not want a procedure that kept the same values it used last time (OK so there are exceptions, but bear with me on this one). Would you want someone after you to go to the ATM and still have all your information in the variables for their withdrawal transaction? When the object variable loses its scope, the instance of the class is destroyed and the `Class_Terminate` event is fired. Remember from Chapter 2 that one of the behaviors of COM objects is that when the reference count is set to zero, the object is destroyed.

User-Defined Events

You may want to have your class create events based upon some occurrence. When an event occurs in a class, we can associate code that will execute in the client. Think of the command button. The command button is actually an object. When we draw a command button on a form, we are creating an instance of a command button class as an object. Now when we go into the code window of Visual Basic, we can see that there are quite a few events that we can write code for and probably the most used is the `Click` event. Therefore, we can write code in the command button's `Click` event procedure to execute when the button is clicked.

Creating an Event

In a class module, we might want to create an event that fires when we have submitted a purchase by calling the `Purchase` method from our client.

1. Bring up the code window for the `CCustomer` class in our `CustomerProject.vbp` and place the following line at the bottom of the General Declarations section of our class. This is called declaring the event.

```
Public Event OnPurchase()
```

2. Now we need to **raise** our event. Raising the event actually generates (known as **firing**) it. Place the following line at the end of the `Purchase` method in the class.

```
mvarDateLastPurchased = dtmDate
RaiseEvent OnPurchase

End Sub
```

3. Now our class is ready to fire the OnPurchase event. We need to prepare our client form so that it will be able to use the OnPurchase event. The first thing to do will be to declare our object using the WithEvents keyword. WithEvents specifies that the object variable we are using to instantiate our object will be able to handle events. Delete the following line of code that declared our object variable:

```
Dim Customer As CCustomer
```

4. Add this line to the General Declarations section of our form:

```
Private WithEvents Customer As CCustomer
```

5. Now look at the code window in our form and bring up our object. We can now see that there is an OnPurchase event that we can write code for:

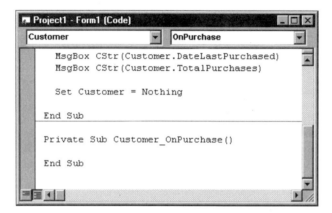

6. We can now write code that will execute whenever the Purchase method is called. Let's add the following line to our Customer_OnPurchase event:

```
Private Sub Customer_OnPurchase()

Debug.Print "A purchase has occurred."

End Sub
```

7. Step through the application using the *F8* key. Notice that when we get to the RaiseEvent statement within our class, the debug line will step out into the client code and execute the code within our Customer_OnPurchase event. If you have the Immediate Window visible, you will see that the code we put in the procedure has been executed:

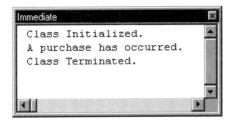

Caveats with WithEvents

There are some limitations when using the `WithEvents` keyword.

❑ You cannot declare an object variable with the `WithEvents` keyword if you are assigning it to an `Object` type:

```
Private WithEvents MyObject As Object
```

❑ You cannot create arrays with an object variable if you are using the `WithEvents` keyword:

```
Private WithEvents MyArray(4) As CArray
```

❑ You cannot declare an object variable `As New` with the `WithEvents` keyword:

```
Private WithEvents MyObject As New CObject
```

❑ You cannot declare an object variable with the `WithEvents` keyword in a standard module (`.bas` file).

The Class Builder Wizard

Visual Basic 4.0 allowed Visual Basic developers to create classes in their applications but it had no tools to create these classes visually or rapidly. A Class Builder Wizard add-in was included in Visual Basic 5.0 to address this problem. The Class Builder Wizard allows us to create a framework for our classes using a pseudo-wizard interface.

Using the Class Builder

1. Load up our `CustomerProject.vbp` project.

2. To enable Visual Basic 6.0 to use the Class Builder Wizard, select **Add-In Manager...** from the **Add-Ins** menu. The **Add-In Manager** will be loaded:

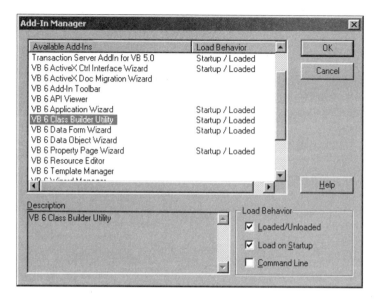

3. Select the VB 6 Class Builder Utility and check the Loaded/Unloaded and Load on Startup check boxes. The Loaded/Unloaded behavior allows you to specify whether an Add-In is loaded or not. The Load on Startup option allows you to specify that an Add-In should be loaded whenever you start Visual Basic. Click on OK to continue.

4. Now you can choose the Class Builder Utility... from the Add-Ins menu. As we already have a class that we created ourselves in our project we see the following dialog:

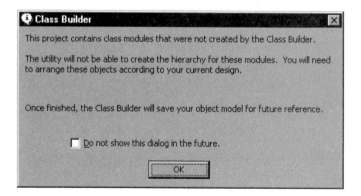

This message is only of concern if you have built an object model hierarchy. You can simply drag your classes in the left-hand pane to build the object model hierarchy.

5. Click on the OK button and the **Class Builder** will appear. Notice that our `CCustomer` class is already in the Wizard for us. With the A̲ll tab selected, we can see all the properties, methods, events and enumerations in our class:

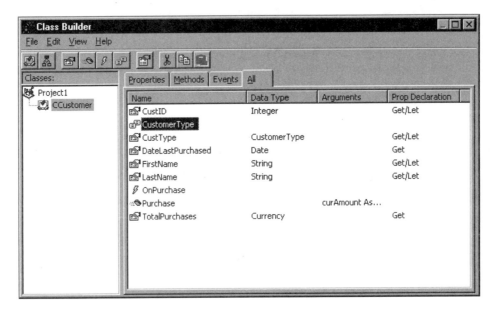

6. To view the enumeration double-click on CustomerType in the right pane:

7. We'll create a new class called `CInvoice`. This class will handle an invoice item. It will have three properties, the item's name, ID and price. We will have a method called `Save Invoice`, which will raise an event called `OnSave`:

Type	Name	Data Type	Get/Let?
Property	ItemName	String	Get/Let
Property	ItemID	Integer	Get/Let
Property	ItemAmount	Currency	Get/Let
Method	SaveInvoice	Boolean	
Event	OnSave		

8. So let's create the `CInvoice` class. Select Project1 from the left-hand side of the Class Builder window. Then select File | New | Class... from the menu. A dialog will appear asking for the Name of the class; you should type in `CInvoice`. The Based On field allows us to specify whether we want to place it in an object hierarchy. We will leave it as (New Class):

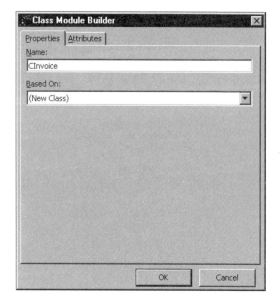

9. Click on the Attributes tab, here we can give a Description of our class. We can also associate a Project Help File and a Help Context ID so that when users of our class need to access the help file regarding the class, you can tell it where to look in the help file. Put in a description as shown:

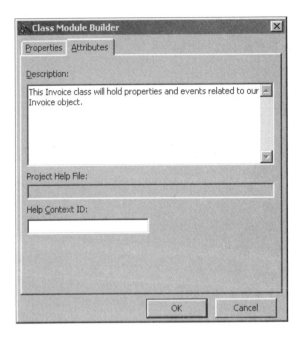

10. Click on OK and now you see we have the `CInvoice` class listed in the Class Builder:

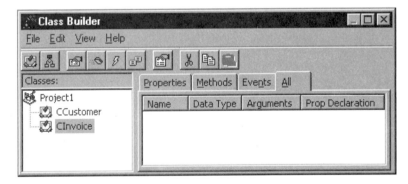

11. Now let's create our properties. We can choose File | New | Property from the menu or we can just click on the Property icon on the toolbar to bring up the Property Builder dialog:

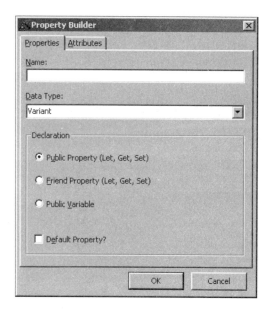

12. Let's create the first property, `ItemName`. Put the property name of ItemName in the Name field. Set the Data Type to String, since this is the data type of `ItemName`. Keep the default Declaration of Public Property (Let, Get, Set). We could specify a Friend Property (which we will touch on later) or create it as a Public Variable. We can also specify whether it is the Default Property; we'll keep this unchecked.

A default property is a property that we do not explicitly have to declare. For example, we can refer to the `Text` property of a text box by:

```
Text1.Text = "some string"
```

or

```
Text1 = "some string"
```

We do not have to state `Text` because it is the default property of the text box. I do not suggest using this, I have found it to cause problems and it makes it difficult for the user to know which property is the default one.

13. We can also go to the Attributes tab and give a description for the `ItemName` property. When you have completed the `ItemName` property click on OK.

14. Now let's create the `ItemID` and `ItemAmount` properties according to the table in Step 7 of this exercise. Once we are finished, our Class Builder should display them on the right-side of the window:

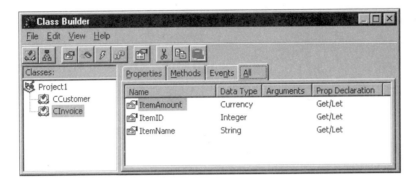

15. To create our `SaveInvoice` method, we can either select File | New | Method... from the Class Builder menu or click on the **Method** icon on the toolbar. The **Method Builder** looks a little different than our Property Builder:

16. In the Method Builder, we can specify the <u>N</u>ame of our method, the A<u>r</u>guments, the Return <u>D</u>ata Type and whether it is a <u>F</u>riend or a <u>D</u>efault Method. Type SaveInvoice into the <u>N</u>ame field. We could add an argument to our method by clicking the + button. We can also delete method arguments or specify their order. We will leave ours blank for now. Select Boolean as our Return <u>D</u>ata Type. That way we can return a True or False value based on whether or not the Invoice was saved. Also, make sure to put in a description on the <u>A</u>ttributes page.

17. To create our `OnSave` event for our class, select either the <u>F</u>ile | <u>N</u>ew | <u>E</u>vent... from the Class Builder menu or click the Event icon on the toolbar. In the Event Builder, type OnSave as the <u>N</u>ame and create a <u>D</u>escription for it on the <u>A</u>ttributes page:

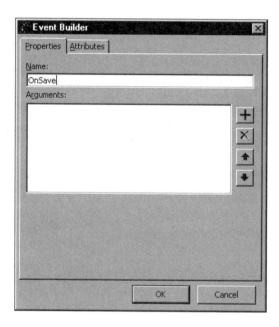

18. Your Class Builder wizard should now look like this:

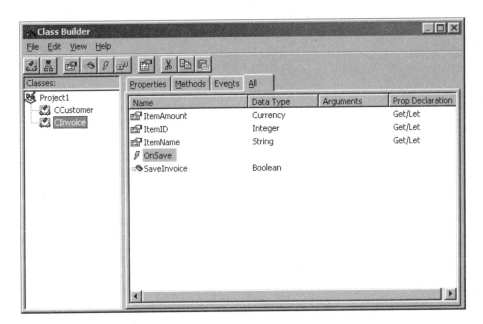

19. Our class has not been added to our project yet. To do this we select File | Update Project and the wizard will now put the framework code for us in the project. Then exit the wizard. You will now see in the Project window that the CInvoice class has been added to our project:

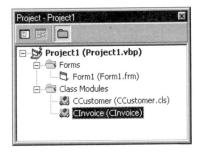

20. Now open the code window for CInvoice. The wizard has generated the following code:

```
Option Explicit

'local variable(s) to hold property value(s)
Private mvarItemName As String 'local copy
Private mvarItemID As Integer 'local copy
Private mvarItemAmount As Currency 'local copy
'To fire this event, use RaiseEvent with the following syntax:
'RaiseEvent OnSave[(arg1, arg2, ... , argn)]
Public Event OnSave()

Public Function SaveInvoice() As Boolean

End Function

Public Property Let ItemAmount (ByVal vData As Currency)
'used when assigning a value to the property, on the left side of an assignment.
'Syntax: X.ItemAmount = 5
    mvarItemAmount = vData
End Property

Public Property Get ItemAmount () As Currency
'used when retrieving value of a property, on the right side of an assignment.
'Syntax: Debug.Print X.ItemAmount
    ItemAmount = mvarItemAmount
End Property

Public Property Let ItemID(ByVal vData As Integer)
'used when assigning a value to the property, on the left side of an assignment.
'Syntax: X.ItemID = 5
    mvarItemID = vData
End Property

Public Property Get ItemID() As Integer
'used when retrieving value of a property, on the right side of an assignment.
'Syntax: Debug.Print X.ItemID
    ItemID = mvarItemID
End Property

Public Property Let ItemName(ByVal vData As String)
'used when assigning a value to the property, on the left side of an assignment.
'Syntax: X.ItemName = 5
    mvarItemName = vData
End Property

Public Property Get ItemName() As String
'used when retrieving value of a property, on the right side of an assignment.
'Syntax: Debug.Print X.ItemName
    ItemName = mvarItemName
End Property
```

Now we have a fully functional class that we can use. We would need to add our `RaiseEvent` statement to the `SaveInvoice` method so that the event would be raised to our client. Notice that the Class Builder wizard uses its own prefixes for variables instead of what you might be used to using. For example, the variables that hold property values all begin with the prefix, `mvar`. The Class Builder wizard code also gives you the syntax and comments on how to make calls to the class.

Creating Enumerations with the Class Builder

The Class Builder makes it easy to create enumerations. The Class Builder wizard that shipped in Visual Basic 5.0 did not support enumerations so they had to be coded manually. But with Visual Basic 6.0, we can let the Class Builder wizard handle the work for us.

Incidentally, if you view one of the enumerations intrinsic to Visual Basic in the Object Browser you'll notice that Microsoft has added descriptions for each enumeration and its constants - there is no facility to do this with the Enum Builder in VB 6 - perhaps in a future version...

1. Select **Class Builder Utility...** from the <u>A</u>dd-Ins menu. Our `CCustomer` and `CInvoice` classes should be displayed. We want to create an enumeration for a parameter of our `SaveInvoice` method. We would like to be able to specify whether the invoice will be saved to a file, a database, or an e-mail. Instead of just assigning an integer like 1, 2, or 3. We can specify constant values that make more sense to the user.

2. Make sure to select **CInvoice** in the Class Builder window so that the wizard knows which class to place the Enum statement in and choose <u>F</u>ile | <u>N</u>ew | E<u>n</u>um... or click the Enum icon on the toolbar.

3. In the Enum Builder type **StorageType** in the <u>N</u>ame field. Leave **StorageType** as <u>P</u>ublic.

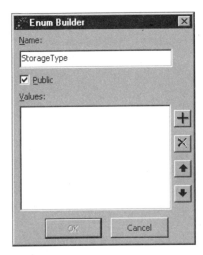

4. We add our constant values by clicking the + button. A new dialog appears. Type in ifile = 1 and select OK.

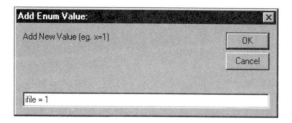

5. Repeat the process with idatabase = 2 and iemail = 3. Then select OK.

6. Our StorageType enumeration now appears in the right-hand side of the Class Builder:

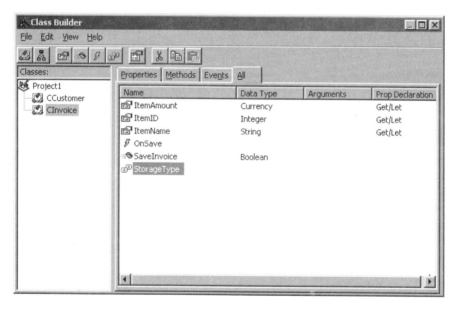

7. Choose File | Update Project from the menu and exit out of the wizard. The wizard has now entered the following code for us in the General Declarations section of our class:

```
Public Enum StorageType
    ifile = 1
    idatabase = 2
    iemail = 3
End Enum
```

8. Unfortunately, if a method has already been created, we cannot go into the Method Builder and create a parameter based on our new enum. If we had created our enum first and then created the method, we could have selected the enum as the data type for the parameter argument. So now we need to go ahead and change:

```
Public Function SaveInvoice() As Boolean
```

to:

```
Public Function SaveInvoice(vData As StorageType) As Boolean
```

This will allow the user to select from a list of constants.

9. Add the following line of code to our `SaveInvoice` method so that our `OnSave` event will be raised:

```
Public Function SaveInvoice(vData As StorageType) As Boolean

RaiseEvent OnSave

End Function
```

10. Now go to the form and create a second command button. Set its `Caption` property and `Name` property to `CInvoice`. Double-click on the **CInvoice** button and enter the following code:

```
Private Sub CInvoice_Click()

    Set Invoice = New CInvoice

    Invoice.ItemID = 1
    Invoice.ItemName = "Floral Arrangement"
    Invoice.ItemAmount = 45.71

    Invoice.SaveInvoice idatabase

    Set Invoice = Nothing

End Sub
```

11. Place the following line in the General Declarations section of the form:

```
Private WithEvents Invoice As CInvoice
```

12. Now enter the following code into the `Invoice_OnSave` event procedure:

```
Private Sub Invoice_OnSave()

    Debug.Print "The invoice was saved."

End Sub
```

13. Finally, use *F8* to step through the code. Values will be assigned to our new properties. Our `SaveInvoice` method is called and raises the `OnSave` event of our `Invoice` object. The `OnSave` event sends a message to the Immediate Window to tell us that the invoice was saved successfully:

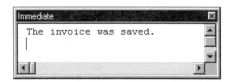

We have now created an `Invoice` object that supports events, allows us to assign values to properties, choose constants for our storage type in the `SaveInvoice` method, and be able to clear the object out of memory.

The Class Builder wizard makes it very easy to create frameworks for our classes. It also has many other great features such as the ability to create collection classes and object hierarchies. I encourage you to explore and use the Class Builder wizard to create your classes. It takes a lot of the coding off your hands.

The Object Browser Returns

When I first used the Class Builder wizard to create my class framework, I diligently created robust descriptions of all my class elements. When I updated a project for the first time I was very disappointed. I thought that it would comment my class code with my descriptions in my classes, but View Code showed no such addition to my code. I thought, it must be a bug!

Well, you know what they say about
assuming things. Fire up the Object
Browser in VB by pressing the *F2* key.
Select the `CInvoice` class from the left-
hand side of our browser. Notice that on
the right-hand side of the Object Browser
we can see all the elements of our class.
But is something missing? What about
our enumeration? Scroll down the left
window and you will find StorageType
by itself with its constant list displayed in
the right-hand window:

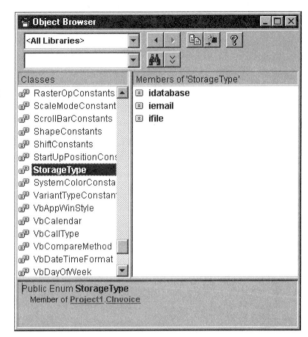

Now go back to the `CInvoice` class.
Notice the window at the bottom? This is
the **Details** pane. The Details pane gives
the name of the class and what it is a
member of. We can actually click on the
hyperlinked objects in the Details pane
and change the view of the Object
Browser to the member you selected.
This is where our descriptions are! So
users of our objects can use the Object
Browser to view the elements of the
classes that we have created. It is
important to place those descriptions for
our classes so that these users can have
an idea of how the property, method, or
event should be used.

Why Use an ActiveX DLL?

We have been talking about classes that reside in a project that we are working in. But what if we wanted to be able to create an object from any project we are working on? Let's say we have a customer object that we want our accounting, marketing, and sales projects to have access to. With just a class file (.cls), each developer for the different projects would have to add the .cls file to their project. There are problems with this method.

Let's take our seasoned developers from the "Frog on a Turtle's Back" garden company's development group. Phil has created a class module for handling customer objects. This class takes customer information and can save it to a database, retrieve it from a database, allow changes to customers and just about anything else that a clerk would like to do with customers' data. Bill is in charge of the accounting project, David is in charge of the marketing project, and Robert is in charge of the sales project. Phil could just hand over the .cls file to the others to include in their projects.

The first problem that occurs is that whenever Phil makes a change to the customer class file, he now has to distribute them to everyone on the team. Second, if the team members were to make changes to the class file once they had received it from Phil, each time Phil made a change, they would have figure out what changes Phil made and incorporate them into their versions. This is a bomb waiting to go off! Third, Phil has no way of keeping sensitive code from Robert who is a temporary consultant brought in to help out. Robert can look through the class code and find information such as log-in names and passwords.

By creating an ActiveX DLL, these issues can be resolved.

Creating an ActiveX DLL

1. Create a new project in Visual Basic and select ActiveX DLL from the New Project dialog:

2. After you click OK, the Project window will have the project name and an empty class for us to work with.

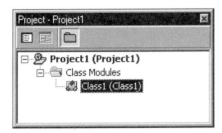

3. Also, note that the Properties window for the class now contains more than just the Name property that the classes we built in our Standard EXE application had:

Instancing

The Instancing property allows the developer to determine if the object that we will create with the class can be used for client applications and if more than one instance of the object can be created:

1 – Private

When the `Instancing` property is set to `1-Private`, no external clients can create the object. The object is only available to other objects of the component. So if we tried to create an object based on a private class, we would get an error. This type of instancing is generally reserved for those classes that will be called by other classes in our DLL and will not be able to be used in a client application.

2 – PublicNotCreatable

When a class is made `PublicNotCreatable`, the class is public, but a client cannot make calls to it until another class in the component has created an instance first. Thus, you cannot use the `New` keyword or `CreateObject` to get to this class.

5 – MultiUse

This setting is the default. It allows for clients to create objects from this class. Also, one instance of the component can create multiple objects. This allows multiple clients to access the object.

6 - GlobalMultiUse

This setting is very similar to the `5 - MultiUse` setting. The difference is that the properties and methods of this class can be invoked as if they were global functions.

Continuing to Create Our ActiveX DLL

4. Leave the `Instancing` property on the default `5-MultiUse`.

5. We will use the Class Builder to create our class framework. Rename the class to `CCustomer`. Then create the following elements of the class:

Type	Name	Data Type
Property	CustomerID	Long
Property	FirstName	String
Property	LastName	String
Property	Address	String
Property	PhoneNum	String
Method	AddToDatabase	Boolean
Event	OnAdd	(not applicable)

6. Update the project from the Class Builder. Open the code window of the `CCustomer` class. You should see this:

```
Option Explicit

'local variable(s) to hold property value(s)
Private mvarCustomerID As Long 'local copy
Private mvarFirstName As String 'local copy
Private mvarLastName As String 'local copy
Private mvarAddress As String 'local copy
Private mvarPhoneNum As String 'local copy

'To fire this event, use RaiseEvent with the following syntax:
'RaiseEvent OnAdd[(arg1, arg2, ... , argn)]
Public Event OnAdd()

Public Function AddToDatabase() As Boolean

End Function

Public Property Let PhoneNum(ByVal vData As String)
'used when assigning a value to the property, on the left side of an assignment.
'Syntax: X.PhoneNum = 5
    mvarPhoneNum = vData
End Property

Public Property Get PhoneNum() As String
'used when retrieving value of a property, on the right side of an assignment.
'Syntax: Debug.Print X.PhoneNum
    PhoneNum = mvarPhoneNum
End Property
```

```
Public Property Let Address(ByVal vData As String)
'used when assigning a value to the property, on the left side of an assignment.
'Syntax: X.Address = 5
    mvarAddress = vData
End Property

Public Property Get Address() As String
'used when retrieving value of a property, on the right side of an assignment.
'Syntax: Debug.Print X.Address
    Address = mvarAddress
End Property

Public Property Let LastName(ByVal vData As String)
'used when assigning a value to the property, on the left side of an assignment.
'Syntax: X.LastName = 5
    mvarLastName = vData
End Property

Public Property Get LastName() As String
'used when retrieving value of a property, on the right side of an assignment.
'Syntax: Debug.Print X.LastName
    LastName = mvarLastName
End Property

Public Property Let FirstName(ByVal vData As String)
'used when assigning a value to the property, on the left side of an assignment.
'Syntax: X.FirstName = 5
    mvarFirstName = vData
End Property

Public Property Get FirstName() As String
'used when retrieving value of a property, on the right side of an assignment.
'Syntax: Debug.Print X.FirstName
    FirstName = mvarFirstName
End Property

Public Property Let CustomerID(ByVal vData As Long)
'used when assigning a value to the property, on the left side of an assignment.
'Syntax: X.CustomerID = 5
    mvarCustomerID = vData
End Property

Public Property Get CustomerID() As Long
'used when retrieving value of a property, on the right side of an assignment.
'Syntax: Debug.Print X.CustomerID
    CustomerID = mvarCustomerID
End Property
```

7. Now add the `RaiseEvent` for our `OnAdd` event to the `AddToDatabase` method.

```
Public Function AddToDatabase() As Boolean

   RaiseEvent OnAdd

End Function
```

8. Also add the line below so that when the method is called we will return a Boolean value of `True`. In your production application you would write the code to actually take the values in the member variables and add them to a table in a database and when we know that it did it, we would have the method send a Boolean value of `True`. For right now though, let's assume it has been written.

```
Public Function AddToDatabase() As Boolean

   RaiseEvent OnAdd

' We would add code here to check whether the record was added.
   AddToDatabase = True


End Function
```

9. Now select Project Properties from the Project menu in Visual Basic. We need to change the Project Name to Garden and the Project Description to Garden Business Server. Then OK the changes:

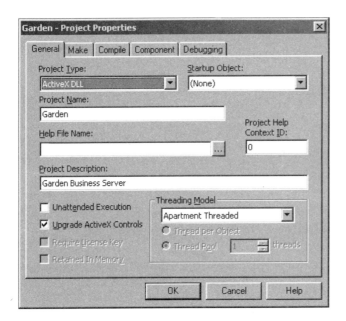

10. Select A<u>d</u>d Project from the <u>F</u>ile menu. Choose Standard EXE as the project type. Now we have two projects opened within our Visual Basic environment. Open the form in the new project and create a command button called `cmdCustomer` with a `Caption` property set to `&Customer`:

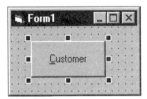

11. We cannot test our ActiveX DLL without setting a reference to it. Select Refere<u>n</u>ces... from the <u>P</u>roject menu and select Garden. Then click OK:

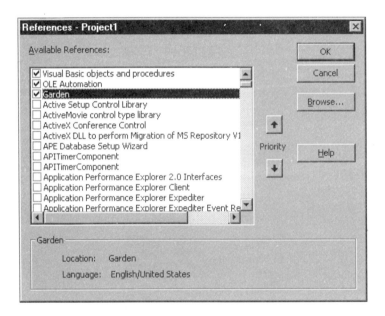

12. Now double-click the <u>C</u>ustomer button on the form and add the following code:

```
Private Sub cmdCustomer_Click()

    ' Create the object as New.
    Set Customer = New CCustomer

    With Customer
      .CustomerID = 1
      .FirstName = "Thomas"
      .LastName = "Lewis"
      .Address = "In the Middle of Nowhere"
      .PhoneNum = "555-555-5555"
      .AddToDatabase
    End With

    Set Customer = Nothing

End Sub
```

13. Place the following code in the General Declarations section of the form:

```
Option Explicit

' Declare the object variable.
Private WithEvents Customer As CCustomer
```

14. Now add the following code to the `Customer_OnAdd` event procedure:

```
Private Sub Customer_OnAdd()

    MsgBox "The AddToDatabase method has been invoked."

End Sub
```

15. Press *F8* to step through the code. You should see the following message box:

If you look at the code, you should realize that it is not different to how we called it when the class was included in the application. We only changed how we work with the object by using the `With` keyword. This keeps us from having to type in `Customer` in front of every property or method assignment. But everything else is the same. If you don't believe me, let's actually create our ActiveX DLL.

16. Now save the ActiveX DLL project as `Garden.vbp` (do **not** save the Project Group or the Standard EXE). From the Project window, select the Garden project. Then select Ma**k**e Garden.dll from the **F**ile menu. Select where you would like the DLL to be written. Visual Basic then compiles the `.DLL` and registers it to be used on the development system.

17. Now let's create a new project to test out our new `Garden.dll`. Select **N**ew Project from the **F**ile menu. When Visual Basic prompts you to save your files click on **N**o. Then create a new Standard EXE project.

18. After we have created a new project, select Refere**n**ces... from the **P**roject menu. Let's choose Garden like we did for our test application. Hmmm. Where is it? Well, once you have actually created the ActiveX DLL, it uses the project description you gave in the Project Properties dialog as the name that appears in the References dialog. So now we want to choose Garden Business Server:

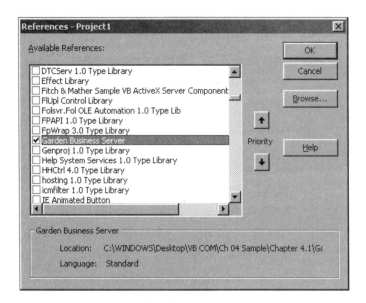

19. Now press *F2* to bring up the Object Browser. In the drop-down box in the top left-hand corner, select Garden. Now we can see the CCustomer object in our ActiveX DLL:

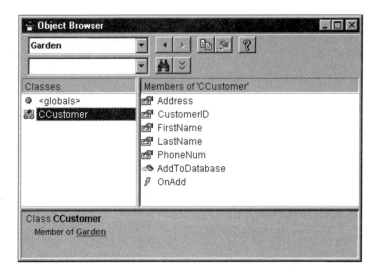

20. Add a command button to Form1. Set the Name property to cmdCustomer and the Caption property to &Customer. Then add the following code into the code window (we've seen this before a few pages back):

```
Option Explicit

' Declare the object variable.
Private WithEvents Customer As CCustomer

Private Sub cmdCustomer_Click()

  ' Create the object as New.
  Set Customer = New CCustomer

  With Customer
    .CustomerID = 1
    .FirstName = "Thomas"
    .LastName = "Lewis"
    .Address = "In the Middle of Nowhere"
    .PhoneNum = "555-555-5555"
    .AddToDatabase
  End With

  Set Customer = Nothing

End Sub
```

```
Private Sub Customer_OnAdd()

    MsgBox "The AddToDatabase method has been invoked."

End Sub
```

21. Step through the code using the *F8* key. Notice that we are able to use the same code to communicate with our class!

This example shows that we can create applications that can call on the functionality of an object inside an ActiveX DLL. We could also create multiple client applications that call upon our ActiveX DLL. Also, we did not have to know how things worked in the ActiveX DLL to actually call the functions of the ActiveX DLL, we just needed to know the interfaces which we could view through the object browser.

So now you can see that if Phil was to create his customer object and wrap it in an ActiveX DLL he could solve some of the issues that he was having. One, the ActiveX DLL can be written to encapsulate business logic that is separate from the user interface. If a business rule changes, he does not have to recompile all the user interface clients. Second, no one can make changes to the class. The only way they can access the component is through the interfaces Phil has set up. This also prevents Robert from acquiring usernames and passwords that he should not be able to get a hold of.

Version Compatibility

It is important that we think about versioning when it comes to our ActiveX components. If you were to create an ActiveX DLL, compile it, then create a client application that called on the objects in our ActiveX components and compiled it, everything would appear to be fine. Then when you went back into your component and made changes to the interfaces such as changing a property or a method parameter and re-compiled the component. You would find that the client would not work anymore. Why does this occur?

Remember in Chapter 2 we discussed GUIDs? When a component is created, it is given a type library, which allows the client to discover these GUIDs. When we change the interface to a class and recompile, the type library is changed to reflect the new interface. Our client on the other hand is still using the old, incorrect type library and thus passes the wrong IID.

For more information on GUIDs, CLSIDs and IIDs see Appendix A - COM and the Registry.

Visual Basic handles the assignment of new GUIDs according to the compatibility settings in the Project Properties dialog:

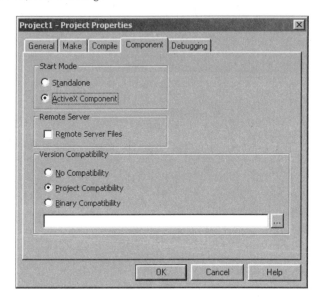

The Version Compatibility frame allows us to choose No Compatibility, Project Compatibility, or Binary Compatibility.

No Compatibility

This option states that there will be no compatibility for your component. Each time the component is compiled, a new set of GUIDs will be created. Therefore, each time you recompile your component, you will also have to recompile the clients that call upon the component. Client applications compiled to use one version can't use subsequent versions. No Compatibility is useful when you want to make a clean break between versions of your component.

Project Compatibility

This option keeps your component's type library identifier the same each time it compiles. It also keeps the previous versions of your CLSIDs (Class IDs) and changes the IIDs (Interface IDs) if they are no longer compatible. In Visual Basic 5.0, all CLSIDs and IIDs changed if a class was no longer compatible, now in Visual Basic 6.0 the CLSIDs are protected.

Use this mode when you are working on the first edition of your component.

Binary Compatibility

Once you have compiled your component, you should change its compatibility to Binary Compatibility. Now if you make changes to a component you will be warned that you are breaking compatibility. If you choose to accept the warning, the type library identifier and the class IDs will be kept. As with Project Compatibility, IIDs that are no longer compatible are updated. If you ignore the warning though, the component will maintain the IIDs. The ability to override the warning is different than what Visual Basic 5.0 allowed. Once you have compiled the component for the first time, set the compatibility to Binary Compatibility, so that you are warned that you risk breaking compatibility in your component.

One of the principles of COM that we discussed in Chapter 2 is that the interfaces, once published for an object, should remain the same. If we do not do this in our components, then we are breaking the rules COM has specified for us.

Making an ActiveX DLL Binary Compatible

1. Open up our ActiveX DLL project, the `Garden.vbp`. Select Garden Properties from the Project menu. Select the Component tab.

2. Change the compatibility to Binary Compatibility. Notice that it already has filled in the file name of our component to be compatible with. Click OK.

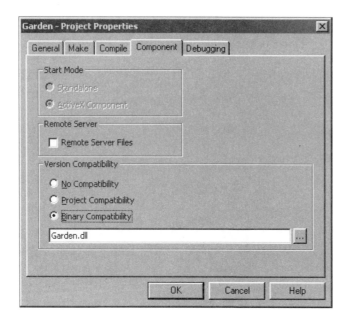

3. Change the method in our class by adding a new parameter in the argument list:

```
Public Function AddToDatabase(BadParam As Integer) As Boolean
```

4. Now try to compile the component. When you do, a dialog appears:

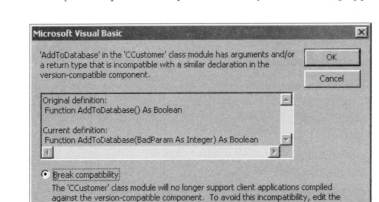

We can now decide to either <u>B</u>reak compatibility or <u>P</u>reserve compatibility. This time though, as we don't want to keep our altered class, select Cancel.

Design also plays a big part in how versioning will effect our programs. We need to make sure that when we design our components, that we take into account that we will have to update them at some point. So it is very important to take versioning into consideration when laying out the design of your component.

ActiveX EXEs

Creating an ActiveX EXE is not much different than creating an ActiveX DLL. An ActiveX EXE is an executable file that contains objects that client applications can call upon. Before we create our first ActiveX EXE, let's consider the differences between ActiveX EXEs and ActiveX DLLs.

Differences Between an ActiveX EXE and an ActiveX DLL

The most obvious difference is the fact that an ActiveX EXE is an executable file. We can actually run the file by double-clicking on the filename in Windows Explorer. The EXE has objects that can be accessed through interfaces that are created for the object. Microsoft Excel is an example of an ActiveX EXE. We saw how it was not only an application, but also had many objects such as Chart and Application exposed through COM-based clients.

An in-process server is an object that runs within the same process space as the client application that is calling it. An ActiveX DLL is an example of an in-process server.

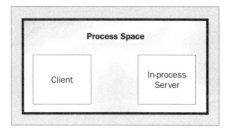

An out-of-process server is an object that runs in its own process space. If an out-of-process server crashes for some reason, it does not take the client application down with it. An ActiveX EXE is an example of an out-of-process server.

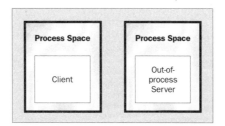

Since ActiveX EXEs are in their own process space, there is a slight performance penalty. Performance is always hindered when an application has to cross a process boundary. But having it run in its own process space allows it to be remotely called on another machine.

Instancing and the ActiveX EXE

You remember that with ActiveX DLLs, we had the following choices on what we could assign the `Instancing` property of the class to be:

Well for ActiveX EXEs there are two more `Instancing` options, `3` `-SingleUse` and `4` `-` `GlobalSingleUse`.

3 – SingleUse

`SingleUse` instancing allows client applications to create objects from the class where a new instance of the component is created each time an object is instantiated. In short, each instance is created in its own process.

4 - GlobalSingleUse

The `GlobalSingleUse` instancing is similar to `SingleUse` instancing except that the properties and methods of the class can be invoked as if they were global functions like those using `GlobalMultiUse` instancing.

Asynchronous Notification

One of the features of the ActiveX EXE that the ActiveX DLL does not have is **Asynchronous Notification**. When a client calls upon an ActiveX DLL to perform an operation the client is not able to complete its operations until the ActiveX DLL is done with its processing. An ActiveX EXE allows you to create events that will run in its own components process.

So you could create an ActiveX EXE that would go and create a long report while your client would be notified when the report is done. There are no special keywords or API calls to make the events you create already have this feature. Your client applications will create code to respond to the event such as:

```
Private Sub oReport_OnFinish()

      Msgbox "The report is finished."

End Sub
```

Visual Basic does the work - you enjoy the benefits.

Creating a Simple ActiveX EXE

1. To create an ActiveX EXE, first create a new project and select ActiveX EXE:

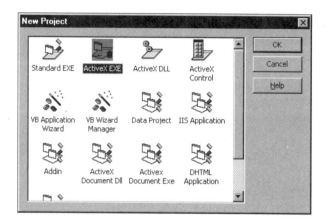

2. Keep the default `Instancing` property of `5 - MultiUse`.

3. Rename the class, `CSimple`.

4. Add the following line to the General Declarations section of our class:

```
Option Explicit

Public Event OnReturn()
```

5. Now add this method to the code window of `CSimple`:

```
Public Function ReturnMessage() As String

  ReturnMessage = "Hello from an ActiveX EXE."
  RaiseEvent OnReturn

End Function
```

6. Select Project | Project1 Properties to bring up the Project Properties dialog. Set the Project Name to Simple and the Project Description to Simple ActiveX EXE.

7. From the File menu, select Make Simple.exe. Now our ActiveX EXE has been created.

8. Now that Visual Basic has compiled and registered the ActiveX EXE for us, open a new Standard EXE project (say <u>N</u>o when prompted to save changes) and set a reference to Simple ActiveX EXE:

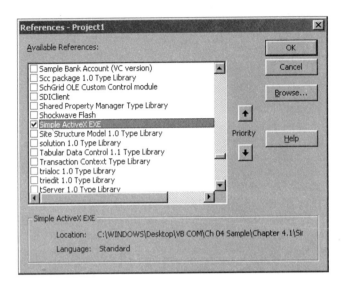

9. Add a new command button to the form. Set its `Name` property to `cmdSimple` and the `Caption` to `&Simple`.

10. Add this line of code into the General Declarations section of the form:

```
Option Explicit

Private WithEvents Simple As CSimple
```

11. Add the following code to the `Click` event of `cmdSimple`:

```
Private Sub cmdSimple_Click()

    Set Simple = New CSimple

    Dim sReturn As String

    sReturn = Simple.ReturnMessage

    Set Simple = Nothing

End Sub
```

12. Add this line of code to the `Simple_OnReturn` event procedure:

```
Private Sub Simple_OnReturn()

    MsgBox "The OnReturn event has been fired."

End Sub
```

13. Step through the code using the *F8* key. You can now see how a client calls upon an ActiveX EXE just as it did an ActiveX DLL.

You may notice that it takes slightly longer to create the object due to the cross-process operation we are doing. In addition to this, starting an EXE is much slower than loading a DLL. However, there is not much difference between creating an ActiveX EXE and creating an ActiveX DLL.

We'll now discuss a tool that is very useful to us when we're working with components.

Visual Component Manager

The **Visual Component Manager** is an add-in with which we can find, reuse and organize our components. These components can be ActiveX DLLs, ActiveX EXEs, ASP pages, HTML, code modules, or just about anything else.

The Visual Component Manager is a visual interface to the **Microsoft Repository**, which is a storage mechanism for components. Microsoft Repository allows our components to be saved to a Microsoft Access or Microsoft SQL Server database.

Storage of components is not the only benefit. Developers can search across multiple databases for objects. So the Internet development team could search the Marketing development team's Repository for a credit card validation component if needed. So now teams across an enterprise can share components.

Adding a Component to the Visual Component Manager

Let's add our ActiveX DLL to the Visual Component Manager (VCM).

1. Make sure that the VCM is loaded as an add-in.

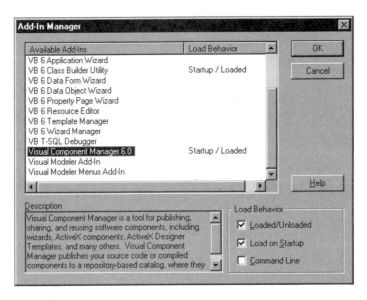

2. Choose <u>V</u>isual Component Manager from the <u>V</u>iew menu in Visual Basic. The VCM will appear:

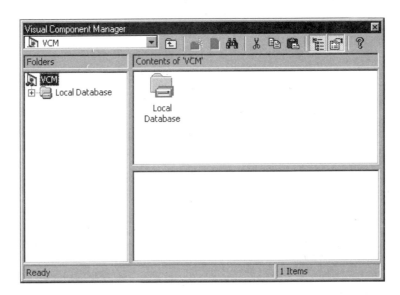

3. Go ahead and expand the Local Database tree node by clicking on the +.When you open the VCM for the first time you'll see the following message box:

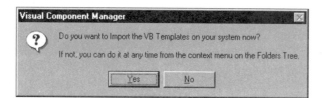

4. Answer Yes. These templates are located in the `Template` directory where Visual Basic is installed. This allows you access to these templates from the VCM.

5. Now we can see all types of components that we could store. Right-click on the COM Servers folder and select New | Component. When the following dialog appears click Next:

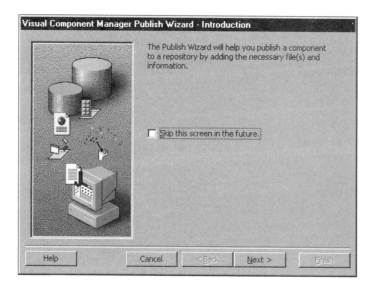

6. The <u>P</u>rimary File Name is the location of the DLL that we created. The <u>T</u>ype is COM Server Library. Fill in the information as shown and click on <u>N</u>ext:

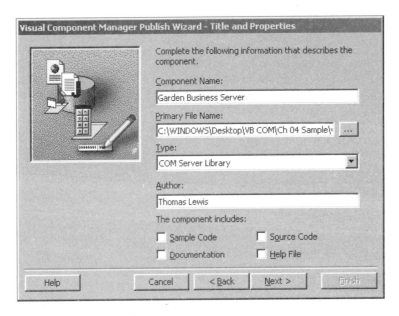

7. In the next dialog, it is important to give a good description of the component. That way it is much easier for a developer who is looking for the component to know what its function is:

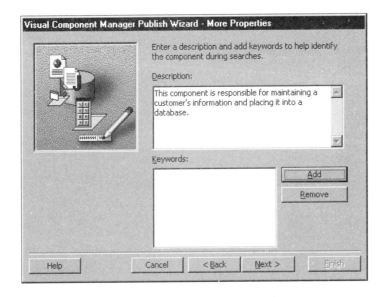

8. We also want to create keywords that a developer can search on to find the component. Click on the <u>A</u>dd button. In the Item Keywords dialog box that appears, select ActiveX and Basic from the <u>A</u>vailable Keywords list on the left and click on the > button to move them to the <u>S</u>elected Keywords list box:

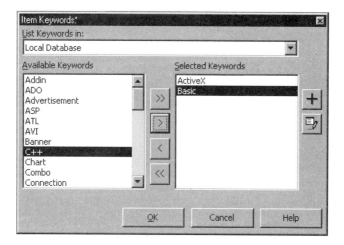

9. Click on the + button so that the Add a Keyword dialog appears. Type Garden into the text box and click <u>O</u>K:

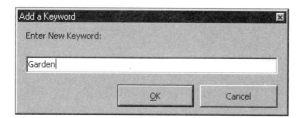

10. Garden now appears in the <u>S</u>elected Keywords list box, click <u>O</u>K and then <u>N</u>ext.

11. Click <u>N</u>ext until you get to the COM registration screen:

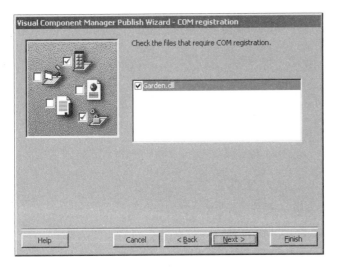

Make sure when adding your component that you choose whether or not to require COM registration for the component. If the DLL is selected to be registered, whenever a developer gets a copy of it from the VCM, it will go ahead and register the DLL for them.

12. Go ahead and click <u>N</u>ext and then <u>F</u>inish the wizard. Once the wizard is done, the VCM will show the component listed in the Contents of 'COM Servers' pane. Notice at the bottom all the information that is included with the component, this is why I suggest being verbose about describing your objects.

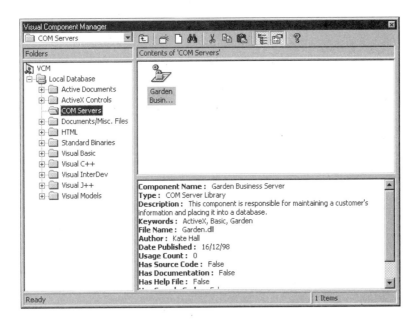

13. Right-click on the Garden Business Server and select <u>B</u>rowse Item Details. We can now see the interfaces of our component:

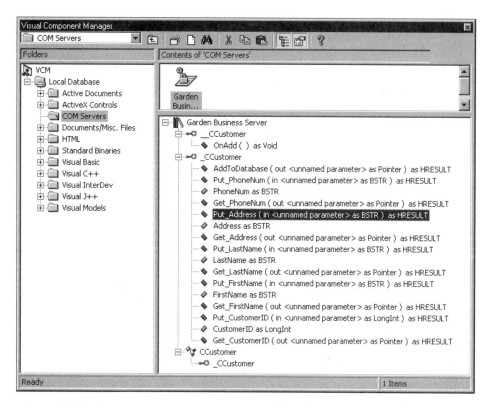

If we wanted to add this component to our project, we could right-click on it and select Add to project.

Finding a Component with the Visual Component Manager

The Visual Component Manager makes it very easy to manage all the components within a team. It allows team members not only to share components but also provides a mechanism by which to search for a component. To search for a component, click on the binoculars icon and it will bring up a Find dialog:

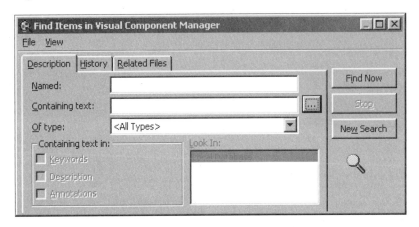

Use the <u>N</u>amed text box to specify the name of the component that you want to find. The <u>C</u>ontaining text box allows you to specify keywords to search for. To browse the available keywords click on the ... button. Our Garden Business Server component is searchable under the keywords ActiveX, Basic and Garden. If you only know part of a name or keyword you can use *, for example entering G* into the <u>N</u>amed text box will find all components that begin with G.

The <u>O</u>f type text box allows us to specify the type of component we want to search for, for instance our Garden Business Server component is a COM Server Library.

To search for a component by the author, person who last updated it or publication date, click on the <u>H</u>istory tab:

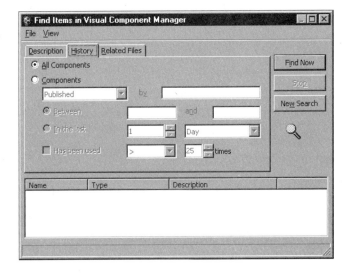

Summary

In this chapter we've seen how, in Visual Basic, the class module is the basic nucleus to ActiveX DLLs and ActiveX EXEs. This can be attributed to one very simple but very important point. You use class modules to define interfaces in Visual Basic.

We covered classes quite comprehensively and explained:

- Private Variables
- Property Statements
- Methods
- Enumerated Values
- User-Defined Events
- Intrinsic Events

We also learned how easy it was to use the Class Builder to create frameworks for our classes. It sure helped the carpal tunnel syndrome! We walked through creating an ActiveX DLL and an ActiveX EXE noticing that creating them was much the same but we could do different things with them.

Also, we used the Visual Component Manager to share the components we created with other members of the development team.

With the knowledge you gained in Chapter 2 you should now have a good idea how you should use ActiveX code components to make the best possible use of the integrated COM support.

Although we've covered both ActiveX DLLs and EXEs together in this chapter they have important and distinct differences which govern how and when you should use each type. In Chapters 6 and 7 we will discover how we can take these components and remote them across a network and how that affects our design decisions.

Now that we know how to build classes and wrap them in ActiveX DLLs and ActiveX EXEs, let's take a look at another of the ActiveX family, and a technology that should be quite familiar: ActiveX Controls.

VB COM

5

ActiveX Controls

Who among us hasn't heard about or already used an ActiveX Control? ActiveX Controls are pervasive in today's Windows software development. While some of the first major press on ActiveX Controls may have been in relation to the browser wars between Microsoft's Internet Explorer (IE) and Netscape's Navigator, ActiveX Controls are not just limited to the Internet. Most of the top Windows desktop software applications, like Microsoft Office, make heavy use of ActiveX Controls both to increase the richness of their end user experience, and to reduce their time to market through component reuse.

The familiar Visual Basic Toolbox presents you with a number of Microsoft and third party ActiveX Controls so that you too can bring a professional look-and-feel to your applications in a much shorter amount of time than if you had to write your entire application from scratch. You are free to focus on the problem at hand rather than on the details of making, for example, a grid or a calendar.

Over time, though, you may write a widget that, "If I could just package it like so..." you could quickly reuse in a suite of applications. Your widget may even have potential mass appeal to software developers in other locales and other languages. Packaging your code as an ActiveX Control may be the perfect solution to your own software development. The great news is that as a Visual Basic developer, you can develop ActiveX Controls as efficiently and as easily as Standard EXEs.

However, the real enabling power behind ActiveX Controls is not Visual Basic or, for that matter, any other programming language. As you'll discover during the course of this chapter, the power is COM! In particular, you will learn:

- ❑ The history of the ActiveX Control
- ❑ How to create an ActiveX Control
- ❑ How ActiveX Controls and their containers interact

❏ ActiveX Controls and their properties and methods
❏ The COM behind ActiveX Controls
❏ Distributing an ActiveX Control

After finishing this chapter, you will be able to create a new tool written in Visual Basic that can work in many different environments, so let's get started!

A Brief History

In the beginning, the Microsoft Visual Basic team decided that there was a need to create controls that would be used in Visual Basic development, but that were separate from Visual Basic itself. These controls took the form of visual tools that the developer could easily drag and drop from the toolbox onto a form. With a double-click on the control, code could be written based on events that the control exposed. Properties could also be called upon from the control.

These **Visual Basic Extensions** (or **custom controls**) were better known as **VBX**s due to their `.vbx` filename extensions. VBXs made it quite easy to create visual applications, and many third parties began creating VBX controls for sale to Visual Basic developers. For example, if you wanted to have a spreadsheet in your application but didn't want to have to program it yourself, you could just find a VBX control developer who had created a spreadsheet control. You would purchase it from them, simply drag it from the toolbox onto a form and write your code. The control could be used in any application you wrote as long as the licensing agreement was adhered to. Talk about code reuse!

It was also cheaper to use VBXs than to do your own development. For example, let's say that at the time, a programmer charged $20/hour, while the VBX component cost $150. Now, if the programmer was to create this component on their own (which, by the way, they would have to do in C++ because you couldn't *create* VBXs with Visual Basic) it might take them 40 hours. It's not hard to see that the pre-built VBX for $150 is much cheaper than the $20 x 40 hours or $800 it would take for the programmer to develop the equivalent functionality provided instantly by the control. The market exploded with all the great VBX tools that a Visual Basic programmer could ever want to use. In fact, there are still companies whose whole business is selling these controls.

VBX controls made it much easier to develop applications but there were still some problems. First, they were not COM-based; they were proprietary to Visual Basic. For the most part, you could not take a VBX control and use it in another language. Second, a Visual Basic developer could not create a VBX with Visual Basic. If you did not know C++, you were out of luck, not to mention that developing controls at the time in C++ was not as easy as the visual tools that Visual Basic developers were accustomed to. Finally, the VBX architecture was dependent on Intel's 80x86 processors running in 16-bit mode. Today we take 32-bit applications for granted, and not every desktop computer has an Intel processor inside. The VBX architecture didn't scale well with the future.

Then came the tidal wave that would change things for the VBX: the Internet. Microsoft needed a technology that could compete with Netscape's plug-in architecture for their Internet Explorer browser, which enabled users to download components that allowed them to view and interact with a variety of features that were not supported by HTML alone. For example, if you had the correct plug-in component installed, you could go to a page and listen to radio stations over the Internet or maybe view animations.

The problem with the plug-in architecture was that if you didn't have the plug-in installed, it simply didn't work. There was no way to have the browser install the plug-in automatically. Worse still, once you downloaded a plug-in, you had to go through an installation procedure and sometimes even reboot the system. This was not very user friendly.

Microsoft released a new specification for controls based on the set of COM technologies known as
OLE (pronounced "oh-lay") in 1994. OLE Controls, the subject of this specification, entered the
Visual Basic scene about nine months later with the launch of Visual Basic 4.0, and are now better
known as **OCXs** due to their `.ocx` file extension. Because OLE Controls were based on COM, there
was support for both 16-bit and 32-bit computing environments. Controls could now be written and
consumed in a variety of languages, not just Visual Basic:

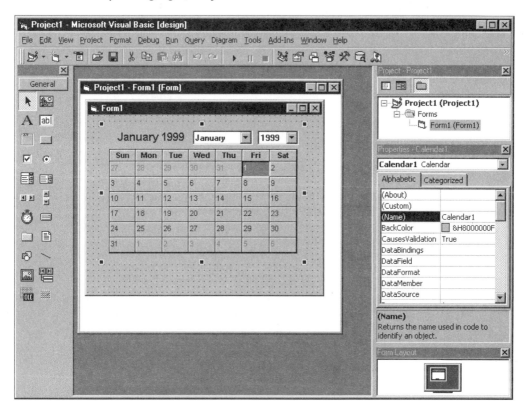

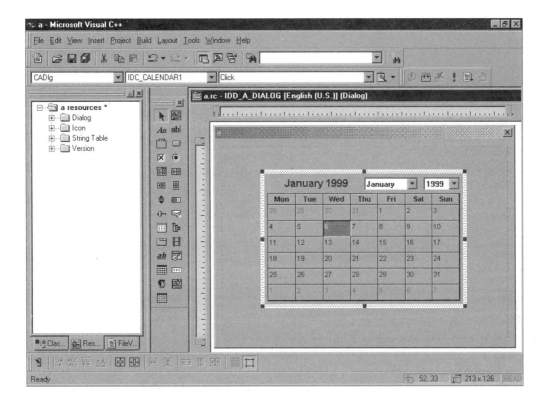

Keep in mind that there is nothing magical about the .ocx *file extension in an ActiveX Control implementation. The bottom line is that an ActiveX Control is simply another kind of COM object. As long as you properly register your in-process server, you may give it any extension you choose. Visual Basic just happens to choose* .ocx *for its ActiveX Control file extension.*

After Visual Basic 4 came the introduction of Internet Explorer 3, and this event gave cause for the marketing department at Microsoft to rename OLE Controls as ActiveX Controls. The important point, though, is that the underlying technology – COM – did not change. All OLE Controls immediately "became" ActiveX Controls, although technically there are a few differences between older OLE controls and modern ActiveX Controls.

IE3 was the first version of Microsoft's browser that supported the embedding of ActiveX Controls in HTML pages. As a result, IE3 and ActiveX Controls were placed in direct competition with Navigator and its plug-in architecture. ActiveX Controls were no longer limited to the desktop and could now be downloaded via the Web:

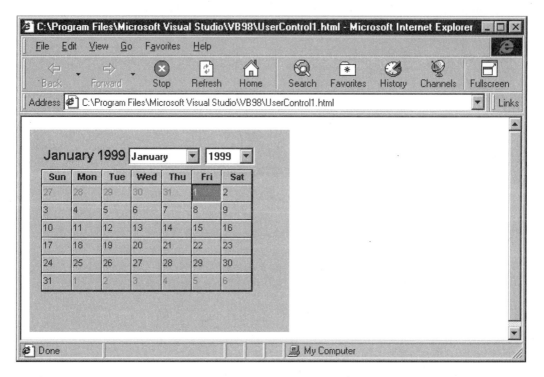

A second specification for ActiveX Controls was released in 1996 (known as OC96 or "OLE Controls '96") which, in the light of burgeoning Internet use, focused on making controls more efficient. This new breed of ActiveX Controls was employed in both Office 97 and Internet Explorer 4. Later, Visual Basic 5 was released, and although it dropped support for 16-bit controls, you'll soon learn that overall, it added a lot more support for controls than it lost.

Since Visual Basic 4.0, the number of ActiveX Controls available on the market has increased substantially. Even the set of controls included with Visual Basic itself has grown. Today, you have immediate access to a significant amount of pre-built functionality that allows you to focus on more important development tasks. The VBX is now a thing of the past (except for those who must still support 16-bit clients; I pray for you) and our toolboxes are filled with all kinds of great, new OCX controls.

Visual Basic 5.0 Control Creation Edition

A few months before the release of Visual Basic 5.0, Microsoft posted the Visual Basic 5.0 Control Creation Edition on its web site for free download. Commonly known as **VBCCE**, this tool allowed Visual Basic developers to create ActiveX Controls in Visual Basic, but nothing else – you were not able to compile applications. This was strategic for Microsoft because VBCCE made it easy to create ActiveX Controls, and because it was free, many developers quickly downloaded it in order to write new ActiveX Controls to put on their web pages. The only flaw was that to create ActiveX Controls, you had to know a little more about Visual Basic than the simple tutorial that came with VBCCE told you. Many developers downloaded it, but some had no idea how to get past writing a simple counter control.

In general, however, the move to release VBCCE earlier than Visual Basic 5.0 release paid off. Not only was there a proliferation of ActiveX Controls created with the tool, but also many budding developers decided that if it was this easy to create ActiveX Controls with Visual Basic, it would be just as easy to write applications. Thus began the wave of new Visual Basic programmers.

ActiveX Control Primer

> An ActiveX Control is just a special type of in-process COM object. In Visual Basic terms, an ActiveX Control can be thought of as an ActiveX DLL with support for an additional set of well-defined interfaces.

Since an ActiveX Control is a COM class, it implements a set of COM interfaces. Remember that interfaces are everything to COM. A control may be written in Visual Basic and its container may be written in C++; to be an ActiveX Control simply means supporting or implementing a particular set of interfaces that allow the control and its container to negotiate user interface real estate and behavior. An ActiveX Control can also expect certain support of its container.

This two-way support depends on a set of interfaces. As long as the control and container each implement particular interfaces, then regardless of language and application, things are satisfactory. As long as a control implements the required interfaces, it can operate equally well in a custom Visual Basic application, Internet Explorer, or a software solution written in C++ or Java.

There is a caveat, unfortunately. Controls cannot be guaranteed to function in exactly the same way in different containers. This is down to interface support, which we'll cover later in the chapter.

ActiveX Controls are a lot like the ActiveX components we wrote in the previous chapter, in that they have properties, methods, and events we can call upon. The principal difference is that ActiveX controls require a container – they cannot run within their own process space.

Creating an ActiveX Control

Now we've had a brief introduction to what an ActiveX control is, we can begin to peel back the covers. However, before we get into our COM discussion, let's create our very own ActiveX control that we can use as the basis for our future discussion. In this project, we are going to create a very simple double text box control that can be used for people's names.

1. Create a new ActiveX Control project and change the Project Properties to resemble the following dialog:

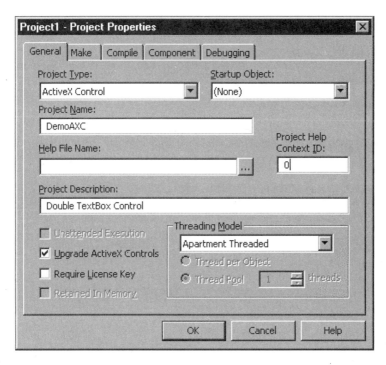

2. Change the name of the User Control to DblTxtBx.

3. Place two text boxes on the frame provided, name them txtForename and txtSurname respectively, and clear their Text properties:

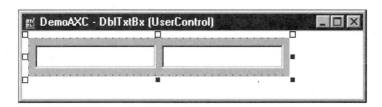

4. We *could* just compile the control as it is, but let's add some implementation of our own. Open the code window and add the following:

```
Option Explicit

Event FieldsComplete()

Public Property Get CompleteName() As String
    CompleteName = Forename & " " & Surname
End Property

Public Property Get Forename() As String
    Forename = txtForename.Text
End Property

Public Property Let Forename(vData As String)
    txtForename = vData
    PropertyChanged "Forename"
End Property

Public Property Get Surname() As String
    Surname = txtSurname.Text
End Property

Public Property Let Surname(vData As String)
    txtSurname = vData
    PropertyChanged "Surname"
End Property

Private Sub txtForename_KeyPress(KeyAscii As Integer)
    If KeyAscii = 13 Then
        If txtForename <> "" And txtSurname <> "" Then
            RaiseEvent FieldsComplete
        End If
    End If
End Sub

Private Sub txtSurname_KeyPress(KeyAscii As Integer)
    If KeyAscii = 13 Then
        If txtForename <> "" And txtSurname <> "" Then
            RaiseEvent FieldsComplete
        End If
    End If
End Sub
```

These are just some basic property routines and event handlers, and we'll be exploring this code in detail throughout the rest of the chapter.

5. Compile the control as an OCX so that we can use it in other projects.

Using an ActiveX Control

Let's create a very simple project to see how to use the control we just created.

1. Start up a new Standard EXE project.

2. Bring up the Components dialog, either by right-clicking on the toolbox and selecting Components... or by using the Project | Components... menu item:

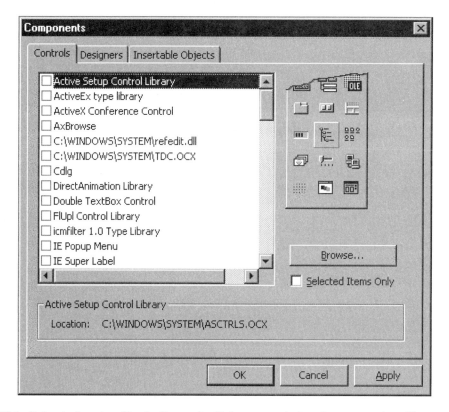

This dialog is functionally similar to the References dialog that we used in Chapters 2 and 3. In fact, it's possible to add a reference to our ActiveX control by using the References dialog, but then you can't use the control as you normally would. What you *can* do is declare object variables of your control type, just as you would with any other ActiveX component.

The significant difference between the two dialogs is that the Controls tab of the Components dialog lists *only* those components registered as ActiveX controls. When you select a control from this dialog, Visual Basic adds it to your toolbox. (See Appendix A for more information on how components are registered.)

3. Scroll down the list of controls until you find our Double TextBox Control component and check the checkbox:

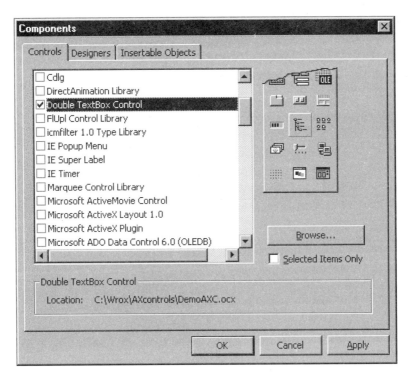

When you close the dialog, you will find a new icon in your toolbox:

This is the default icon for an ActiveX Control. You can replace it with something more meaningful if you wish by using the ToolboxBitmap *property.*

4. Double-click on the icon to draw an instance of our control on the form; you will see that Visual Basic gives the control instance the default name `DblTxtBx1`.

5. Open the code window so that we can put some code behind the `FieldsComplete` event we defined earlier:

```
Option Explicit

Private Sub DblTxtBx1_FieldsComplete()
    MsgBox DblTxtBx1.CompleteName, , "Fields Complete!"
End Sub
```

6. Now run the project and enter values into the two text boxes. Press *Return* and you will get a message box:

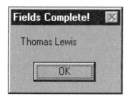

Although we'll revisit the project a few times later in the chapter to improve its functionality, the basics of the control are complete. Now that our control is in place, we can move on to discussing some of the COM that underlies ActiveX Controls.

An ActiveX Control's Interfaces

In Chapter 2, we saw how Visual Basic provided eight extra interfaces for our ActiveX DLL that it thought might be of use to us. It does much the same thing again when we compile an ActiveX control, but this time it doesn't just implement eight interfaces – it adds 25!

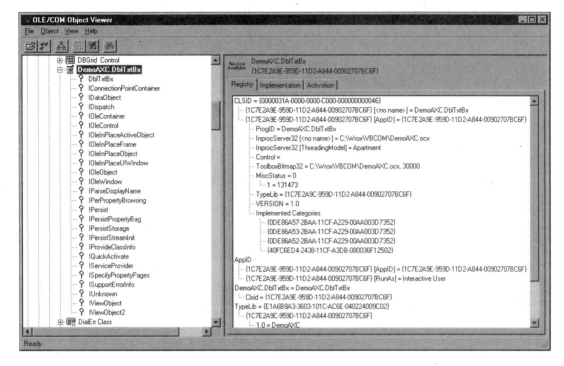

Why on earth should an ActiveX Control need so many more interfaces? Some of them, such as `IDispatch` and `IUnknown`, we've seen before but there are a whole slew of interfaces that are new to us. Again, as with the ActiveX DLL, we don't actually *need* all these interfaces – they are just Visual Basic's best guess as to the support that we might require, and we'll only have to look more carefully at a few of them in this chapter.

One of the principal reasons why so many interfaces can be required is to handle the relationship between container and control, which is more complicated than the typical client-server relationships we've seen so far. There is a great deal of bi-directional communication and many of these interfaces are devoted towards implementing and maintaining this complex interaction.

ActiveX Control Objects

It's about time we took a look at the some of the innards of an ActiveX Control. Unlike ActiveX DLLs or EXEs, where you only really have to deal with the objects that you define yourself, there is a group of default objects that are an integral part of ActiveX Control programming. These are:

❑   Your Control object

❑   The UserControl object

❑   The Ambient object

❑   The Extender object

❑   Constituent Control objects

The **Control** object is the only one that you have to implement yourself, and it's here that you define your control's interface in the same manner as you would for standard ActiveX components. From this Control object, you have access to the functionality provided by all the other objects.

The **UserControl** is the base object that Visual Basic uses to create ActiveX Controls. A lot of the basic control handling, such as activation and focus, is already implemented for you. This is yet another example of Visual Basic making your life easier.

We'll discuss the **Ambient** and **Extender** objects in more detail shortly, but for now you just need to know that they provide a mechanism by which your control can interact with its container.

Finally, **Constituent Control** objects are any controls that you use *within* your own ActiveX Control. For example, our `DblTxtBx` control contained two constituent text box controls. You use these objects in almost exactly the same manner as you would normally use controls. The COM mechanics of this are quite interesting and have general relevance to all COM programming, so we're going to spend some time examining the COM considerations of constituent and composite controls.

Constituent and Composite Controls

In our `DblTxtBx` example, we took the easy route and based our control on two text boxes. Our control could then be said to be a **composite control** and the two text boxes are its **constituent controls**. Essentially, what we have here is three COM objects: our `DblTxtBx` control and two text boxes. They are not on an equal footing, though: the two text boxes are contained within our `DblTxtBx` control:

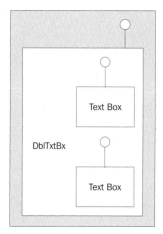

In fact, the UserControl is also contained within our Control, but I haven't included that here because it's not part of this discussion and I didn't want to clutter the diagram.

We are effectively reusing the text box component in a different setting (albeit only a *slightly* different setting on this occasion), demonstrating the power that COM provides for reusing components. Our `DblTxtBox` can be said to be composed of the other controls – or rather, it **contains** the other controls. In order for a client to access any of the properties or methods of the constituent controls, we need to delegate down from our own Control object.

Containment and Delegation

Containment and delegation are good examples of COM's ability to allow us to use and reuse components dynamically in the systems we build.

Containment is when we dynamically create other COM object instances at runtime in order to use their services, such as when we create instances of text boxes for each `DblTxtBx` instance. Containment is easy on the client, because it doesn't have to know about the existence of the contained object.

Delegation is when we call a method on a contained object in response to a call on the component that contains it. In other words, instead of handling the implementation for this in the container component, we are delegating or passing on this responsibility to a contained object. The client never knows that its request has been delegated down to another object, as it only ever interacts with the interface of the "outer" component.

We've implemented just such a relationship with our `DblTxtBx` control:

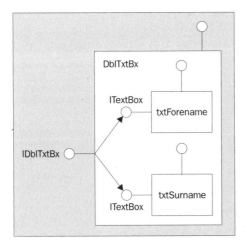

By default, all the properties, methods and events of our constituent controls are hidden – another example of encapsulation. However, it makes sense for a client to be able to access the text from either of the text boxes, and there are a number of ways that I could have chosen to do this. We could have added some routines whose purpose was to read the value from the `Text` properties of the text boxes, and then to pass this value out to the client. We could even have added some code to change the value if we didn't like it. By far the simplest thing to do, though, is to delegate the call down to the text boxes themselves. In COM terms, we are **exposing** the `Text` property of the constituent text box controls:

```
Public Property Get Forename() As String
    Forename = txtForename.Text
End Property

Public Property Get Surname() As String
    Surname = txtSurname.Text
End Property
```

Exposing constituent control events involves a different procedure, as you might have noticed from the code. We'll cover this later when we discuss events and outgoing COM interfaces.

You might think this is a rather labor intensive task. After all, if there are a lot of properties and methods that we want to expose, we'll need to code a lot of interface routines. Wouldn't it be simpler to expose the constituent control itself? That way, the client would have complete access to the constituent control's full range of functionality:

```
Public Property Get txtForename() As TextBox
    Set txtForename = txtForename
End Sub
```

Well, to start with, the above code won't compile because `TextBox` isn't a public data type. However, there are some more theoretical, COM-based reasons why this is a bad idea.

Imagine that the above code *does* compile. From an OOP perspective, the client now has direct access to the constituent control's state and behavior, bypassing any validation code you might want to implement. It would be quite possible for a client to resize one of the text boxes, something that you almost certainly wouldn't want them to be able to do.

This technique also restricts your ability to modify your control's implementation at a later date. We might decide, for example, that it would be better to use a rich text box control than the intrinsic version, but this would automatically break any client code that expected only an intrinsic textbox to be present.

The ActiveX Control Interface Wizard

Earlier in the chapter, we created the COM interface for an ActiveX Control, writing the properties, methods and events for this control manually. You can see that if we were creating a very complex and detailed control, it would take quite a while to create all the properties, methods, and events that our control would need.

Do not despair: our good friends at Microsoft have realized this and created **the ActiveX Control Interface Wizard**. Perhaps a better name for this Wizard, though, would be the ActiveX Control *COM* Interface Wizard, because it allows control developers to assemble the COM interfaces of their controls quickly. It's not designed to assist in creating the visual aspects of a control. We will use this Wizard to create the infrastructure of properties, methods, and events that lies *behind* what we present to an end user.

Recreating our ActiveX Control

Let's recreate our control using the ActiveX Control Interface Wizard. Not only will we see once again how easy it is to create COM interfaces with Visual Basic, but also we will add some additional functionality that our original code was lacking, but which we need for later discussion.

1. Open the `DemoAXC` project. Then, either right-click on the project window or use the Project menu to add a new, blank UserControl to the project. Name it `DblTxtBxWiz`.

2. Position two text boxes on the form and set their properties as we did before.

3. Now we do things differently. From the Add-Ins menu, select the Add-In Manager... and load the VB6 ActiveX Ctrl Interface Wizard:

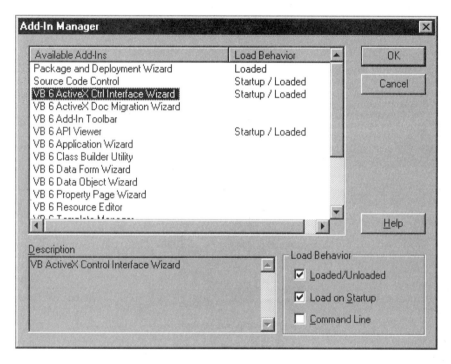

4. Now if you open the Add-Ins menu again, there will be an item for the ActiveX Control Interface Wizard. Run it.

The Introduction screen instructs the user to create all the interface elements (constituent controls) before running the Wizard. This is important, because the Wizard will need to know what they all are so that their properties, methods, and events can be mapped correctly. I don't recommend running the Wizard multiple times to create your control because it does not seem to include any custom changes that you make to it.

5. Once you've clicked the Next > button, you will need to instruct the Wizard to use the `DblTxtBxWiz` control:

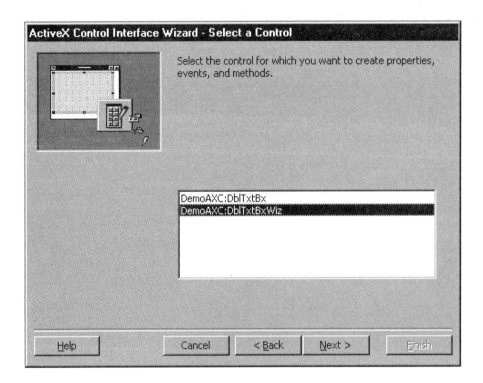

6. The next screen allows you to select your interface members:

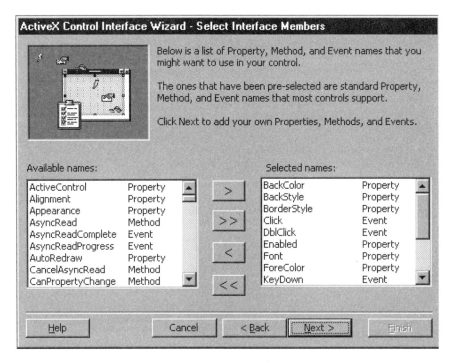

7. The list box on the left contains a list of behaviors that Visual Basic has deduced that you could support by examining the constituent controls, including the UserControl.

The list box on the right contains the list of behaviors that you want the control to implement, and therefore want the Wizard to create in your control's interface. You'll notice that the Wizard has already created a list of behaviors that it thinks you will want to implement; again, this is based on the constituent controls.

Microsoft recommends that you implement a common set of properties in the ActiveX Controls that you create, and this is a good idea because the users of your control will expect it to have a minimal set of functionality in addition to the custom behavior that you want to provide. For example, it aids for a better user experience if they see properties such as BackColor that they may have used before.

In fact, most of the behaviors in the earlier example *were* custom, apart from the KeyPress event that is already in the list. We really ought to leave the list as it is and accept the Wizard's suggestions, but this would create a lot of additional code that would only serve to confuse the issue. Therefore, use the < button to move all the behaviors except KeyPress from the right-hand list to the left:

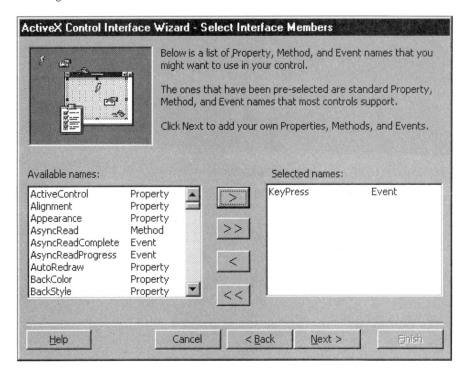

8. The next dialog allows us to define custom behaviors. We need to add the `Forename`, `Surname` and `CompleteName` properties, plus the `FieldsComplete` event. To do this, hit the Ne<u>w</u>... button, enter the name of the behavior and use the option buttons to select the type:

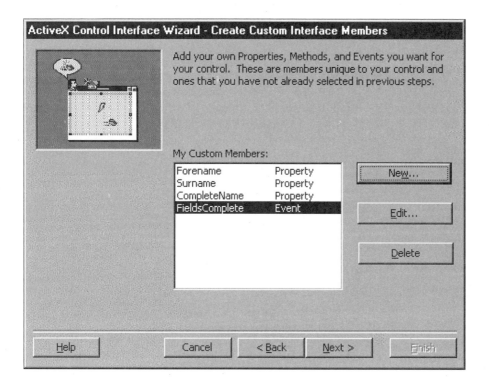

9. The next page of the Wizard allows us to map or delegate behavior down to one of our constituent controls. We need to map our custom properties `Forename` and `Surname` to the `Text` properties of `txtForename` and `txtSurname` respectively. To do this, select the custom property from the list box, and use the two combo boxes to map it to the respective `Text` property:

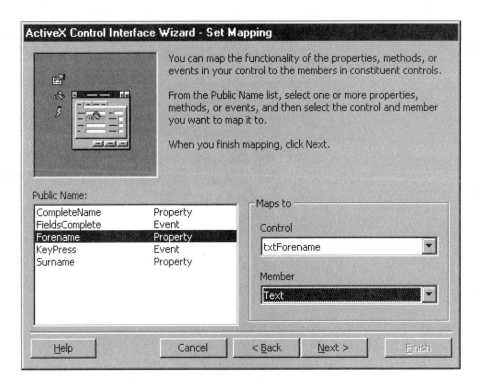

10. After clicking the <u>N</u>ext > button again, the Set Attributes screen becomes available, and it is here that we can handle the members we were unable to map. In fact, you will *only* see those members listed here. The member we really need to set is the `CompleteName` property; do it like this:

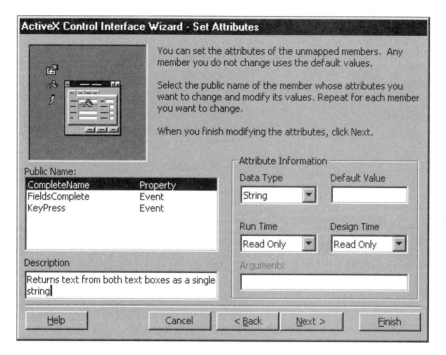

11. Once you've pressed the <u>N</u>ext > button for the last time, the Wizard is ready to go away and generate the code that you've specified. Hit the <u>F</u>inish button and the Wizard will crank away, grinding out code for our control. When it's finished, the Summary appears, which gives us instructions on how to create a program to test our control. It also allows us to save the summary to a text file. The unfortunate part is that there is no 'Print' button on the form, so you can't print it out without saving it first.

12. Go to the code window of the control and have a look at the code it has created:

```
Option Explicit
'Default Property Values:
Const m_def_CompleteName = ""
'Property Variables:
Dim m_CompleteName As String
'Event Declarations:
Event KeyPress(KeyAscii As Integer)
Event FieldsComplete()

'WARNING! DO NOT REMOVE OR MODIFY THE FOLLOWING COMMENTED LINES!
'MappingInfo=txtForename,txtForename,-1,Text
Public Property Get Forename() As String
    Forename = txtForename.Text
End Property

Public Property Let Forename(ByVal New_Forename As String)
    txtForename.Text() = New_Forename
    PropertyChanged "Forename"
End Property

'WARNING! DO NOT REMOVE OR MODIFY THE FOLLOWING COMMENTED LINES!
'MappingInfo=txtSurname,txtSurname,-1,Text
Public Property Get Surname() As String
    Surname = txtSurname.Text
End Property

Public Property Let Surname(ByVal New_Surname As String)
    txtSurname.Text() = New_Surname
    PropertyChanged "Surname"
End Property

'WARNING! DO NOT REMOVE OR MODIFY THE FOLLOWING COMMENTED LINES!
'MemberInfo=13,1,1,
Public Property Get CompleteName() As String
    CompleteName = m_CompleteName
End Property

Public Property Let CompleteName(ByVal New_CompleteName As String)
    If Ambient.UserMode = False Then Err.Raise 387
    If Ambient.UserMode Then Err.Raise 382
    m_CompleteName = New_CompleteName
    PropertyChanged "CompleteName"
End Property

'Initialize Properties for User Control
Private Sub UserControl_InitProperties()
    m_CompleteName = m_def_CompleteName
End Sub

'Load property values from storage
Private Sub UserControl_ReadProperties(PropBag As PropertyBag)
    txtForename.Text = PropBag.ReadProperty("Forename", "")
    txtSurname.Text = PropBag.ReadProperty("Surname", "")
    m_CompleteName = PropBag.ReadProperty("CompleteName", m_def_CompleteName)
End Sub
```

```
'Write property values to storage
Private Sub UserControl_WriteProperties(PropBag As PropertyBag)
    Call PropBag.WriteProperty("Forename", txtForename.Text, "")
    Call PropBag.WriteProperty("Surname", txtSurname.Text, "")
    Call PropBag.WriteProperty("CompleteName", m_CompleteName, m_def_CompleteName)
End Sub
```

As you can see, most of the code is very similar to ours, with the addition of two private routines that deal with property persistence, which we'll come back to in a while.

13. Two things the Wizard hasn't done are to provide the code to raise `FieldsComplete`, and to create the `CompleteName` property. Copy the routines we used in our original control into this one.

I want to draw your attention to the `Property Let` routine for `CompleteName`:

```
Public Property Let CompleteName(ByVal New_CompleteName As String)
    If Ambient.UserMode = False Then Err.Raise 387
    If Ambient.UserMode Then Err.Raise 382
    m_CompleteName = New_CompleteName
    PropertyChanged "CompleteName"
End Property
```

If you recall our original code, we made the `CompleteName` property read-only simply by omitting a `Property Let` routine. The Wizard, on the other hand, has included just such a routine, except that because we specified that the property should be read-only, it has added two lines that use the Ambient object we'll be discussing shortly:

```
    If Ambient.UserMode = False Then Err.Raise 387
    If Ambient.UserMode Then Err.Raise 382
```

These two error messages are Property Set not permitted and Property Set can't be executed at run time, respectively. Whenever you try to set this property, you'll get an error message depending upon the state of the environment. Either way, you can't set this property through code.

The Container-Control Relationship

Developing an ActiveX Control is not quite as simple as developing other ActiveX components. The customer for your ActiveX Control may be a user working with it at runtime, or another developer interacting with it at design-time. You need to provide support within your control for both possibilities. Also, the level of interaction is likely to be different for design-time and run-time use, and so you need some mechanism that you can code into your control that can detect how it is being used.

Fortunately, ActiveX Controls provide just such functionality for you in the shape of the Ambient and Extender objects, but it is up to you as the author of the control to use these exposed objects appropriately.

The Ambient Object

We can use the Ambient object to determine information about the container of our control, and so it is even possible to arrange for the control to function differently depending upon the type of container it's in. Before you get too confused, this works because the Ambient object is not implemented by your ActiveX Control, but rather by its container. The properties of the Ambient object are accessed via the AmbientProperties object, which is in turn accessed through the `Ambient` property of the UserControl object.

Ambient properties reflect values that the container wants to communicate to the control so that the control can better integrate with its environment. While these values are recommendations from the container rather than edicts, controls should accept container advice of this kind whenever it's appropriate to do so.

According to the Visual Basic Object Browser, the Visual Basic runtime library supports the following standard ambient properties through its AmbientProperties object:

Property	Description
BackColor	A color that contains the suggested interior color of the contained control.
DisplayAsDefault	Returns a Boolean value that indicates whether the control is the default control for the container, and should therefore display itself as such.
DisplayName	A string containing the name that the control should display for itself.
Font	Returns a `Font` object.
Forecolor	A color that contains the suggested foreground color of the contained control.
LocaleID	Returns a long value that contains the locale identifier (language and country) of the user.
MessageReflect	Returns a Boolean value stating whether the container handles message reflection to the control automatically.
Palette	Returns/sets an image that contains the palette to use for the control.
RightToLeft	Returns a Boolean value that indicates text display direction (for instance, Hebrew and Arabic versions of Windows have text running from right-to-left) and controls visual appearance on a bi-directional system.

Property	Description
ScaleUnits	Returns a string value that is the name of the coordinate units being used by the container.
ShowGrabHandles	Returns a Boolean value stating whether the control should show grab handles.
ShowHatching	Returns a Boolean value stating whether the container should show hatching over an inactive control if needed.
SupportsMnemonics	Returns a Boolean value stating whether the control's container handles access keys for the control.
TextAlign	Returns an enumerated value of type TextAlignChoices stating what kind of text alignment the container would like the control to do.
UIDead	Returns a Boolean value indicating whether the control should be responsive to the user or not.
UserMode	Returns a Boolean value indicating whether a form designer or a form user is using the control.

Containers do not have to support all these properties, and their implementation may vary from container to container. The AmbientProperties object provided by the Visual Basic runtime is kind enough to provide default values for any standard ambient properties not implemented by a control's container. This means you don't have to worry about getting error messages when using an ambient property that is not available. Alternatively, some containers may implement custom ambient properties, and unlike standard ambient properties (which are early-bound), container-specific ambient properties are always late-bound due to the lack of a type library. Container-specific ambient properties aren't visible in the Object Browser either; you must rely on the container documentation for usage details in these cases.

To return to the code generated by the Wizard:

```
If Ambient.UserMode = False Then Err.Raise 387
If Ambient.UserMode Then Err.Raise 382
```

We can see that the UserMode property is being used to determine what state the control is in. Since CompleteName is read-only at both design- and run-time, we raise an error either way.

The UserControl has an event called `AmbientChanged` that fires whenever an ambient property value has changed. For example, whenever the color of the container changes, we would probably like the color of our ActiveX control to change as well. It would not look very professional to have the container one color and the control a different color:

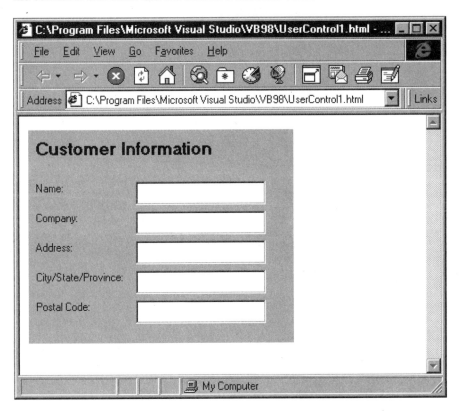

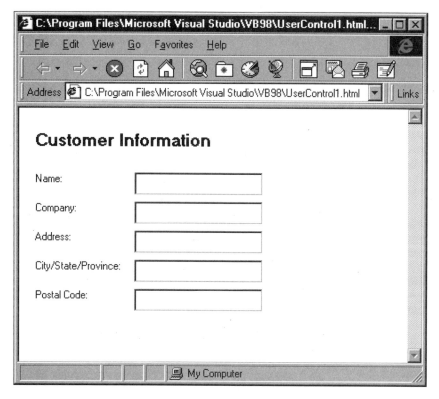

To have the `BackColor` of a control match the `BackColor` of the container, we could add the
following to our UserControl code:

```
Private Sub UserControl_AmbientChanged(PropertyName As String)
    Select Case PropertyName
        Case "BackColor"
            UserControl.BackColor = Ambient.BackColor
            ' Add other ambient properties...
    End Select
End Sub
```

You can see that whenever an ambient property changes, the UserControl's `AmbientChanged` event
is fired, and a variable called `PropertyName` is passed to the event. This variable stores the property
that was changed, and allows you to decide how you are going to handle it. Here, I've used a `Select
Case` statement that determines whether `BackColor` is the property that changed. Then we need to
get the `Ambient` property's `BackColor` value, and assign it to the UserControl's `BackColor`
property so that they match up. A `Select Case` statement is the best choice here because normally
there would be more code to handle the other ambient property changes that can occur.

The Extender Object

If you look at the Properties window for either of our `DblTxtBx` controls, you'll see a whole list of properties that we didn't add ourselves:

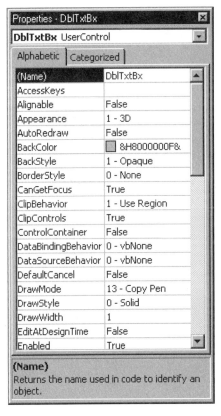

These are properties that *seem* to be part of your control, but are actually provided at runtime by the container – quite literally, they *extend* the functionality of the control. They also provide a way for the container to provide standard functionality. Keep in mind that the parent Extender object is owned by the container, not the control.

> **The difference between properties supplied by the Extender object and those supplied by the Ambient object is that ambient properties are for use by the control's author, while extended properties are only used by someone developing *with* a control.**

When you design a control, be sure to consider what containers it is likely to be placed in, and how each container implements its Extender object. Implementations are free to vary from one container to the next. You should provide robust error handling in case your container's Extender object does not behave in the way you anticipated.

To the developer, it seems as if the Extender's properties and your Control's properties are as one – they appear as a single interface:

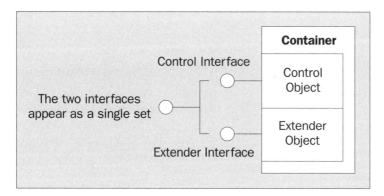

When you reference a control programmatically, you are really referencing its Extender object. Thus, when the user gets or sets a property, or invokes a method on the control, they do so through the interface of the outer Extender object, not the inner Control object. If the Extender object recognizes the property or method as one of its own, it performs the actions required. Otherwise, the control itself is called upon to satisfy the user's request.

The ActiveX Control specification states that the following extended properties should be provided in all containers:

Property	Type	Access	Defined
Cancel	Boolean	Read-only	Will be true if the control is the cancel button of the container.
Default	Boolean	Read-only	Will be true if the control is the default button of the container.
Name	String	Read-only	The name assigned to the control instance.
Parent	Object	Read-only	Returns the object reference to the container.
Visible	Boolean	Read/write	Will be true if the control is visible.

ActiveX Control Properties

It would be inconvenient, to say the least, if you had reset all the properties on your controls every time you reopened the project that contained them. Happily, another thing that sets ActiveX Controls apart from other ActiveX components is their ability to save information about the state of the control *at design-time*. This is known as **property persistence**.

Persisting Properties

An ActiveX Control is able persist its properties through the use of yet another object called the **PropertyBag**. This object is provided by the UserControl object, and all access to it is through the UserControl.

The PropertyBag Object

The PropertyBag object has these basic behaviors as exposed through UserControl:

- ❑ `InitProperties` event
- ❑ `WriteProperties` event
- ❑ `ReadProperties` event
- ❑ `WriteProperty` method
- ❑ `ReadProperty` method

We saw these in practice earlier in the code implemented by the ActiveX Control Wizard:

```
'Initialize Properties for User Control
Private Sub UserControl_InitProperties()
    m_CompleteName = m_def_CompleteName
End Sub

'Load property values from storage
Private Sub UserControl_ReadProperties(PropBag As PropertyBag)
    txtForename.Text = PropBag.ReadProperty("Forename", "")
    txtSurname.Text = PropBag.ReadProperty("Surname", "")
    m_CompleteName = PropBag.ReadProperty("CompleteName", m_def_CompleteName)
End Sub

'Write property values to storage
Private Sub UserControl_WriteProperties(PropBag As PropertyBag)
    Call PropBag.WriteProperty("Forename", txtForename.Text, "")
    Call PropBag.WriteProperty("Surname", txtSurname.Text, "")
    Call PropBag.WriteProperty("CompleteName", m_CompleteName, m_def_CompleteName)
End Sub
```

From this code, you can also see that our `CompleteName` property has a default value called `m_def_CompleteName`. Default values should be used whenever possible, because they will help to make your control run more efficiently. Visual Basic only persists a property if it has changed from its default value, so providing a default value will save on unnecessary save operations.

Property values are saved to the `.frm` file that corresponds to the form in which the control is sited. If the developer wishes to save values between sessions, they need to save this file to disk.

PropertyBag Events

InitProperties

The `InitProperties` event occurs only in a control instance's first incarnation, when an instance of the control is placed on a form. It's where you would set up any default property values:

```
Private Sub UserControl_InitProperties()
    m_CompleteName = m_def_CompleteName
End Sub
```

WriteProperties

The `WriteProperties` event is fired when an instance of a control needs to save its property values. This happens when a design-time instance of a control is being destroyed, provided that at least one property value has changed. It is here that you need to write data to the `.frm` file:

```
Private Sub UserControl_WriteProperties(PropBag As PropertyBag)
    Call PropBag.WriteProperty("Forename", txtForename.Text, "")
    Call PropBag.WriteProperty("Surname", txtSurname.Text, "")
    Call PropBag.WriteProperty("CompleteName", m_CompleteName, m_def_CompleteName)
End Sub
```

ReadProperties

The `ReadProperties` event fires when loading an old instance of an object that has saved property values. This occurs on the second occasion that a control instance is created, and on all subsequent re-creations. In this event, you retrieve the control instance's property values from the in-memory copy of the `.frm` file belonging to the form the control was placed on:

```
Private Sub UserControl_ReadProperties(PropBag As PropertyBag)
    txtForename.Text = PropBag.ReadProperty("Forename", "")
    txtSurname.Text = PropBag.ReadProperty("Surname", "")
    m_CompleteName = PropBag.ReadProperty("CompleteName", m_def_CompleteName)
End Sub
```

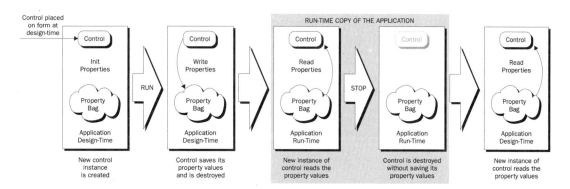

PropertyBag Methods

WriteProperty

The `WriteProperty` method is what's actually used to store a property value into a PropertyBag. Its syntax is:

```
PropBag.WriteProperty(DataName, Value[, DefaultValue])
```

We saw it being used in the `WriteProperties` event handler:

```
Call PropBag.WriteProperty("CompleteName", m_CompleteName, m_def_CompleteName)
```

This code writes the value of `m_CompleteName` to the `.frm` file, and associates the value with the string `"CompleteName"`. However, the value is only written if `m_CompleteName` is different from `m_def_CompleteName`.

ReadProperty

The `ReadProperty` method is used to return a saved property value and set up the control accordingly. Its syntax is:

```
PropBag.ReadProperty(DataName[, DefaultValue])
```

We saw it being used in the `ReadProperties` event handler:

```
m_CompleteName = PropBag.ReadProperty("CompleteName", m_def_CompleteName)
```

Essentially, this code works like the `WriteProperty` method in reverse. It uses the string `"CompleteName"` to find a property value associated with that string in the `.frm` file and sets the `m_CompleteName` variable accordingly. If no entry is found then the default value is used.

Mapping to Multiple Controls

As you can perhaps begin to see, relating persisted data to strings rather than to any particular property provides us with a great deal of flexibility. It means, for example, that we can map a property value to more than one control by exactly the same method.

Take our `DblTxtBxWiz` control. Let's add a `BackColor` property that maps to the `BackColor` properties of the two constituent text boxes. Add the following code:

```
Public Property Get BackColor() As OLE_COLOR
    BackColor = UserControl.BackColor
End Property

Public Property Let BackColor(ByVal New_BackColor As OLE_COLOR)
    txtForename.BackColor = New_BackColor
    txtSurname.BackColor = New_BackColor
    UserControl.BackColor() = New_BackColor
    PropertyChanged "BackColor"
End Property
```

Now, whenever we set the `BackColor` of the UserControl, we are also setting the `BackColor` of both text boxes.

Note the call to `PropertyChanged`. This method is important, as it notifies the environment (the Visual Basic IDE, for example), that the property value has changed. This means that displays such as the **Properties** window can be updated.

COM Interfaces for Persistence

From a COM perspective, an ActiveX Control implements a series of `IPersist` interfaces that allow the control to persist its properties. The OLEView screenshot earlier in the chapter showed that we were implementing several of these `IPersist` interfaces, but the only one that we shall discuss is `IPersistPropertyBag`:

`IPersistPropertyBag` works in conjunction with another interface called `IPropertyBag`, which provides the PropertyBag object used for persistence. The basic mechanism is that a container tells the control to save or load its properties through `IPersistPropertyBag`. In order for this to happen, a PropertyBag object is required. Therefore, for each property, the control calls the container's `IPropertyBag` interface, which supplies a property bag to the control.

The methods on the `IPersistPropertyBag` and `IPropertyBag` interfaces are directly comparable with the methods and events that we have been using to persist properties. `IPropertyBag` implements two methods, `Read` and `Write`, which relate to the `ReadProperty` and `WriteProperty` methods. `IPersistPropertyBag` has three methods – `Init`, `Load` and `Save` – which relate to the `InitProperties`, `ReadProperties` and `WriteProperties` events.

Property Pages

We often access a control's properties using the Properties window, but there's a rather obvious limitation here. The window is specific to Visual Basic, yet our control is not necessarily restricted to being sited in a Visual Basic application. **Property pages**, therefore, provide a container-independent method of displaying/changing a control's properties.

In Visual Basic, when you use an ActiveX Control that has property pages in the creation of another project, you can access those pages via a (Custom) button in the Properties window:

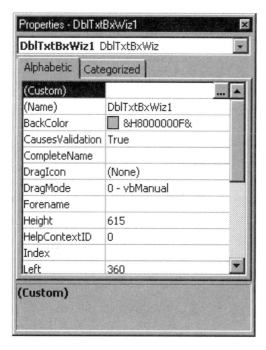

Property pages are implemented using the `IPropertyPage` interface, and each of the tabs in the dialog represents a separate COM object that implements `IPropertyPage`. This means that a control can divide up its properties as it wishes among several property pages. Also, because each page is a separate COM object, it's possible to share common pages with other controls.

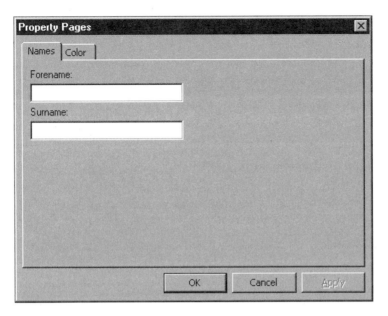

To support property pages, controls implement the ISpecifyPropertyPages interface, which has a single function called GetPages. A container can call GetPages in order to retrieve a list of the property page objects supported by the control. When the container wants to display the property pages it creates a property frame, and then creates instances of each of the page objects. Each page object represents a tab on the dialog box.

If a property is changed through a property page, the change is first communicated from the container's property frame to the page object, and then the property page object uses Automation to pass the changes on to the control itself.

Of course, whenever you ask to see the property pages for a control, all these COM operations take place transparently. As a Visual Basic developer, all you need to worry about is which properties belong in which pages. In fact, it's even easier than that, because Visual Basic provides a Wizard to help us create our property pages.

The Property Page Wizard

In this example, we're going to add some property pages to our control.

1. Either use the <u>P</u>roject menu or right-click in the Project window to add a property page to our DemoAXC project. We'll use it to set the Forename and Surname properties, so call it Names, and set its Caption property to Names as well:

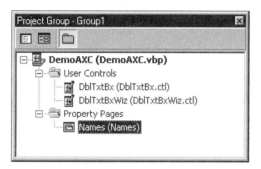

2. The Property Page Wizard can be accessed either through the <u>A</u>dd-Ins menu, or by adding another property page. First, you will need to specify which control the page corresponds to. Select our DblTxtBxWiz control:

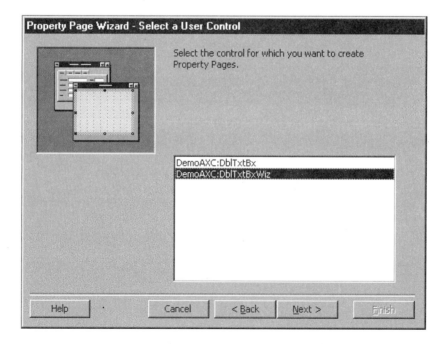

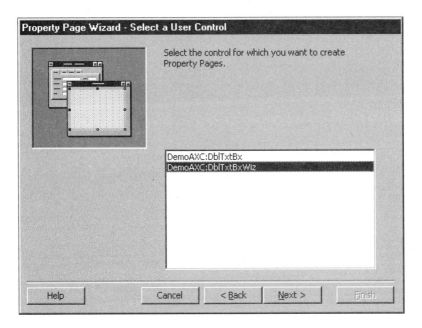

3. Next, we need to choose which property pages to add to our control. You can see that our Names page is there, but so is another called StandardColor:

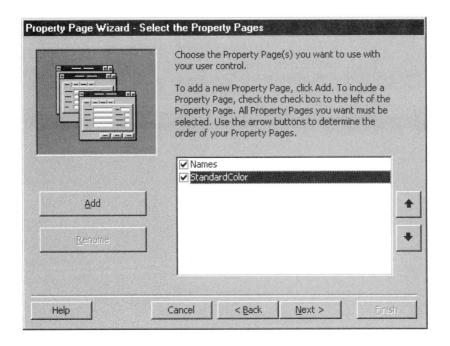

There are two types of property page in Visual Basic: custom and standard. Custom pages are ones like our Names page that we create ourselves, while standard pages are pre-constructed pages that are used for setting things like colors and fonts. We want both pages, so check both boxes.

4. The next page allows us to separate our properties onto different pages. Notice that our BackColor property is already on the Standard Color page tab. We do, however, have to specify that the Forename and Surname properties belong on our custom Names page:

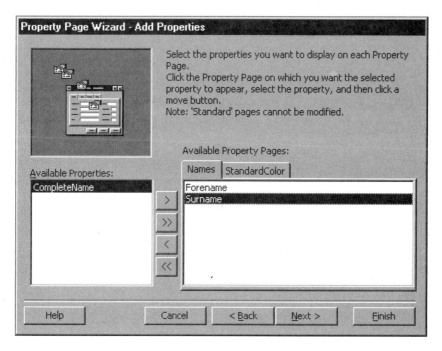

5. You can now step through the last few steps and then Visual Basic will go away and create our property pages for us.

If you open the custom property page, you will find it's little more than a couple of labels and text boxes. The code is also very simple:

```
Private Sub txtSurname_Change()
    Changed = True
End Sub

Private Sub txtForename_Change()
    Changed = True
End Sub

Private Sub PropertyPage_ApplyChanges()
    SelectedControls(0).Surname = txtSurname.Text
    SelectedControls(0).Forename = txtForename.Text
End Sub

Private Sub PropertyPage_SelectionChanged()
    txtSurname.Text = SelectedControls(0).Surname
    txtForename.Text = SelectedControls(0).Forename
End Sub
```

The two routines to note are the `SelectionChanged` and `ApplyChanges` event handlers. The `SelectionChanged` event occurs when the property page is displayed, and when the list of currently selected controls changes. In other words, all this routine does is load the property pages with the current values.

The `SelectedControls` collection is simply an array of all the controls currently selected in the container. If a property page is shared by more than one type of control, then the collection may contain controls of different types.

The `ApplyChanges` event fires when either the OK or Apply buttons are pressed, or another tab is selected. This event does the opposite of `SelectionChanged` by copying the new property values back to the control.

Events and COM

Although events are not exclusively limited to controls, we are far more used to coding event handlers that *are* connected to controls.

> *We saw how to use events with ActiveX DLLs and EXEs in the previous chapter, through the use of the* `WithEvents` *keyword.*

When we coded our control, we added a line in the Declarations section to declare an event:

```
Event FieldsComplete()
```

Then, when we wanted to raise this event, we simply used the `RaiseEvent` keyword:

```
RaiseEvent FieldsComplete
```

But how can our client know that this event has been raised and respond accordingly? The answer lies in a type of interface we haven't come across before: an **outgoing interface**. In COM diagrams, outgoing interfaces are symbolized differently from ordinary interfaces:

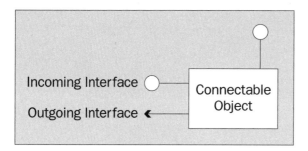

Normally, clients make requests of a component by calling **into** its properties and methods. Events, on the other hand, are raised by the *component* calling out to event handlers in clients. In COM terminology, this is called the **connection point** model, and a component that uses an outgoing interface is called a **connectable object**.

Connection Points

So: now you know that an event is really a function call made by the component. What we need to cover next is where exactly this call is made *to*. Well, common sense tells us that connections have two ends, or **points**. When you're dealing with COM events, these connection points are between a **sink** and a **source**.

Outgoing interfaces are not implemented by the component, but they certainly have to be implemented *somewhere*, and that somewhere is on the client itself. More precisely, the client creates a **sink object** that implements the interface:

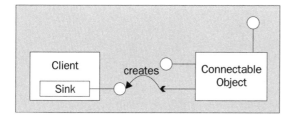

When the source (in this case, the component) needs to raise an event, it calls a function on the interface on the sink. From the sink's perspective, *it* is acting as the server and the component is acting as the client.

In order for this to function successfully, the client needs to implement the interface that the component is expecting. The client 'knows' what interfaces it needs to implement from the component's type library, but it makes sure that the container is aware that it's implementing them by calls to **connection interfaces**.

Connection Interfaces

COM implements connection points through the use of two interfaces:

- ❏ IConnectionPoint
- ❏ IConnectionPointContainer

You've already seen one of these interfaces, at least by name. In the OLEView screenshot earlier in the chapter, you can see that Visual Basic added the IConnectionPointContainer interface to our ActiveX Control:

The presence of this interface indicates to a client that the component has outgoing interfaces that need supporting by a sink. The client uses the IConnectionPointContainer interface to request a pointer to another interface called IConnectionPoint on the component. By calling a method on this interface, the client provides the component with a pointer to the sink interface. Thus, whenever an event needs to be fired, the source has a pointer to the sink where the interface handler lies:

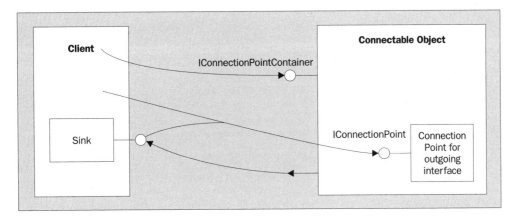

A connectable object also publishes information about its source interface in its type library. If we look at the type library for our DemoAXC control, we can see this in action:

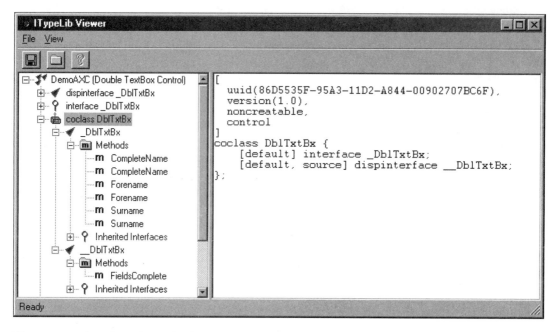

You can see that the only method of the source interface __DblTxtBx is our FieldsComplete event. It is also marked as a **dispinterface**, which means that the methods contained within it are only accessible through the Automation interface IDispatch. Because of this, events in Visual Basic are slower than standard vtable method calls – they have to go via the Invoke method on the client side.

My final point regarding events is that (as you can see) the __DblTxtBx interface is defined as the [default, source]. A Visual Basic client can *only* ever hook up to this default source interface. This means that you cannot include events in your custom interfaces that are implemented across different classes. You will need to declare events in each class separately so that they are compiled into the default source interface.

Distributing an ActiveX Control

Now that we have a good idea of what's going on within our ActiveX Control, let's finally prepare it for distribution.

Of course, our control isn't really ready for distribution quite yet – it has fairly minimal functionality – but for the purposes of this book it's ready enough. Just don't go using it in your applications and then come running to me when you find it too awkward to use!

Distributing a new ActiveX Control is not as simple as compiling it and copying it to a disk. There are three basic areas we need to concern ourselves with:

- ❑ Licensing
- ❑ Versioning
- ❑ Deployment

The following sections apply equally well to all ActiveX components; not just controls.

Licensing

Using Visual Basic, ActiveX Controls can be licensed so that other developers cannot use them in creating their own controls. Licensing prevents other developers using any programming language from using your control without consent. This keeps them from using your control as a constituent and selling it as their own.

A **license** is a registry key that allows a developer to use a control in the design-time environment. That way, even if someone has got hold of your .ocx file and registered it for use, they won't be able to use it because they don't have the license key.

What happens when a developer who *has* the key creates an application that includes your ActiveX Control and distributes the application to their customers? The license key is compiled into the ActiveX Control, but it's not added to the registry of the user. This keeps the user from using a programming language to use the ActiveX Control on their machine. A developer *must* have the key added to the registry before they are able to use your ActiveX control.

Now, it may just be that you develop ActiveX Controls for the love of it, and you don't mind who uses them, but that's OK too: you can specify that there is no need to have a license for an ActiveX control.

When you create a control with licensing switched on, a .vbl file is created. This is the file that holds the licensing information. If you must license a control for the *Internet*, a **license package** needs to be created, and this will have a .lpk extension. You must use the Lpk_Tool.exe program to create a license package that can be used from the Microsoft Internet Client SDK. Once the file has been created, a reference needs to be made to the license file on the HTML page it is sited on, via an <OBJECT> tag that knows how to read license packages.

We'll see how to add a license key to our ActiveX Control project in a short while.

Versioning

We discussed this topic in the previous chapter. Versioning enforces **backward compatibility**, which means that no established contracts between our COM object and its clients are broken. The COM interface of our ActiveX Control is the contract in question, and this means that in order to maintain backward compatibility with our existing client base, the existing properties, methods and events of our control's public COM interface cannot change.

Visual Basic uses your component project's compatibility settings to support robust versioning of your component. In particular, setting your component project to Binary Compatibility ensures that our existing clients will continue to work with newer versions of our component. I suggest that you set binary compatibility once your component's interfaces are reasonably mature, or as soon as your first client is distributed. Hopefully, clients won't be implemented until all component interfaces are well defined!

Once your component is ready for binary compatibility, I further recommend that you create a reference copy of your component housing, because Visual Basic wipes out old versions of the target OCX, DLL or EXE during its build process. I have a habit of creating a `RefCopy` folder under my Visual Basic project folders, and once I'm satisfied that my project's interfaces are reasonably mature, I make a final build with Project Compatibility selected. I then copy the newly created component to the `RefCopy` folder. Finally, I set Binary Compatibility for my project, specifying the reference copy as the OCX, DLL or EXE to use for the compatibility integrity check.

As with an ActiveX DLL or an ActiveX EXE, it's important that when a developer updates an ActiveX Control, it should be able to run just as it did before. A client application should not break if a control it employs has been updated. How many times have you been burned when you went and got the latest and greatest ActiveX Widget control version 2.0 and found that your application broke because Widget 2.0 doesn't support the features you used in Widget 1.0? You can put your hand down now.

With versioning, we can make sure that our component – in this case, an ActiveX Control – *will* be backward compatible. It works just as it did for ActiveX DLLs and ActiveX EXEs.

Deployment

Some thought and effort also needs to go into the actual deployment of an ActiveX Control. We could simply compile our control and then distribute it as a collection of related files, but this is not a very user-friendly method, and leaves such things as registering the control up to the user.

Although you do come across setup programs that are no more than compressed ZIP files, it is far more common (especially with professional applications) for setup to be controlled by a special installation executable that's been created by another program, such as InstallShield or WISE. Fortunately, Visual Basic provides yet another Wizard that helps us to deploy our Visual Basic applications.

The Package & Deployment Wizard

We will now create a distributable for our ActiveX control with the **Package & Deployment Wizard**, which was a new feature in Visual Basic 6.0 (it was formerly called the Setup Wizard). We will also handle some licensing and versioning issues along the way.

1. First, we need to go the Project Properties dialog of our ActiveX control project and make sure we have checked the Require License Key option. Now, when we create our setup program, it will include functionality to handle the licensing of our control:

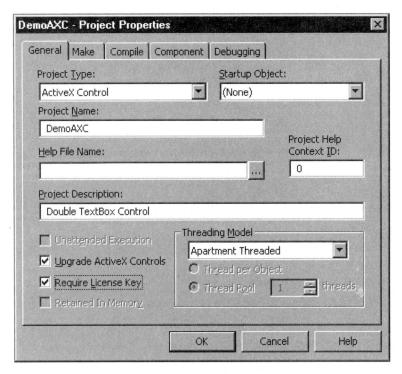

2. Recompile our .ocx file so that we can set up the versioning.

3. We need to make sure that any changes made to the ActiveX control retain backward compatibility. Go back to the Project Properties dialog and select the Component. Change the Version Compatibility to Binary Compatibility. This will now notify you whenever you change the control in such a way that will break backward compatibility:

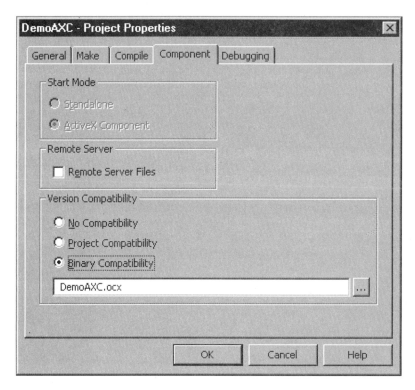

4. From the Add-Ins menu, select the Package & Deployment Wizard. If it does not exist on the menu, you must go into Add-In Manager and add it.

5. The project path will automatically be entered in the introduction screen of the Package & Deployment Wizard. Go ahead and click the Package button so that we can create our package:

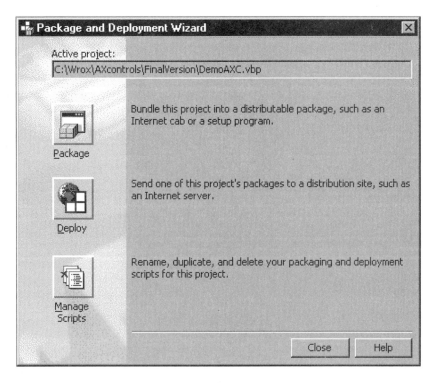

6. You will be prompted if you want to recompile the control, because we changed the versioning property. Select Yes:

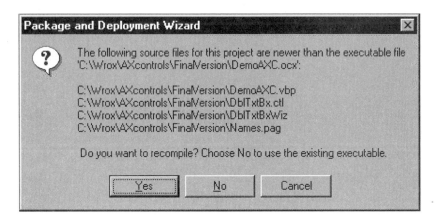

7. The Package Type screen allows you to choose whether you want to create a Standard Setup Package, an Internet Package, or a Dependency File. A standard package is the typical package you are probably used to from Visual Basic 5.0 or earlier. An Internet package allows you to save your distributable in a .cab file, which is a Microsoft file format. The dependency file option creates a .dep file that contains type information about the files in a project.

8. Dependency files are important if your component is dependent on the functionality of another. If for example, you are using ADO in your control then you will need to include some dependency information in case the user doesn't have ADO registered on their machine. We will use a Standard Setup for now:

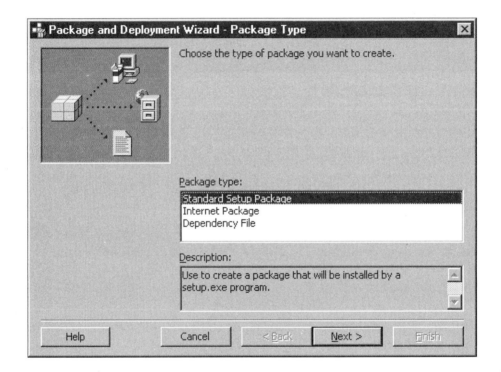

9. Now follow the rest of the screens and make changes as appropriate. You may be asked if you want to include the Property Page DLL with the package:

In our case, since our control is underdeveloped, we probably ought to select <u>N</u>o but it doesn't really matter.

10. You will also be asked if you want to share the .ocx file:

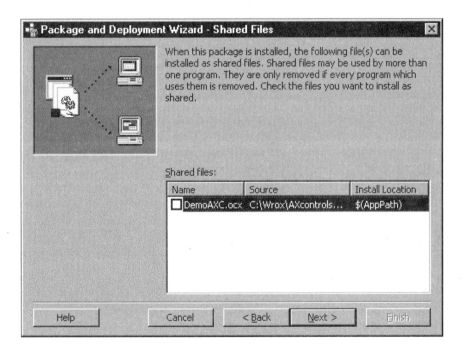

Normally you will want to tick this box, because it is quite possible that a developer might want to use our control in multiple applications.

11. Finally, you will reach the Finished! setup screen. Click the Finish button to create the setup program:

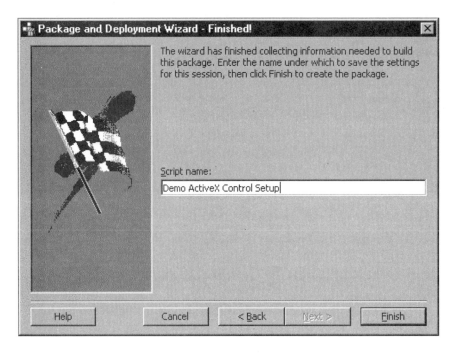

Make sure to enter a script name of your own – don't just use the default. This script name will be used when we are ready to deploy our control.

12. Once finished, the Wizard will churn and crank for a while until the setup application has been created. Now it is ready to be deployed. At the introduction screen, click the Deploy button. A screen will appear asking which package you want to deploy, and you should select the one you just created. (Now do you see why I told you to put in a script name?)

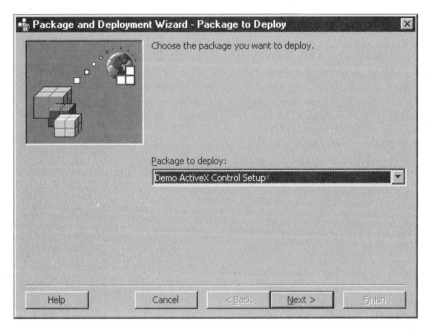

13. From here, we are asked to choose a Folder deployment or Web deployment, of which the former is the standard. In Visual Basic 6.0, we are given the choice to deploy our setup files on a web server and install the application or control from there with a click of a button.

14. Now we can browse to the folder specified and find the setup files needed to deploy our control to our users.

I have kept this example of the Package & Deployment Wizard simple, but the techniques you have learned here should be fine for small applications. However, if you need some more creative things included in your setup, you may want to think about a third party tool.

I always recommend that some time be spent with installation issues. Usually, installation is thought about at the last minute, but remember that a user who has to go through a buggy installation to get your program running tends to have little confidence in the application itself.

Summary

In this chapter, we started out discussing how ActiveX Controls came into being – how Microsoft released the Visual Basic 5.0 Control Creation Edition to spur growth for ActiveX Controls not only within Visual Basic, but also in other containers such as Internet Explorer.

We then created our own very simple ActiveX Control, and used it as the starting point for an exploration of the COM mechanics that occur behind the scene. We saw that, despite its relative simplicity, Visual Basic implements a great many COM interfaces for us. During the chapter, we encountered several of these interfaces in relation to property persistence and events.

Finally, you saw an example of how to package and distribute your control using the Package & Deployment Wizard, including coverage of issues such as versioning and licensing.

In the next chapter, we will go back to the ActiveX DLLs and ActiveX EXEs we've looked at in earlier chapters, and examine how we can use them remotely.

VB COM

6

Distributed COM

Overview

Microsoft's **Distributed COM** (**DCOM**) enables components to interact with each other remotely across a network in a secure fashion. In Chapter 4, we created COM components that would communicate with each other on the same machine. Now, more and more, developers are finding that there is a need to host components on different machines all over the network, to provide more scalable solutions. In recent years, the requirement for the development and deployment of scalable distributed intranet/Internet-based systems has been the main drive. DCOM provides the architecture to do this and a lot more.

DCOM is most commonly described as "COM on a longer wire".

In this chapter, we will cover:

- ❑ An explanation of DCOM
- ❑ The architecture of DCOM
- ❑ Consideration of using DCOM
- ❑ How DCOM works with Visual Basic
- ❑ DCOM Security
- ❑ Handling DCOM problems

I should warn you that to use DCOM you need a minimum of two machines networked together. It is also preferable if at least one of these machines is using Windows NT rather than Windows 9x. Although you can use DCOM on Windows 9x platforms, NT provides a greater level of functionality, especially with such issues as security. Finally, you really need the Enterprise edition of Visual Basic in order to create distributed components.

Fundamentals of DCOM

DCOM extends COM in a transparent fashion, such that any existing COM object can be remotely used without ever changing a single line of code. Although this seamless extension is great, as it protects your existing investments in component based development, it is important to understand from day one, that a COM object written without any consideration to DCOM specific issues, probably won't be efficient or scalable. We will discuss some of these points like network round-trips later in the chapter.

The Story So Far

COM servers (ActiveX DLLs, ActiveX EXEs etc.) allow a developer to package reusable components in such a way that they can be used by any number of applications, provided that an application knows the component's class (CLSID), and the interfaces it exposes. So far we have talked about ActiveX DLLs that run in the process space of their clients, and ActiveX EXEs that run in their own process space, either way both clients and components have been located on the same machine:

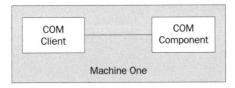

With most desktop applications this approach works fine. We build a client and a component preferably using Visual Basic (because it generally provides more rapid development), use the Package & Deployment Wizard to distribute it to our users and we are done.

Using DCOM

Let's go back to Phil and his software dilemma. The order-entry application that they have been working on is complete. Phil and his team have written a great application using COM components. They used the Package & Deployment Wizard to create an install program that they will use to install the components on all 100 users' machines. They even came in on the weekend to do it so that they would not interfere with an individual's day to day business. The users are happy and Phil gets to take a couple weeks off, right? Wrong!

Unfortunately, it turns out that there is a bug in the component they created for handling inventory business rules. Whenever an order is updated and resubmitted, inventory levels are not correctly adjusted. So Phil and his team need to fix the bug which should only take a half-hour. However, now they have to go back and re-install the 100 clients with the updated DLL. What a hassle!

How could this situation have been remedied? Could Distributed COM help?

COM Objects Do Not Always Make Good DCOM Objects

DCOM allows you to create an object from a remote machine, without any additional programming effort. The object runs on the remote machine, and is accessed across the network by the client. So how would this help Phil?

By taking the ActiveX DLL and placing it on only a single machine on the network, when his team made the change, they would only have to distribute it to one server machine instead of 100 clients. This would have given Phil a quick solution, as only the implementation of his component was changed and not the component's interfaces.

Although Phil's new solution using DCOM solves his initial problem, it is not an ideal solution. He failed to consider some important and initially more subtle issues that DCOM introduces.

DCOM mandates a new way of thinking about design. We will gradually expand on these points through this chapter. However, it would be beneficial to briefly discuss some of these issues that Phil overlooked.

EXEs Not DLLs

Using an ActiveX DLL remotely is not really a wise solution for Phil. A DLL is an in-process server and as such needs a process space to run in. However, if the DLL resides on a remote machine it will no longer have access to the process space of Phil's application. Therefore, Phil would need to configure and use a **surrogate process** in which the in-process server could run. This approach should generally only be used when handling legacy in-process servers, or if you have a specific reason why the server has to be in-process. As this is a brand new system, Phil should have used an ActiveX EXE server, and saved himself the hassle of understanding and configuring surrogates. As surrogates can be useful for some applications, they are discussed later in this chapter.

Roundtrips

When a COM object is remotely created and accessed using DCOM, **every** single call to **every** single function, and **every** single access of **every** property results in a message being sent across the network. Given that a network round-trip (the logical distance between the client and the component and back again) is relatively expensive and takes a lot longer (around 1000 times depending upon the network speed), Phil could end up with an overloaded network and the worst performing component in the known universe. Not something Phil's team would be proud of, more so his upper management! From day one Phil needs to have considered these round-trips and reduced them to a minimum.

Type Libraries

One final point is that Phil could still have the same update and maintenance problems, even with the ActiveX DLL configured to run only on the server machine. Assuming Phil does *not* use late bound interfaces, he will have to register the type library for the component on each client. If any of the interfaces for Phil's components changed after its initial release, each client would still need to be updated with a new type library. So him and his team would still have to update all 100 clients.

To get around the client update problem Phil could use late bound interfaces. By using late bound interfaces Phil wouldn't have to install a type library on each client, because the only interface his client and component would be using is `IDispatch`, for which COM/DCOM provides all the plumbing. So where is the down side?

This approach makes the life of the programmers using his component more difficult because IntelliSense no longer works. More importantly, the overall performance between the client and component will become even slower, and network traffic will increase, due to the extra roundtrips needed by `IDispatch`.

Logical Distribution of Components

A nice feature of DCOM is that components can run on a machine that complements the component. If we had a component that performed intensive database operations, it would make sense to locate that component on the same machine as the database itself. Each request to the database server would not require another network roundtrip, so its overall performance is likely to be a lot quicker.

Similarly, Phil may have a component that checks call statistics on one machine which only occurs once an hour and another component that is responsible for updating orders which can happen once a second! Phil would probably want a better machine, with more memory and faster CPU, to host the *Orders* component rather than the machine that gets used just once an hour.

DCOM enables distribution of components on one or more machines like this.

Load Balancing

DCOM can also be used to provide a basic method of **static** and **dynamic load balancing** through explicit configuration, and/or programming.

If business booms, especially around Valentine's Day, Phil and his team could find out that the *Orders* component might not be able to keep up with the demand. A solution would be to install the *Orders* component on a second system and change some of the clients to point to the new server (static load balancing). This is not an ideal solution, as the configuration of the clients would have to be done on each client machine by Phil and his team, but it would work.

To take this approach one step further, and to remove the need for his team to perform the configuration manually each time an overload occurred, Phil could write some new COM components to perform dynamic load balancing. The new **broker** component could monitor how many clients are using each server, and with a few changes to his original application, could be used to allow his clients to dynamically decide which server a client should connect to. Although not an ideal solution, as it involves a reasonable amount of programming, this handcrafted load balancing gives you an idea of the power of DCOM.

Later in the chapter, we will discuss component load balancing approaches, should you decide that you want to do this.

COM+

Later in Chapter 8, when we talk about COM+, you will see how COM might one day soon provide services like true load balancing and transaction processing for free using 'attributes' and declarative programming. For this reason, you should seriously consider whether it's worth investing your time and effort into load balancing.

Architecture of DCOM

So how does DCOM actually work? Earlier in the chapter, we saw a diagram showing the client and server component communicating with each other on the same machine. With DCOM, a client can be on one machine, and a COM server hosting the component on another. Despite this extra distance between the client and component, the programming model inside VB is still the same, except now the object reference is passed a little further. This encapsulation of the distance of communications is known as **location transparency**.

Proxies and Stubs

If a client and an object are located on different machines, **proxies** and **stubs** are used to facilitate the communications between the two.

The proxy and stub are responsible for intercepting function calls between the client and component, and passing them back and forth across the network transparently. A proxy is created for the client, whilst a stub is created for the server:

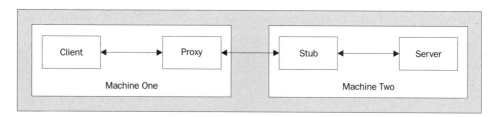

The proxy and stub shown above are COM objects. The proxy, as far as the client is concerned, is the original COM object that it asked to be created. It does not know that it is talking to an imposter. This is possible because the proxy implements an identical interface to the original component, and because COM enforces encapsulation, the component doesn't know about the lack of implementation. The server component doesn't care that a stub, and not the original client, is using it. It makes no assumptions on who consumes its services.

Marshalling

When a client invokes a function on a proxy object, the proxy packages up an identifier for the function called and the function's parameters, into a buffer and sends it to the stub. The stub then unpacks the buffer, and invokes the function on the real component. The stub then packages up any parameters to be sent back to the proxy (`ByRef` parameters, more generally known as 'out' parameters) and the function's return code. The proxy unpacks the stub's response, and returns the output to the client. This packaging and unpacking of information is known as **marshalling**.

Marshalling is a common term used when discussing COM component interaction. **Standard marshalling** describes the default communication mechanism implemented by COM on your behalf. All VB COM created components use standard marshalling.

Custom marshalling describes a user-defined implementation that allows complete flexibility of how a client-proxy and component-stub communicate. With custom marshaling, you basically implement the proxy and stub yourself, with some help from the standard interface `IMarshal`. Unfortunately, this is out of the realms of Visual Basic, so you'll have to stick with standard marshalling, unless you are prepared for a lot of work.

RPC Channels – How Proxy and Stub Objects Communicate

When the client of a COM object invokes a function of a COM object on another machine, the proxy object sends a message to the stub via an **RPC** (**Remote Procedure Call**) channel. Think of this RPC channel as a connection between the proxy and stub created by the COM runtime. Once this channel has been established, the proxy can send data down it describing the function it wants the stub to call. We'll discuss RPCs in more detail later.

Proxy Manager

An interface proxy object or **facelet**, is created for each different interface (IID) that is requested using `QueryInterface`. So if a component has 10 interfaces, and the client is using 4 of them, there will be 4 interface proxy objects.

As each proxy is a COM object in its own right, the COM runtime has to ensure that if you query an interface from one proxy, that a new proxy is only created if there is not one already around.

All of the proxies for a component are managed by
what is known as the **proxy manager**. This gives the
impression to the client that they are only interacting
with one COM object (a single identity), no matter how
many interfaces they request. This trick of making
several COM objects each with their own identity
appear as one object, is performed using aggregation:

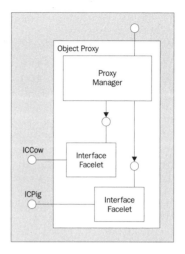

Aggregation is a specialized case of the containment
and delegation that we saw in the previous chapter.
The difference here is that the containing object, now
called the aggregator, exposes interfaces of the
aggregated objects, now called aggregates:

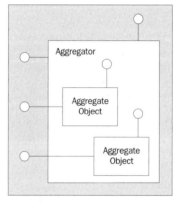

Putting it All Together

This diagram gives you a basic idea of how proxies, stubs and the channels work all work together:

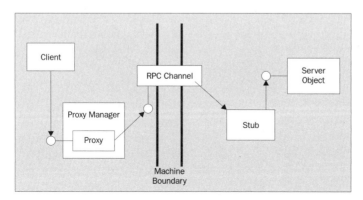

As you can see, a proxy and stub communicate with each other using an RPC (Remote Procedure Call) channel. The channel is used to send the packets of data across between the two.

Microsoft's RPC Implementation (MS-RPC)

DCOM uses RPC as one of its foundation building blocks for enabling remote component communications. RPC is part of the Open Software Foundation's (OSF) Distributed Computing Environment (DCE). RPC basically enables function calls to be remoted in a 'standard' fashion from one machine to another. Given that this is the main goal of DCOM, and that Microsoft has implemented RPC on nearly all versions of Windows, using RPC as the foundation for remote components' interoperation makes a lot of sense.

Because RPC is based upon functions rather than objects, Microsoft extended it and came up with ORPC. ('O' for Object) ORPC is basically a thin layer on top of RPC.

Remote Object Creation

So what is happening when an object is created remotely? First, the client requests that the COM Library create an instance of server. The COM library uses its SCM (Service Control Manager) to determine the location of the component, using the CLSID passed to it by the client. If the component lives on a remote machine, the SCM on the client machine converses with the SCM on the server machine to actually request the services to create the component. Once the server object is running, an object reference is passed back through the COM library, and the client is given the object reference so that it may call upon the services of the component object:

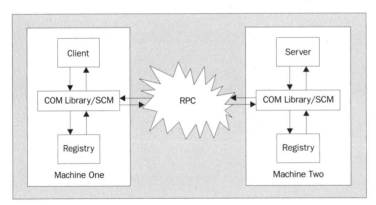

Because COM enables a client to use a component in an identical fashion whether it is created locally or remotely, it's possible for a developer to focus purely upon implementing business solutions. However, if a component is going to be used remotely, it is **essential** to consider network traffic and performance.

Considerations with DCOM Architecture

Some of the other factors in DCOM to consider include:

- ❑ Bandwidth Issues
- ❑ Network Issues
- ❑ Fault Tolerance
- ❑ Language Neutrality
- ❑ Load Balancing
- ❑ Location Independence
- ❑ Platform Neutral
- ❑ Scalability
- ❑ Security

Bandwidth Issues

When we are working with objects over the network or the Internet, we have to concern ourselves about two types of bandwidth usage. We can only force so much data down a wire at a time. With distributed objects, we must consider what we are sending back and forth across the wire. For example, if we had created an ActiveX Control and placed it on a website, we would want to make sure that it was as small in size as possible, since modems these days can only download data so fast. The same goes for the DCOM components we create.

> *I want to point out that a DCOM component is the same as a COM component. I use the term DCOM component merely to indicate that the component is to be created and used on a different machine.*

When creating DCOM components, and indeed any COM object, care must be used to make sure that minimal data travel is required. An example would be keeping the roundtrips to a minimum. Let's take an *Inventory* object that has 3 properties, *ItemID*, *ItemName*, and *ItemCount* that are used to increase or decrease an inventory. When the client calls the object, data is transferred three times, once for each property:

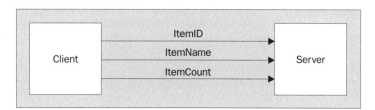

Reducing Bandwith

A Single Method Call

A way to save trips is to create a method that takes a user-defined type or has three parameters passed into it. Then, within the server, there is routine that takes this type or accepts these parameters, and updates the relevant member variables with just one call. This reduces the number of roundtrips from three to one:

Passing Parameters ByVal

Another way of reducing overhead, when passing properties within a method, is to specify `ByVal` or `ByRef` for your parameters. For example, look at the following code:

```
Public Function UpdateInventory(ByVal ItemID As Long, ByVal ItemName As String, _
    ByRef ItemCount As Integer) As Boolean

    ' Update Inventory and return a successful boolean value.

End Function
```

The code above represents an `UpdateInventory` function. You will notice that the function is declared with a data type of `Boolean`. This is so that we can return whether or not the function update was successful. So if we wanted to pass back the inventory count for that inventory item, how can we do that? By using `ByRef`.

`ByRef` is a keyword that allows a client to pass the address of an argument (using a pointer) to the server instead of passing a value. That way, the server can access the variable `ItemName` and change its value. This change is then sent back to the client and reflected in its variable. Passing a pointer to a memory location obviously has no meaning when passed between two machines or indeed two processes, so once again the COM runtime is providing another great facility for free.

If you use `ByVal`, you can pass the value of the argument instead. That way the server is only getting a copy of the variable. The variable's value does not change after the function has been called.

So after the function has been called, a Boolean value is returned to the client to tell the client if it was successful, and `ItemCount` is updated within the client.

It is best to send items `ByVal` if you can, since your components do not have to send the data back again to the client if it is unnecessary. If you do not specify `ByVal` or `ByRef` explicitly, Visual Basic defaults to `ByRef`.

Data Types

But what if you want to pass back more than just one value in the arguments list? Make each parameter `ByRef`, or add a data type of type `Variant`. This will allow you to create an array of variants. Is this the most efficient way? Not necessarily, but it will allow you to store the data in one argument (such as a small recordset) and pass it back to the client:

```
Public Function UpdateInventory(ByVal ItemID As Long, ByVal ItemName As String, _
    ByVal ItemCount As Integer, ByRef ItemRecordset() As Variant) As Boolean

    ' Update Inventory and return a successful boolean value.

End Function
```

Another increasing popular way of passing data is to use ADO disconnected recordsets, which are optimized for use with COM/DCOM.

Remember that data types come in different sizes. Here's a table showing the byte size of the main Visual Basic data types:

Data Type	Byte Size
Byte	1
Integer	2
Boolean	2
String	See below
Single	4
Long	4
Double	8
Date	8
Currency	8
Variant	16

String data types behave somewhat differently. You can have two types of strings: **variable length** and **fixed length**. Variable length strings are 10 bytes long plus the character length of the string. A fixed length string, on the other hand, is only the character length of the string. However, it's not quite that simple because COM and Win32 environments use **Unicode**. Therefore, each character in the string actually consumes 2 bytes of memory. Thus, a fixed length string of 13 characters is actually 26 bytes long (the variable string length would be 36 bytes).

You may not think that a few extra bytes here and there would make much difference but consider the difference of using an integer and using a long. The long is double the size of the integer. That's double the amount of data that has to go down the network pipe. Although these values are quite small, when in an intensive data-driven component, those two bytes take a lot more time to be passed across the network. Be careful which data types you are marshaling over the network.

> **The size of a DCOM remoted function call is about 200 bytes plus the function parameters. Given the typical size of a network packet (around 1k), you shouldn't worry too much about what data types you use, except in large arrays etc.**

You should also be aware that if you combine data types in a user-defined type that some data types are longword aligned. This means they only start on a 4-byte boundary. If you are not careful, you can easily end up with a type that's larger than you think. You can use the LenB() *function to test the length of your user-defined type.*

Referring – The 3rd Object

DCOM has a feature called **referring**. Referring is another way that DCOM reduces the bandwidth of data sent across the network. Referring enables a client component to call upon a referring component to create a reference to a third component. The referring component is responsible for finding the best component for the client to use then it goes away. So now the client does not have to talk with the referring component to get to the third component, they talk directly to each other. This keeps from having frivolous trips back and forth between a middle component.

To understand why referring is used, let consider an example of its application:

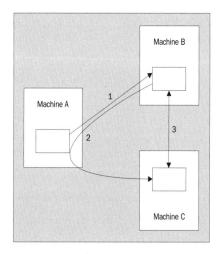

We have three machines, A, B and C. A client on machine A creates a component on machine B (1.). The client on machine A then passes a reference to the component created on machine B, to another component running on machine C (2.). When the component on machine C uses the component created on machine B, passed in from the client on machine A, DCOM will ensure that the component on machine C talks directly to the component on machine B (3.). In more technical terms, a proxy object never talks to another proxy object. A proxy object always communicates with a stub.

Network Issues

Network Protocols Used by DCOM

A network protocol defines how data is carried across the network. DCOM uses different network protocols to send data depending upon the operating system. With Windows NT 4.0 Service Pack 4, you can choose the order in which protocols are used by using the DCOMCNFG tool (this tool is discussed later in the section on DCOM security):

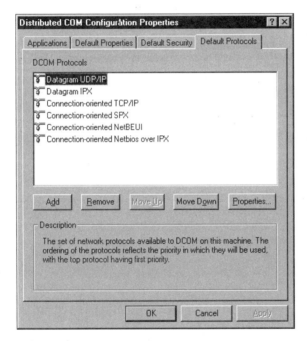

DCOM will try to establish a connection to a remote object using each of these protocols until it is successful. If you ever find that it takes an age to create a remote component, try changing the order of this list.

If you do not specify a protocol, NT will by default use Datagram UDP/IP. Win9x *only* uses Connection-oriented TCP/IP, so if a Win9x client tries to activate a NT object there will be a pause until NT dynamically changes the protocol from UDP to TCP. Thus, if the object will be run on NT and the clients *may be* Win9x it is a good idea to configure the object to use TCP.

TCP/IP

Some useful points about TCP/IP:

❑ **TCP** (Transfer Control Protocol) is a connection-based protocol for sending **IP** (Internet Protocol) packets across a network

❑ TCP/IP is used by most Internet protocols such as HTTP for sending data, as it provides reliable delivery of data in the sequence in which it is sent

❑ TCP/IP is the transport protocol that Windows 95/98 uses by default for DCOM

❑ It is the only protocol that is 'officially' supported by Microsoft for Windows 95/98

UDP/IP

Some basic points about UDP/IP:

❑ **UDP** (User Datagram Protocol) is a connection-less based protocol for sending **IP** (Internet Protocol) packets across a network

❑ UDP/IP does not provide guaranteed delivery or sequencing of data packets

❑ Any confirmation of delivery or data packet ordering must be implemented by the application

❑ UDP/IP is the transport protocol that Windows NT uses by default for DCOM

❑ UDP/IP is preferred over TCP/IP because it is consumes fewer resources and does not have a connection establishment overhead

Protocol Neutral

When dealing with networks and distributed architectures, the network protocol becomes a large issue to deal with. You will find that other distributed architectures require certain network protocols. But what do you do if your company has standardized on TCP/IP, but the new distributed architecture package your company spent thousands of dollars on requires NetBIOS? You have just created a migraine for your IT department.

DCOM is protocol neutral so you do not have to concern yourself with the transfer protocol that you are using; DCOM can work with TCP/IP, UDP/IP, IPX/SPX, or NetBIOS. Each version of Windows defaults to the most appropriate and commonly used protocol.

Network Connections

Due to different types of network protocols and networking software, network connections are not always reliable. In addition, when a component uses a network connection it is using a resource. If a component is not using the connection or has gone idle, it's a good idea for there to be a way to disassociate the connection so that another process can use the connection. DCOM uses different methods such as reference counting and pinging to handle network connections.

Reference Counting

DCOM keeps a reference count of all connections between components much like COM does between components and their clients. When a connection is created to an object, the reference count is incremented. Whenever a client decides to release the object, the reference count is decremented for the object. DCOM keeps these reference counts organized so that it knows when objects are in use or not. Once the reference count is zero, the object releases the network connection resource that can now be used for another process. If you were using TCP/IP as the transport mechanism for DCOM, at this point, the connection would be closed.

How does DCOM make sure that a client process has not stalled or quit without notifying the server? It uses a pinging mechanism.

Pinging

DCOM uses a **ping** to ensure that a client that is connected to a component remotely is alive. A ping is a small message sent between two machines that ensures that the network connection between them is still alive. These "pings" are sent periodically to tell the server that the client is still there. That is how it knows if a hardware or network failure has occurred between the two. The ping is sent from the client to the server. If the server receives a ping then it knows the client is still there.

If there were 10 components on the server that the client was using, would 10 pings occur each time? The answer is no. DCOM uses a single ping to check on all 10. DCOM uses what is called **delta pinging**. Instead of sending 10 separate pings, DCOM creates **meta-identifiers**; these meta-identifiers are an abstraction of the 10 connections. If a connection state changes due to hardware failure, a ping occurs to make sure that the connection is there.

When a sequential series of three pings has occurred where there is no response, DCOM steps in and decrements the reference count. If the reference count is zero, the object is released, along with the network connection if TCP/IP is in use. The interval between each ping is two minutes. This means it can take up to six minutes for DCOM to perform this **garbage collection**. If a component indicates it is still alive after the second ping, the ping counter is reset back to zero.

DCOM does not currently have any mechanism for enabling a client to re-connect to the same object once a connection to it has been lost. This means that a client must recreate any components after the server has not received the 3rd ping. A client is not informed that a connection to its object has died until it tries to invoke a method of the proxy. The proxy will at that stage indicate an error to the caller. This may sound bad, but to date I've never actually had this problem, well, not very often at least.

Fault Tolerance

Fault tolerance allows for errors to occur and determines how gracefully a system can put itself back together and run correctly. DCOM uses its pinging mechanism to provide basic fault tolerance. For example, let's say that DCOM is pinging away at client objects to make sure they are still up and available and that the network goes down very briefly. DCOM allows 3 pings to occur before it starts decrementing reference counts. If the network comes back up, the object reference is not lost, the **same** objects can continue talking to each other.

Language Neutrality

DCOM is simply an extension of COM. It's an extension to the binary specification that describes how the components interact across machine boundaries. DCOM does not effect what programming language you use when creating your COM components, or any of the other basic principles we discussed in Chapter 2. You do not have to have something like Visual DCOM 1.0, you can use different types of programming languages such as Visual Basic (my choice) or Visual C++, and any other programming language that supports the development and creation of COM objects. This allows you to decide the tools to use when developing DCOM components.

Load Balancing

Load balancing refers to allocating resources based on the level of production. For example, whenever you go to a fast food restaurant, do they only have one queue for you to stand in? No, they typically have multiple lines that you can choose from. You will normally choose the shortest one to stand in. This is the theory of load balancing. DCOM provides mechanisms that can be used to facilitate load balancing, but does not actually implement load balancing. Load balancing is the methodology of how to distribute the load equally over multiple servers.

There are two types of load balancing: static and dynamic.

Static load balancing is like attending registration at a conference. They probably have designated booths by the first letter in your last name for you to register. That way the A-C people go to one booth while the U- Z go to another. Why does the U – Z contain more letters than the A – C? Because more people have last names that start with A, B, or C than U – Z. You can see that by balancing it out this way, it's a lot faster to register rather than having only one registration booth for everyone to come through.

In the DCOM realm of things, we can create clients that point to any server we like. So we could put our *Inventory* component on multiple servers. Why do that? Let's say we have 500 clients that need to use the *Inventory* component, if all 500 were to use one *Inventory* component on one machine, that machine and component would get bogged down very quickly. What we can do is to have the *Inventory* component registered on 5 different machines and break up our clients into increments of 100 and specify which server machine to use. Now only 100 clients can hit any one component at a time.

We could also use our referral object to achieve the same thing. We could write code in the referral object to distribute out connections to servers. It's not as easy as the previous example, but would provide the static load balancing we need to achieve.

Dynamic load balancing works a little differently than static load balancing. Static load balancing was based on the premise that the client is assigned a server to work with. With Dynamic load balancing, we now use methods that decide for us which server to use based on the level of loads the servers are maintaining.

An example of this is a typical bank. When you go into a bank, instead of just many tellers taking first-come-first-serve, the bank puts up a series of ropes that you queue up in. Then when a teller becomes available, the first person in the queue approaches the teller booth. So no one is assigned a teller when walking in the door, they are placed in queue and directed to a teller when they are available.

Our referral object can implement this type of load balancing. For example, a referral object could get a request from a client, then the referral object could determine which server to attach the client to, based on reference counts. So if *ServerA* had a reference count of 12, *ServerB* had a reference count of 15, and *ServerC* had a reference count of 18, the referral object would establish a relationship between the client and *ServerA* since its load seems to be the lowest.

> *Do not be fooled by my simple example. Building these load balancing applications is not easy. That is why companies are able to charge quite a lot of money for applications and hardware that supports this dynamic load balancing. You might argue though, that MTS is the exception to this rule. We cover MTS in the next chapter.*

Location Independence

An advantage that DCOM has is location independence. When you build your client or server, you are not forced to put in lots of code to handle location issues with your components. The client is not aware that a component it is calling is even on a remote machine. Even though we must make considerations for things such as bandwidth when designing components, we do not have to write "plumbing" code for our components. This makes it quite easy to move our server components to whatever machine best suits the component.

Due to this location independence, we can place a server component on a machine that supports more of the component's functionality. So we could place a server component on a higher bandwidth segment of the network if bandwidth is an issue, or a component may be placed on a database machine if it needs to do a lot of lookups, then just pass what the client needs.

With location independence, components can be placed within an **application server** at any time. An application server is a sophisticated application that runs on a machine that helps manage components. These application servers come in a wide variety of functionality and price. But DCOM allows us to take a server component running on one machine and place it into an application server on the same or another machine.

Platform Neutral

I know you are thinking, "DCOM comes from Microsoft, how can it be platform neutral?" Remember earlier when we discussed RPC (remote procedure calls) which was a standard created by a group, other than Microsoft. The plumbing within the RPC architecture was created so that it could run on any platform.

This is a lot like the Java virtual machine. If you look at the fundamental basis of the Java VM, it will work across all platforms. However, each Java VM can be enhanced and extended for the platform it will be deployed on. DCOM works the same way; the RPC technology was extended by Microsoft to provide more features.

Right now Microsoft has developed DCOM to run on Intel/Alpha based machines and has looked to third-party providers like Software-AG to implement DCOM on other platforms such as Unix. There is also now available an implementation of DCOM written purely in Java!

Scalability

Scalability relates to the way that you can adapt your application so that as more clients fight for a server's resources, it can continue to handle all these requests. If for example you have 10 clients trying to gain access to a server's resources, what do you think happens whenever your client base grows to 1000? You will probably find that the server component is slowed down considerably.

DCOM helps in two ways. First, it is an architecture that has been designed to work well and scale with multiple processors on a machine. DCOM can handle simultaneous requests and deal with all the issues associated with it. This makes it very easy for the developer to take advantage of since DCOM handles all of this under the covers.

Second, DCOM with its location independence allows the developer or project leader to decide how to deploy components so that it takes advantage of scalability issues. We will cover four different types of scalability deployments: universal handler, pyramids, fall-out queues, and front-lines.

Universal Handler

The **Universal Handler** deployment model uses a component to handle all requests from clients and direct them to the appropriate server:

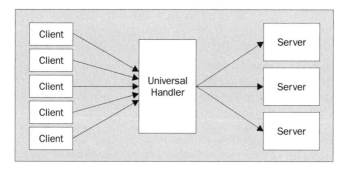

The Universal Handler component is responsible for taking requests from the client and attaching it to the appropriate server, then stepping out of the way so that the client talks directly to the server. This is what I discussed earlier about referring; the Universal Handler refers the client to the server, then gets out of the way. This is commonly known as dynamic-load balancing.

This works well in situations where your client is not aware of which service to connect to before the call. This scheme is good for fault tolerance because the Universal Handler can see which servers are available. Also, the Universal Handler could decide that since the database server is down, it should refer the client to a messaging server to create a queued message, which will be placed in the database once it becomes available.

Pyramids

The **Pyramid** scheme makes use of a **Broker** component:

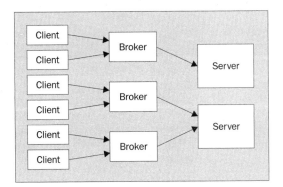

The pyramid scheme works well in multi-client environments with many clients. Since you have quite a few clients trying to gain access to servers, it might be a good idea to send them through Broker components. The broker component takes requests from many clients, and then decides how and which server to call based upon some load-balancing algorithm. This schema especially helps when network traffic is at high levels or the servers themselves can only handle light loads due to memory or hardware constraints.

Fall-Out Queues

A **Fall-Out Queue** uses a series of middle-management components:

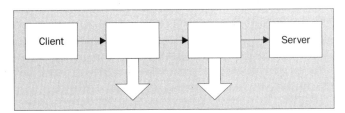

Although not used as often as other schemas, in a Fall-Out Queue schema, middle-management components take requests from the clients and drop them if the request does not follow a certain criteria set by the middle components. This works best in security situations where a client may try to gain access but the middle component will let them fall out since they do not have access. I am not a big fan of this schema but it works well in very niche solutions, especially if you can not use or rely upon NT security.

Front-Lines

This schema gets its name from the old war movies where there was a **Front-Line** to an attack, whenever someone was killed or more people were necessary, the generals could easily integrate more fighters into the front line:

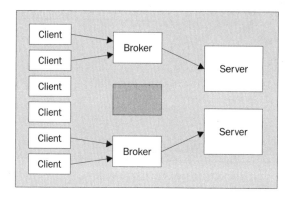

In the Front-Lines schema, when the clients call for resources on servers, the middle components are brought in and out of service and only used when necessary. In the above diagram, we see that 2 middle components work fine but if the client load were to escalate, we would probably need to add more middle components. This is quite similar to the Pyramid scheme, but the difference is that the middle components are not static, but dynamic. This type of scheme is usually supported by an application server that can determine when there is a need to add or subtract middle components as necessary, based on client and server levels of production. This type of schema is more difficult to program, as the relationship between the components is more dynamic and complex.

The four schemas are not cast in stone. Some projects may require a combination of all four. The project will determine which schema fits best with your solution. It can depend on what tools you have already. The Front-Lines schema requires an application server to support it, so it may not be the easiest solution to implement. So spend time designing the solution; keeping these schemes in mind will help with scalability issues.

However, just like with load balancing none of these schemas are easy to implement so we won't be discussing them further.

Security

Security is very important in a distributed environment. A server can be unaware of those clients accessing its services, if security is not taken into consideration. We want to make sure that our servers are not used by persons or other objects that are not supposed to have access to them.

DCOM does provide a layer of security for distributed components. For the Visual Basic developer, the bonus is that you do not have to provide the plumbing within your components to provide security. DCOM security is conceptually wrapped around your component instead of having to implement it within the code.

DCOM uses Windows NT security methods. Windows NT security on a high-level view is based on an access control list. This access control list is a listing of people and groups (many people can belong in one group) that can be assigned to certain resources. For example, you could set up a directory where only those individuals who are a part of the Marketing group set up in NT security could look at the directory.

For DCOM on other platforms such as Unix, an NT-like security system is used.

So how does a client call another server using the NT security model? First, DCOM figures out what the username and password is for the client. This can be the person currently logged in or you could set up an account for that client component. Then, once the request gets to the server machine, DCOM checks the access control list to see if the client component has the rights to the server component. If it does, then the client is able to use the component, if not, then DCOM dumps the request and sends an error back to the client.

A Small Aside on Security

Before DCOM there was no security in COM. Given the damage that could be caused by creating and using components remotely, this was changed. Being a VB programmer, you don't have to worry about security too much. However, it is useful to understand the terms, **authentication** and **authorization**.

When a client attempts to create an object (or optionally, every time it accesses an object depending upon the configuration in DCOMCNFG.EXE) the client account is *authenticated* - that is, DCOM makes sure that the client is who it says it is. Once the account is authenticated it must have *authorization* to perform the requested action and this is where **access control lists** (ACLs) come in. Access control lists basically describe who can do what to an object.

> *Note that if the server is running on Win9x, you can use DCOMCnfg to specify an NT machine to authenticate accounts - Win9x does not have native security. Also note that it is not possible to remotely launch a server for security reasons.*

Where to Get DCOM

You might be saying to yourself, "This DCOM sounds great, now how do I get my hands on it?" If you are running Windows NT 4 or Windows 98, then you already have it, although for Windows NT it is likely to be out of date. If you have Windows 95, you have to download it from the Microsoft site and install it.

DCOM can also be found on most of the newer development tool CDs from Microsoft. The latest version (1.2) should be located in the DCOM98 directory on your Visual Studio CD. This version states it is for Windows 95 and Windows 98 users.

For users of NT 4.0 and above, you should download and install at least Service Pack 3, better still, Service Pack 4, from Microsoft.

For users of NT 3.51 and below, I'm afraid you're out of luck. DCOM from Microsoft is not supported, although Java implementations of DCOM are said to be available.

Like most installs that upgrade core components of the operating system, you will need to reboot your machine after the installation.

DCOM and Visual Basic

DCOM and Visual Basic work very well with each other. The benefit of using Visual Basic is that we get all the great features, such as debugging, in the Visual Basic environment, and DCOM enables us to use our components in a distributed fashion. There is no need to put in code to handle specific DCOM functionality, because DCOM takes care of it for us. The only real downside to VB and DCOM is that we do not have the same level of programmatic control over security. However, MTS and the future COM+ do address this problem.

To demonstrate this we are going to build a simple component that we can distribute remotely.

Creating a Simple DCOM Server Component

1. Create a new ActiveX EXE project in Visual Basic. This is simplest type of server to create remotely. We will discuss how we could also use an ActiveX DLL server later in the chapter when we discuss surrogates.

2. In the code window, put in the following code:

```
Public Sub Display(Message As String)

  MsgBox Message

End Sub
```

3. Change the Name of the class to CDCOM and then set the Project Properties to look like this:

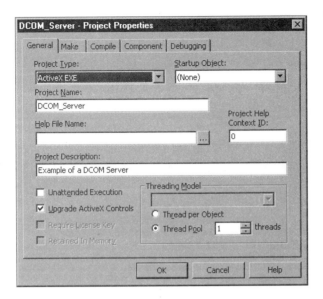

4. Then go to the Components tab and select Remote Server Files:

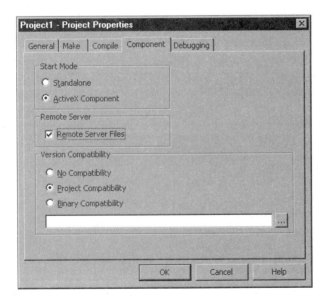

Note that Version Compatibility is set to Project Compatibility. Remember from our discussion on ActiveX DLLs and ActiveX EXEs that when we are creating a component for the first time, we use Project Compatibility, but after we have distributed it for the first time, we then need to change it to Binary Compatibility.

5. Go ahead and select Ma<u>k</u>e DCOM_Server.exe... from the <u>F</u>ile menu to create the executable. If you go to the folder where you created the executable, you will notice that there are three files created: the executable (Application), a .TLB file (Type Library), and a .VBR (Remote Automation Registration File) file:

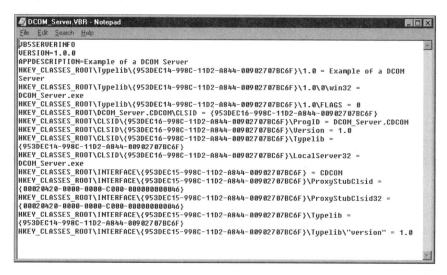

The .TLB file is the type library file and the .VBR file provides the information on how to set up the server remotely using CLIREG32.EXE, without having to have the ActiveX EXE on each client (remember Phil's problem earlier). These two files were created because we checked the R<u>e</u>mote Server Files on the Compon<u>e</u>nt tab in the Project Properties dialog.

The VBR file contains a list of the registry entries that are added to a machine that wants to use our component remotely. The VBR file is a text file for our new server, which looks like this:

Yes, this is quite a simple DCOM project but it stresses the point that we do not have to concern ourselves with writing distribution code or registration code to enable DCOM to work. We just have to remember to consider other important issues such as network roundtrips. So far, all we have done differently from how we previously created COM objects is to set the Remote Server Files setting. That's all!

Distributing a Component

Once we are done with the server and we have saved and compiled it, we need to create an install routine for it. This is quite simple - we will use the Package & Deployment Wizard to create one.

Creating an Install for Distributed Components

1. Open the Package & Deployment Wizard. Depending on how you loaded it before, it may be in the Add-Ins menu or you may need to reload it using the Add-In Manger.

2. Make sure that our DCOM_Server.VBP file is the Active Project (if you haven't saved your project then the wizard will prompt you to do so).

3. Click the Package icon.

4. Choose the Standard Setup Package option, and decide where you would like your server files to be created.

5. You will most likely be prompted if you are going to be using Remote Automation server:

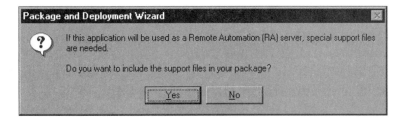

Select No. Remote Automation is a different method of distributed component access. It was thrown into version 4.0 of Visual Basic because DCOM was not ready for prime time yet. Visual Basic 6.0 supports it, but you are better off using DCOM, unless you are targeting a 16-bit platform or operating system such as NT 3.51 that does not have DCOM support.

Remote Automation isn't DCOM, nor is it as efficient or flexible. Only the IDispatch *interface can be remoted with it.*

6. In the Included Files dialog you need to add the .VBR file that was created. Click the Add... button and select the DCOM_Server.VBR file. Once this is done, the Included Files dialog lists the .VBR and .TLB files:

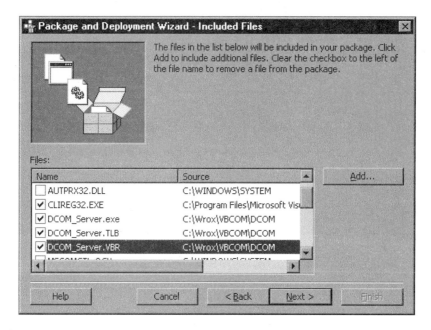

These two files enable us to use our component from a remote machine, without having to install the component on that machine.

7. The Remote Servers dialog shows our .VBR file and its settings:

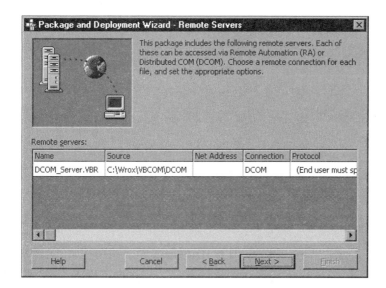

Property	Description
Name	Name of the Server file.
Source	File name.
Net Address	The network address of the machine that the server will be installed on. Typically an IP address or machine name. If this is left blank, the user will need to specify an address when installing the server.
Connection Type	The connection type allows the user to choose whether to use DCOM or Remote Automation.
Protocol	Will be blank since we are using DCOM. Remote Automation allows you to choose from a list.
Authentication	Only available for Remote Automation.

Unless you know the Net Address of the server, you don't need to do anything in this dialog.

8. Accept the defaults through the rest of the Package & Deployment Wizard. You now have a DCOM server that you can distribute to any server that will be hosting the component.

Registering on the Server

Now that we have an install, we can set our server up to run the component. The easiest way is to simply run the `setup.exe` file that the Package & Deployment Wizard created on the server.

This will take care of all the registration details for you and copy the `.TLB` and `.VBR` files into the `System32` directory.

When developing components you may not want to go through the laborious process of creating an install file every time you need to test a new version; there is a way to manually register and unregister components.

Manual Registration

You first need to unregister the current version of your component. To do this, go to the Run dialog from the Windows Start menu. Then you need to run your EXE but using the `/unregserver` switch:

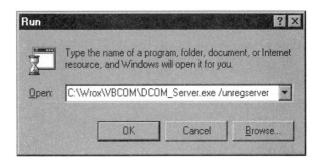

Now we can register the new version using a similar technique. Using the Run dialog you need to run your new component but this time with the `/regserver` switch:

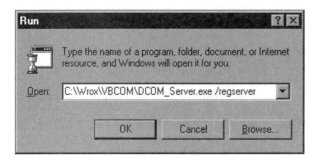

Now that we have registered our component on the server, we still need to configure some additional DCOM settings before we can use it from a client. This requires a detour into security.

DCOM Security

Security is very important to distributed components. DCOM makes it easy to implement security for those distributed components. DCOM provides the security inside the COM runtime, and does not require you to implement a propriety mechanism yourself. However, you do still need to set up the appropriate security settings for your components.

DCOMCnfg

`DCOMCNFG.EXE` will become your best friend when you are setting up security for your components. You can find `DCOMCNFG.EXE` in the SYSTEM directory, so you can execute it using the Run dialog found on the Start menu:

> As Windows 95/98 provides less security options than Windows NT, you may find slight variations in the options you have available. This also applies to the other dialogs shown in this section.

The Applications Tab

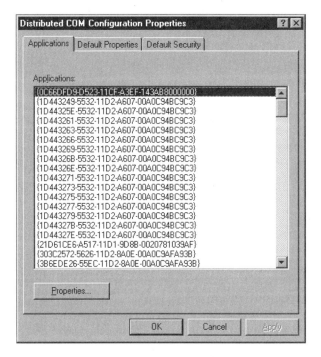

The Applications tab displays the default value of the CLSID key from the registry (see Appendix A) for all COM components that are listed under `HKEY_CLASS_ROOT/AppID`. VB6 adds an entry to this key for your application, and uses the programmatic identifier (ProdId) of your component to describe the entry. We see that our component is listed and the class name is shown. The fact that it shows a class name is not important since the entry is for the whole component, not on a class by class basis.

Property Page

By using the Properties... button you can access the DCOM property pages for the server. You can view information about the server, decide where the server will run, and who can gain access to the server. Properties can be set up individually for each server. This makes it very easy to set up security on a per server basis.

The General tab simply displays information about the component, including its name, whether it is running 'local' or 'remote' and the path to the component itself:

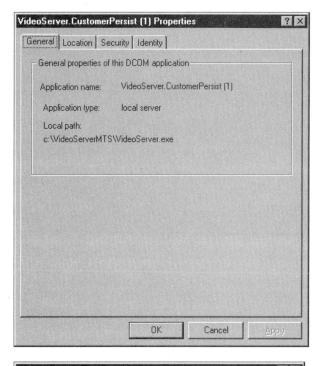

The Location tab allows you to specify on which machine the application should be run:

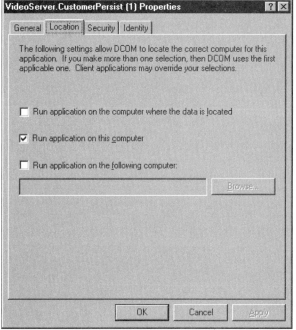

The Security tab allows you to set which users or groups can launch, access and configure your component. We'll be using this tab shortly to set up the security for our DCOM_Server component:

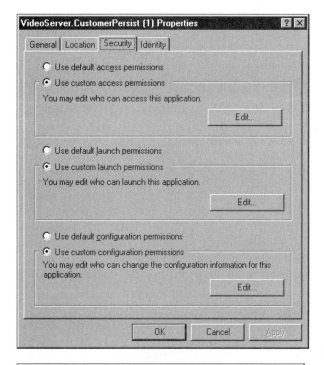

Finally, the Identity tab specifies the user account that the server will use to run the component under:

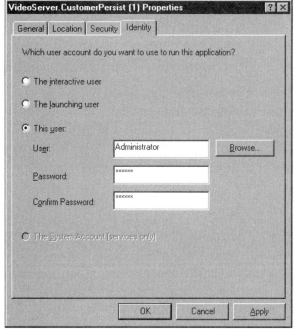

It's a very good idea to set a user ID and password for the server so that it does not depend on the client for an identity. If you do not do this under Windows NT, you will end up with a WinStation for each client. These are a limited resource, and each one requires around 1/2 Mb. If you specify The interactive user, then you are under the account of the person logged into Windows NT. The launching user is the user that instantiated the server. Finally, The System Account is a system account that has almost unrestricted access to the local machine.

The Default Properties Tab

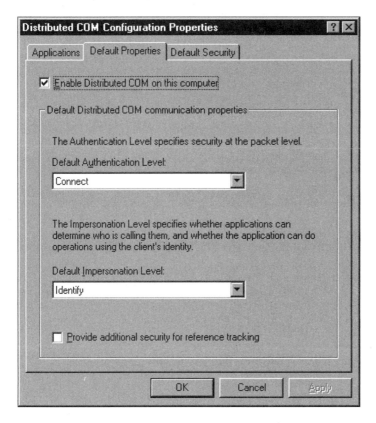

This tab allows you to enable DCOM on a machine. When you first run into a problem using DCOM, I suggest you immediately go to this tab and make sure that Enable Distributed COM on this computer is selected. Although this seems quite obvious, myself and many others have wasted quite a few hours trying to decrypt error messages just because this option wasn't selected. If this is not selected, then DCOM objects cannot be instantiated on the machine. Once you have changed this setting, you will need to reboot the system.

> **This option is NOT checked by default under Windows 95/98. It is checked under Windows NT.**

Authentication Level

You can also decide the Default Authentication Level at the packet level. Packets are the small packages of data that are sent back and forth across the network. This setting effects the entire machine, so generally you shouldn't change it. *Never* use a machine wide value of (None). You will rarely want to increase it from Connect - if a component needs a higher level then the component's server should do this on a by-server basis.

The bad news is that setting the packet level is only available under Windows NT 4.0 with SP4. If you increase the authentication level on a machine-wide basis then calls will take longer (due to authentication traffic); this is only reasonable if the majority of the components on a machine require increased authentication.

Authentication Level	Description
(None)	No authentication is used at all.
Connect	Authentication occurs when the connection is made between the client and the server.
Call	Authentication occurs if the server accepts a remote procedure call.
Packet	All data is authenticated, based per packet.
Packet Integrity	Authenticates data to make sure that it is from the client and that the data has not changed en route.
Packet Privacy	Encrypts the packet.
Default	Implemented per operating system.

If you are using DCOM for Windows 95/98, then your only choices will be (None) and Connect.

Impersonation Level

You can also set the Default Impersonation Level, this is used for when no security has been implemented at the server level. So DCOM defaults to the Impersonation Level chosen here. Impersonation allows the server to impersonate another account with a different level of access. The choices for impersonation level are:

Impersonation Level	Description
Identify	The server can impersonate a client to check permissions within the access control list in Windows NT. Unable to access systems objects.
Impersonate	The server can impersonate the client and has the same access rights to system objects. This means that the server could, for example, access files that the client has access to.

Table Continued on Following Page

Impersonation Level	Description
Delegate	Allows the server to also impersonate calls to other server machines on behalf of the client.
Anonymous	The client is anonymous.

The last attribute is Provide additional security for reference tracking. When this is selected, the server makes sure that connected clients are tracked using a reference count. The reason you may want to use this is so that a rogue client cannot kill a server by setting its reference count to zero. The only drawback is that it will use more memory keeping track of the reference count, and may thus have a slight impact on performance.

The Default Security Tab

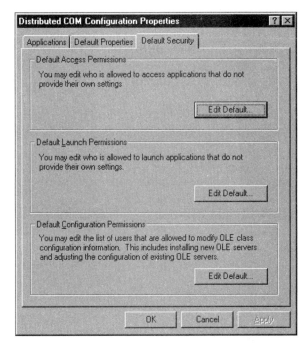

The Default Security tab is similar to the Security tab for each component except that it allows you to set the default settings. Whenever a new component is registered as DCOM enabled it starts off with the access, launching and configuration settings as described by this tag.

Setting the Security for our Component

Now we've explored `DCOMCnfg` in some detail, let's see how to use it by setting the security for our DCOM_Server component.

1. The first thing we need to do is make sure DCOM is enabled on our server machine. From the Default Properties tab make sure that <u>E</u>nable Distributed COM on this computer is selected. If you have to change this option, you will be prompted to reboot the machine.

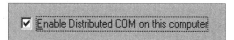

2. From the Application tab scroll down the list of applications until you find our DCOM_Server.CDCOM. Open its <u>P</u>roperties:

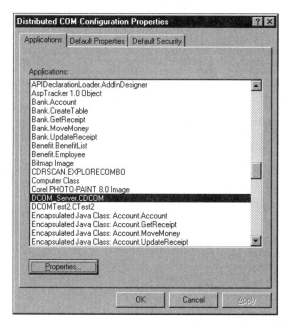

3. On the Security tab we need to change the access and launch permissions. By default, only users that are local to the server can access the components. We can set the permissions as required by a specific environment but the easiest thing in our case is simply to allow everyone access.

4. Change the access permissions to custom and press the Edit... button:

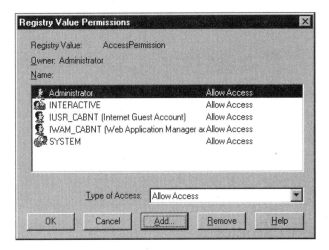

5. Click the Add... button to bring up the Add Users and Groups dialog:

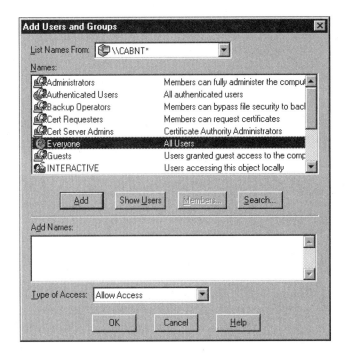

6. Select the Everyone group and make sure the Type of Access is Allow Access. Hit the Add button in this dialog and then OK. The result should be that the Everyone group has been added to the list of users who can access our component:

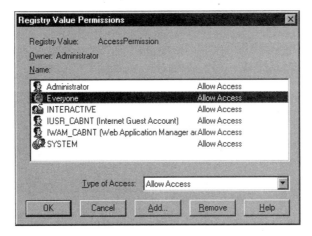

7. Repeat the last three steps for the launch permissions.

8. Now switch to the Identity tab. By default, the user account is set to The launching user. This means that our server application will be run under the user account of the user logged into the client workstation. If the user has no account on our server then they won't be able to run our server application.

We need to set it to the The interactive user, otherwise the message would not actually be visible to us and the code would appear to hang:

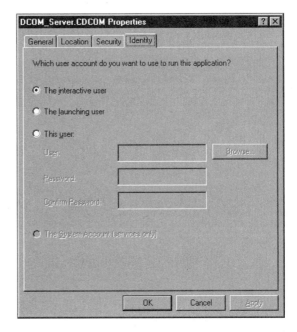

Using The interactive user option is not generally recommended except for test application such as this. You would normally want to specify a specific user account.

9. Click OK and we're all ready to go.

So as you can see, we did not have to make any changes to our server's code to allow DCOM to work its magic. DCOM just wraps around our object to provide security and distributed communication between our components.

Testing the Server

Now we want to make sure that our client can talk to the component. We could build a test client application or we can use a tool provided by Visual Studio called OLE View.

If you don't already have OLE View installed you can download it for free from Microsoft.

Appendix A explains the features of OLE View in great detail so I'll only step you through the process here.

1. Open OLE View and expand the **All Objects** node:

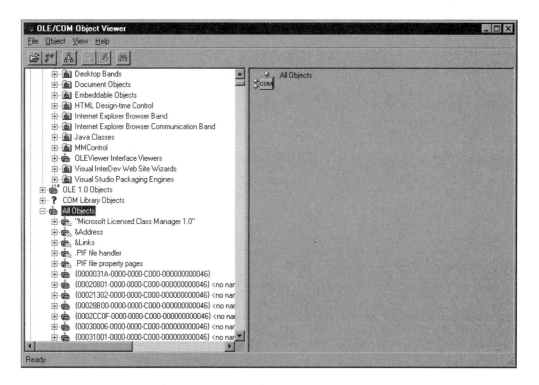

This shows a list of all the COM objects currently registered on your machine.

2. Browse down the list until you find our DCOM _Server component:

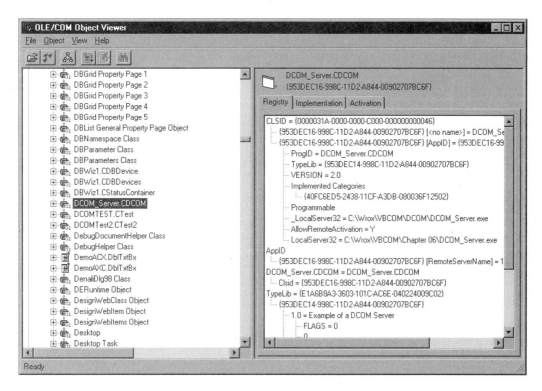

3. Either right-click on our component or use the <u>O</u>bject menu to select Create Instance On... This will bring up a dialog asking for the name of the server on which you want to create an instance of the component on:

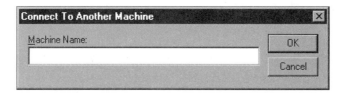

4. Enter either the name or the IP address of your server and hit OK. After a short while you will see a list of interfaces that the component supports. This means that you have successfully instantiated an instance of our component on the remote machine.

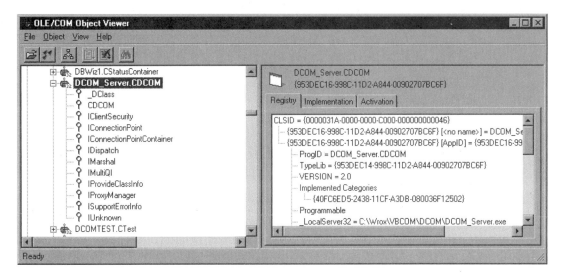

5. If you now go to the server machine and view the processes running in Task Manager (press *Ctrl + Alt + Del*), you should see the DCOM_Server.exe listed:

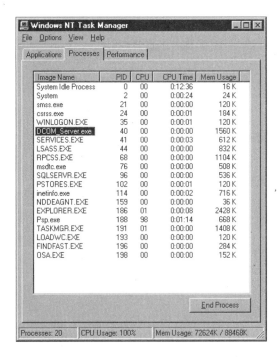

6. Either right-click on the component or use the <u>O</u>bject menu to select Release Instance. This will destroy the object instance.

Creating a Client Application

Now we can create a client application that calls a remote server. In order to do this we will make use of an optional argument of `CreateObject` new in Visual Basic 6. We shall also be using our DblTxtBx ActiveX Control that we built in the previous chapter.

1. Create a new Standard EXE project in Visual Basic and call it `DCOM_Client`.

2. Using the References dialog set a pointer to the type library for our DCOM_Server component:

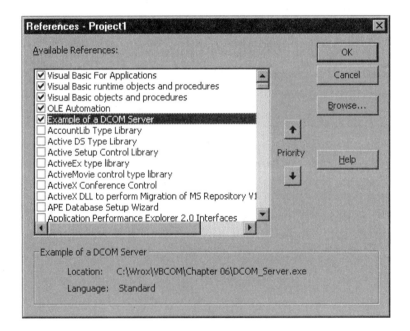

3. Using the Components dialog add our `DemoAXC` OCX to the project:

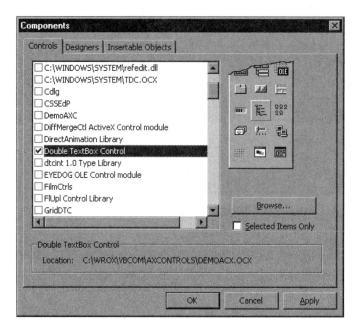

4. Place one of out DblTxtBx controls on the form with a command button called `cmdSend`:

5. Double-click on the command button and enter this code into the `Click` event handler:

```
Private Sub cmdSend_Click()

  Dim objServer As CDCOM

  Set objServer = CreateObject("DCOM_Server.CDCOM", "DCOMSERVER")

  objServer.Display DblTxtBxWiz1.CompleteName

  Set objServer = Nothing

End Sub
```

> **You need to specify the name of your server machine in the** `CreateObject`
> **call in place of my** `DCOMSERVER`**.**

6. Run the project and providing everything has been set up properly, when you enter a name
into the control and hit the Send button you should get a message box on the server:

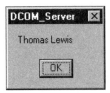

In this example, we requested that the object `DCOM_Server.CDCOM` be created on a server machine.
If the server name is not provided, the object will be created on the local machine.

Running Into Brick Walls

Unfortunately, using DCOM is not always so easy. It's really easy to run into brick walls when
working with DCOM. Hopefully, this section will help alleviate some of the problems you may
encounter.

Potential Errors

Error 429 : ActiveX component can't create object

You may think that your client is communicating with a DCOM server component. It sits there and
churns away for a while and then pops up the infamous Error 429. This occurs because the server is
trying to read the registry but the user account that the server is impersonating does not have
permission to do so. While this is going on, the CPU utilization is at 100%.

To fix this, you can either change the user account to the appropriate level using DCOMCnfg or hack
into the registry and make the appropriate settings.

Error 70: Permission Denied

This is usually the error that occurs when you do not have DCOM running on the server machine.
Make sure that you have Enable Distributed COM on this computer selected on the Default
Properties tab of DCOMCnfg. Also, make sure that the default access permissions is set to allow your
clients to contact the server.

Doesn't Seem to Work on Windows 95/98

Make sure to look in the registry under:

```
HKEY_LOCAL_MACHINE\Software\Microsoft\OLE\EnableRemoteConnect
```

It should have the value "Y". If not, change it to "Y" and reboot the machine.

Error 70 : Permission Denied when using the WithEvents keyword

This error can occur when a remote server is being invoked by a client using the WithEvents keyword:

```
Dim WithEvents objLocal As DCOM_Server.Test
```

This occurs if the server does not have access rights for the client or the custom access permissions on the server are not set properly. When the server tries to raise an event on the client, the error occurs.

Run-time error –2147023174(800706ba): Automation Error – RPC_SERVER_UNAVAILBLE

Isn't that a mess! What it really means is that RPCSS.EXE, which is responsible for the plumbing of DCOM, is not running. This can occur if the client is trying to access a server before the RPCSS.EXE application is running.

Read the README Files !

Microsoft is known for adding last minute important information to read me files. When you install Visual Studio or DCOM98, search the installation directory for the file README.TXT. I know you shouldn't have to do it, but you will find it helps solve those obscure problems that occur from time to time.

Upgrade your DCOM

With the new DCOM upgrades (known as DCOM98 under 95/98 and Windows NT Service Pack 4 under NT), the following have been fixed:

- ❑ Does not permit older versions to overwrite newer versions of DLLs
- ❑ Provide Visual Basic 6.0 data types support
- ❑ Array parameters in Visual Basic 6.0 can be greater than 64K
- ❑ Issues with marshaling concerning Visual Basic 6.0 have been fixed
- ❑ Many more...

Most Important, turn DCOM on!

Once again, learn from the many who have lost many billable hours just to find out that it was not turned on to begin with. Again, make sure that you have Enable Distributed COM on this computer selected on the Default Properties tab of DCOMCnfg.

Surrogates

When a client creates a component on a remote machine, the component must execute within the process of an application.

So with our DCOM_Server that was an ActiveX EXE server, the first thing that the SCM of the remote machine did was to launch that EXE. That gave the component a process in which to execute.

Next, the application was asked to create the component specified by the CLSID. This created the component within the application's process.

Finally, the reference to the resultant DCOM object was returned to our client, via the local SCM.

If, however, our simulator was contained within an ActiveX DLL (in-process component), whose process space would the component be hosted in?

Because a DLL can only be loaded and used within an EXE, that is, it doesn't have its own process, we need a surrogate EXE to perform this role.

DLLHOST.EXE

The role of a surrogate is simply that discussed above. It provides a process space enabling in-process components to be created and used remotely.

As well as just hosting one or more components, the surrogate also has some other benefits:

❑   The component is isolated in the surrogate application. If the component crashes for any reason, only the surrogate process will die, and not any part of the client process.

❑   A surrogate can host one or more components for one or more clients. This helps reduce the resources, as otherwise there would be an EXE running for each component.

❑   Enables the in-process component to have security attributers associated with it.

Security and Surrogates

When a component is created remotely, the security attributes of the COM server will by default determine whether or not in can be hosted in an already existing surrogate. If the security identities (name of the remote user in simple terms) are different, another surrogate will be created, assigned the associated permissions, and used. This is important as it ensures that a powerful remote client (an administrative user for example) could not have its surrogate's power misused.

If a disgruntled employee wrote a component that deleted critical information from a shared drive, unless he had delete access to the files, he couldn't actually cause much. However, if he could get his component to run remotely in a surrogate that had the permissions needed, he could cause some serious damage. This is why each remote client basically has its own surrogate, unless you specify a named account using DCOMCnfg.

If you only ever want one instance of a surrogate per COM server (multiple components can of course live within that), you can configure the component to run under a specific user account (security identity), via the Identity tab within DCOMCnfg, rather than user the identity of the remote client.

Summary

I began with an example with our intrepid hero Phil and showed how distributed components can solve some basic business issues, and how we can either solve them the right way, or the wrong way. I then discussed how DCOM works to allow communication between components without having to implement code to support the distributed functionality, but with consideration about the new factors DCOM introduces, such as network roundtrips.

You saw how easy it was to create a Visual Basic server and implement it into a DCOM environment. Again, DCOM shields you from having to work with plumbing issues and allows you to stick to solving business problems, but it does require some additional thought when designing your components.

I also walked you through the DCOMCnfg application and showed you how to set up security for your components.

I gave you some tips on how to get around some of the brick walls that occur when working with DCOM. I hope you have found something that will save you hours of frustration.

Although DCOM if often called 'COM on a longer wire' as we've seen its significance to our components is far greater. Components that are going to be used remotely require a different design approach to those that are just used locally. Such factors as round-trips and bandwidth need to be considered if we want to design effective and efficient DCOM components.

In the next chapter, we will talk about enhancing and deploying our objects using Microsoft Transaction Server (MTS). We will discuss what it is, and how it makes the development of scalable component-based systems a lot easier. See you there!

VB COM

7
MTS

Overview

In the previous chapters we have seen how you create components that can be located either on the same machine as the client or on a remote machine and accessed remotely using DCOM. In this chapter, we will discuss how you can write more scalable, robust and secure server applications that could be used by potentially 1000s of users, with a little help from **Microsoft Transaction Server**.

In the first half of the chapter we'll discuss the basic concepts and architecture of MTS, and how it generally helps in the development of scalable applications. In the second half of the chapter you will see how you can develop and deploy a simple component in MTS, essentially using MTS as a super surrogate.

In this chapter, we will cover:

- ❑ What Transaction Processing is all about
- ❑ The Basic Architecture of MTS
- ❑ The Benefits of using MTS
- ❑ Using MTS and the MTS Explorer
- ❑ Developing an MTS object in Visual Basic

Like with Chapter 6, you should be aware that MTS is really intended for Enterprise development, and as such you really need to be using Windows NT. Although it is possible to run MTS on a Windows 9x platform, it is missing several key features and the MTS Explorer looks different.

MTS is a complex subject and all I can ever hope to do is give you a brief idea of some of the capabilities of MTS. It you would like to learn more then I suggest you look at *Professional MTS and MSMQ with VB and ASP* by Wrox Press.

What is MTS?

MTS is essentially a component-based run-time environment that makes it easy for you to develop and deploy scalable Enterprise applications. Its key goals are to relieve you of the pain of developing the basic infrastructure required for such applications, whilst helping to shield you from the many complexities of multi-user development, such as concurrent access to resources and distributed transaction processing.

The end result of using MTS is that you can focus on developing the business objects to solve your business problems, rather than spending 40% of your development time implementing the framework required just to host your objects. Indeed, writing a truly scalable system in Visual Basic is probably not possible without MTS. Even in C++, creating your own scalable infrastructure would be fairly silly, given that somebody else has already done the hard work and is giving it away for free!

MTS is built entirely around COM, and you should think of it as an extension of the existing functionality that COM provides. Probably one of the most important features of Windows 2000 is the unification of the COM and MTS programming models, bringing context and activity-based concurrency management directly into the COM runtime. The unification means that your investment today in MTS won't be wasted with the advent of the next generation of Windows operation systems.

MTS - Name Confusion

Microsoft marketing made a really good decision and a really bad decision. The good decision was to give away MTS for free. Do not think this was just a flippant decision, other server applications that do the same thing can cost thousands of dollars. Microsoft in their generous nature (or aggressive market-share strike) decided that MTS would be free and included it in all versions of Windows NT since it's part of a strategy for distributed development known as Windows DNA (which I will address in the next chapter). Currently, MTS is included with Windows NT Server 4.0 Standard Edition, Windows NT Workstation 4.0 Edition, Windows NT 4.0 Enterprise Edition, Windows NT 4.0 Option Pack, Windows 9x when you install Personal Web Server services, and MTS can be downloaded for free off the Microsoft Web Site. Microsoft says it will ship with every operating system (could there be one for Windows CE in the future?) they release from now on.

The bad decision Microsoft marketing made is the name, Microsoft Transaction Server. It would be like calling Microsoft Office, Microsoft Word Server. Transaction Processing is only one of the features of MTS. MTS also provides a myriad of other services including database connection pooling, process isolation, and state management. It seems that at every Microsoft conference, they either apologize for the name, or say that it should be called 'Microsoft Component Server' or 'Microsoft Application Server'. For right now we are stuck with the name. But remember MTS is more than just transaction processing, as you will soon see.

Origins of MTS

MTS is not an application that Microsoft has invented from scratch. It is based upon well established mainframe transaction processing systems that have been evolving over the past 30 years, and object request brokers that have been around since the earlier 80's, and of course, some of their own systems. Let's discuss these terms, as you'll find people often use them in the MTS/database world.

Transaction Processing Monitors

Microsoft describes MTS as **middleware**; software that generally makes the development of scalable distributed applications easier. Its functionality is a combination of a **Transaction Processing** (TP) monitor and an **Object Request Broker** (ORB), with a few extra bits thrown in. The end product is best described as a 'Distributed Object Broker and Transaction Monitor'.

A TP monitor has two main functions. Firstly, it enables business applications to scale by multiplexing system resources such as processes and threads (we'll talk a little about what these are later in the chapter). If we had 5000 clients each with their own system process, Windows NT would probably either crash or use 100% of its CPU swapping, because a process under NT needs a fair amount of memory, roughly 540k. If instead we had say 100 processes, each servicing 50 clients, we would have a better system, because a typical NT system these days can quite happily support 100 processes. This basic concept of sharing resources between multiple clients can also be applied to threads, database connection and many other types of resources, as we will discuss later when we talk about MTS resource dispensers and resource pooling.

The second main function of a TP monitor is to ensure that work is executed correctly and the results are accurately recorded by using transaction protocols. These protocols essentially coordinate the work being done by different elements of a system.

Object Request Brokers - ORBs

Object Request Brokers (ORBs) enable the deployment of distributed applications, and generally make the development process of component software easier. ORBs create objects for clients, know where objects are located and how to create them, and generally provide the basic plumbing and services to perform such tasks with code that is separate from the components you develop. COM/DCOM is essentially a type of ORB.

When Should You Use MTS?

MTS can host any COM component contained in an ActiveX DLL. To provide any real benefit though, you need to understand the basic philosophy of MTS, use some of the COM objects and interfaces it provides, and understand how special design considerations need to be made when developing certain types of components. If you design a system using traditional OO design tools it will probably fail miserably under MTS, in the same way a DCOM application without any consideration for network round-trips does. Just like DCOM, MTS mandates a new way of thinking if you are going to use it successfully.

Generally speaking, using MTS is a good idea when your application has some or all of the following requirements:

❑ Requires scalability - Support for a large number of clients, 10s, 100s or potentially 1000s

❑ Needs the ability to perform localized or distributed transactions across one or more databases, or other such durable resources such as message queues

❑ Requires multi-user support and/or concurrent access to components

❑ Would benefit from the ability to monitor activity in the system and view statistics

❑ Secure access to components via a simple programmatic interface

❑ Easy deployment of DCOM client installations

❑ Remote Creation of ActiveX DLL components

MTS is Not Just for Database Oriented Applications

One point that needs to be made clear early on, is that many developers that have heard about MTS have not used it, thinking that it's a service that only helps develop database application servers. Although database applications will certainly gain more with the current set of features provided with MTS, any application that wants better concurrency, multi-user functions and simplified development model can also gain from using it.

The Architecture of MTS

Now that we have briefly covered what MTS is and when it might be useful, let's discuss how its architecture works. We will gradually build up a picture of the architecture, by looking at the features MTS provides and how it implements them.

Transaction Processing

The most powerful feature of MTS is **transaction processing**, hence its name, Microsoft **Transaction** Server. If you've ever used a relational database, when you read the word transaction your mind probably interprets it to think of database transactions. Whilst this interpretation is correct in many ways, it's important to realize that MTS is designed to deal with transactions for many types of data sources, and not just databases.

What is a Transaction?

A transaction is best described as one or more actions that are either all performed as a whole or none of them are performed at all. Sticking with one of the world's most frequently used analogies, think of a bank account, and how funds are transferred between accounts.

If Phil wanted to pay his friend Dave $200, he could dial up the Internet and use his home banking system to transfer the funds. He would go to his account, enter the amount to be transferred, and then specify the account to which the funds should be transferred. Behind the scenes, the bank system performs a transaction that involves:

- ❑ Updating several database tables to move the funds from account A to account B
- ❑ Creating activity journals so that his next bank statement shows the funds transfer
- ❑ Manipulating various objects performing other types of processing that banks generally require

Most of this activity will either be performed or not, that is, it will be done within a transaction, and will either complete as a whole, or fail as a whole. It might of course be done in several transactions, but that really depends on how the bank's system has been designed.

If a transaction was not used, the bank systems could potentially take $200 from Phil's account, after which they could encounter an error and crash, loosing any record of the $200. Phil probably wouldn't be very happy about this, and his friend Dave might not buy the story. If a transaction were used, then when the error occurred the system would reset everything back to how it was, so Phil would get his $200 back.

ACID Properties

A transaction **must** have four properties known as **ACID**. These four requirements are:

Atomicity

Atomicity dictates that a transaction must execute completely, or not at all. If the process breaks down in the middle, based on atomicity, everything that occurred before the breakdown should be rolled back. So in the example above, Phil wouldn't lose his $200.

Consistency

Consistency dictates the persistent state reflects that which the business rules had intended. In other words, the transaction must not break any rules laid down in the environment by the business rules. That means in our above example, that once the transaction occurred, there should money added to Dave's account, and money removed from Phil's account. We wouldn't expect money to be added to any other account.

Isolation

Isolation refers to how concurrent transactions are not aware of what each other is doing. The end point of the transaction would be the same no matter what the outcome of the individual transactions. In the above example, imagine if Dave's friend Mark was also transferring money to Dave's account at the same time as Phil. The two transactions would be unaware of each other, but would still successfully result in two sets of funds being added to Dave's account, and a set of funds being removed from Phil and Mark's accounts.

Durability

Durability states that when updates have occurred to a resource, only then should the client be notified that a transaction has occurred. If the system failed for any reason after the notification, then the changes would still be reflected once the system was restarted. This allows the user to know that a transaction has been successfully completed even if there is an error later. So relating to the above example, Phil would not think that the money had been transferred when in fact it hadn't.

MTS Manages Resources

One of the real powers of MTS is that the basic principles of transaction processing can apply to any number of data sources of varying types on one or more machines. For example, a transaction could be made up of these actions:

❑   Update multiple databases/tables on machine A
❑   Create and modify several files on machine A
❑   Update multiple databases/tables on machine B

If it's possible to change so many different types of data in a single transaction, how does MTS manage the committing or aborting of the transaction when so many different data sources are involved? The answer is **resource managers** and **resource dispensers**.

Resource Managers and Resource Dispensers

Resource managers in MTS are responsible for implementing transactions over a specific data source such as a database. They manage **durable** data, that is, data that is persistent. Resource managers *must* keep the data they are responsible for in a *consistent* state when it's used and manipulated by an object. They do this by implementing transactions that have the ACID properties discussed earlier.

Resource managers have a close relationship with **resource dispensers**. Resource dispensers are responsible for managing and sometimes pooling **non-durable** shared resources such as database connections, that are needed by an object to manipulate the durable data maintained by a resource manager.

Resource Pooling

Together, resource managers and resource dispensers are the major players in the scalability game. Resource dispensers enable limited resources to be efficiently shared among clients by pooling them. In more traditional non-scalable systems, clients would typically allocate resources they needed during the lifetime of the application at the start of it, and then free them at the end. For precious resources such as database connections that are often very limited, this severely limits the number of clients that an application can have, as it's not possible to have more clients than you have available database connections.

MTS uses resource pooling to enable potentially thousands of clients to share a relatively small pool of resources. Rather than allocating resources as the start of an application, clients demand resources as they need them, use them, and then release them when they have finished with them.

Resource Pooling and Scalability in More Detail

Resource dispensers pool and re-use the resources they give out to objects in order to aid performance and scalability as discussed:

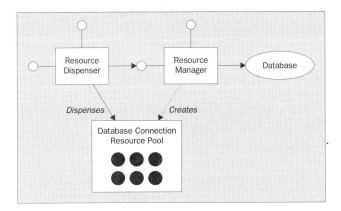

If we take the above diagram, the resource dispenser is responsible for giving out database connections to MTS objects. When an object releases a database connection, the dispenser places it back into a resource pool. When another object comes along and asks for a connection, the resource dispenser can first check its pool to see if there is connection that can be re-used. If a connection has the same attributes, (e.g. user id, password, transaction attributes etc.), the dispenser can give out a connection much more *quickly* than by asking the resource manager to create a new one. Pooling database connections is much quicker because creating a database connection is an expensive process that takes time.

The real beauty of this resource pooling and transaction enlistment is that it's all done *transparently* and *automatically* for you.

One important point to note about resource dispensers is that resources can only be involved in a transaction when they are returned to the pool. Such resources cannot be re-used by objects within the same transaction until the transaction is committed.

How does MTS relate to COM?

You should picture MTS as a logical extension to the COM runtime. The services it provides will one day soon form part of COM+, so with the event of Windows 2000, you'll probably find that the name MTS disappears, and the functionality of MTS overlaps with that of COM+.

MTS essentially extends COM with the following features:

- ❑ Just In Time activation of COM objects
- ❑ As Soon As Possible deactivation of COM Objects
- ❑ Automatic component based transactions
- ❑ Statistics and activity monitoring
- ❑ Interception

When a client application uses MTS they are just using another COM object. Client applications or installations *do not* require MTS be installed locally. If you remember back to Chapter 6 when we discussed how proxy and stubs enable a component to be used remotely via DCOM, the same principles still apply in MTS:

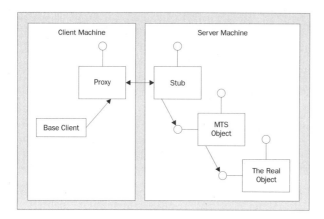

The base client accesses a proxy object that remotely calls to the remote machine. On the remote machine the stub interacts with the MTS object. The stub knows nothing about MTS. As far as it is concerned it is just another COM object that conforms to the well-defined binary specification. The MTS object that the stub is interacting with is the Context Wrapper object.

The Context Wrapper Object

When a base client first creates an object hosted in MTS, they get a reference to a **Context Wrapper** object returned, not the real object:

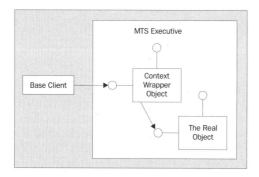

On a small aside, in MTS terms, a client outside of MTS that uses an object hosted inside of MTS is known as a base client. An object inside of MTS, that uses another object inside of MTS, is simply referred to as a client. So when you see base client, think 'runs outside of MTS'.

As the client interacts with this object transparently, MTS can intercept methods calls and perform Just In Time activation when the first one is called, activating the real object. This process is known as **interception**. Now you may have noticed that I've used the word **activating**, rather than **creating**. This is because the first base client to create an MTS object actually causes the real object to be created, although it is not activated until the first invocation of a method on one of its interfaces. When a transaction is completed, any objects involved within it are deactivated and the real object is subsequently destroyed. It is then recreated when a client invokes another method.

The MTS Executive

The MTS executive provides the run-time services that MTS components use. The code for the executive is located in the DLL `MTSEX.DLL`. The executable `MTS.EXE` is also used if you configure MTS such that your components run in their own process space. This executable is essentially a surrogate like those discussed in Chapter 6.

MTS Object Activation and Deactivation

When a client creates a component hosted in MTS, the component is not actually activated until the first method of an interface is invoked. This is known as **Just In Time (JIT) Activation**. This means any initialization code that might cause a server's resources to be consumed, is delayed until they are really needed. This is a nice idea, because it means that a client can create a component earlier on in an application's life, and use it much later, without having to worry about resources being consumed prematurely.

By the same principles, an object is deactivated as soon as possible. This enable MTS to release the memory and resources consumed by the object, whilst the client still thinks it maintains a reference to the real object, without knowing that it has been destroyed. This is known as **As Soon As Possible (ASAP) Deactivation**.

> **MTS extends COM to allow objects to be activated and deactivated such that client references are still maintained, i.e. the client is unaware of the objects being activated and deactivated. This makes server applications potentially more scalable by allowing server resources to be used more efficiently, depending upon the type of object.**

When a transaction is executing, it implicitly locks out other users from modifying any state that it is using that might cause any inconsistency, violating the ACID principles discussed earlier. It is therefore essential to keep transactions as short as possible. A component does this is by using the `SetComplete` and `EnableCommit` methods of the Context object.

The Context Object

Just In Time Activation, As Soon As Possible Deactivation, implicit transaction processing enlistment, transaction monitoring and statistics are just some of the features enabled by the **Context object** in conjunction with the MTS Executive. The Context object is different to the Context Wrapper object discussed earlier.

The Context object is responsible for maintaining state that is implicitly associated with an object hosted inside of MTS. It is sometimes called the shadow object, because every MTS object has one, containing information about the object's execution environment. This includes information such as the identity of the object's creator, security information, and, optionally, the transaction encompassing the work of the object if one is active.

So, the base client interacts with a Context Wrapper, and the real object interacts with the Context object:

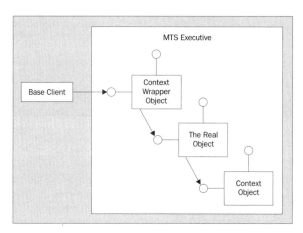

The Context object is essentially the key to how the most of the functionality of MTS works.

The ObjectContext Interface

A Context object implements the `ObjectContext` interface. We can easily access this interface from within any MTS object by calling the `GetObjectContext` function:

```
Dim objContext As ObjectContext

Set objContext = GetObjectContext
```

The `ObjectContext` interface has the following methods; we shall see some of them in action later:

Name	Description
CreateInstance	Creates another MTS object within the activity of the callee. We will discuss activities shortly.
DisableCommit	Changes the object's internal state to indicate that it has not finished its current work, and that its transactional updates are in an inconsistent state.
EnableCommit	Changes the object's internal state to indicate that its work isn't necessarily finished, but its transactional updates are in a consistent state. This is the default state for a newly created object.

Name	Description
IsCallerInRole	Indicates whether the object's direct caller is in a specified role (either directly or as part of a group).
IsInTransaction	Indicates whether the object is currently executing within a transaction. This method can be used to enforce the transaction requirements of a component.
IsSecurityEnabled	Indicates whether security is enabled. MTS security is enabled unless the object is running in the client's process, or MTS is running under Windows 9x.
SetAbort	Declares that the object has failed to complete its work and can be deactivated on returning from the currently executing method. It should be called to indicate that transactional updates are in an inconsistent state or that some sort of unrecoverable error occurred. This means that the transaction in which the object was executing must be aborted. If any object executing within a transaction returns to its client after calling SetAbort, the entire transaction is doomed to abort.
SetComplete	Declares that the object has completed its work and can be deactivated on returning from the currently executing method. For objects that are executing within the scope of a transaction, it also indicates that the object's transactional updates can be committed. When an object that is the root of a transaction calls SetComplete, MTS attempts to commit the transaction on return from the current method.

> An object should never pass its ObjectContext to another object. Doing so invalidates the reference.

Life Time of the Real Object

The creation, activation, deactivation and destruction of an object is done transparently to the client, but it does require a certain amount of participation from your components hosted in MTS.

Any *good* component under MTS implements the custom interface ObjectControl. This interface informs an object when it is activated and deactivated.

The ObjectControl Interface

This ObjectControl interface has just three methods:

Name	Description
Activate	Called when this object is Activated

Table Continued on Following Page

Name	Description
Deactivate	Called when this object is Deactivated
CanBePooled	Called when an object is deactivated to see if it can be pooled. MTS 2.0 does not implement object pooling.

These methods are all fairly self-describing, and essentially reflect the lifetime of the real object, so let's discuss when they are called by MTS.

The `Activate` method is called the first time a client invokes a method exposed by one of the object's interfaces. In this method a component should perform any useful initialization that is global to all of the methods in the component. If, for example, all of the methods of the object used a database connection, and the component always executed within a transaction, it could be used to allocate the connection and perform any error handling. The connection would then be freed in the `Deactivate` method when the transaction ends.

> **Any initialization code that you previously put in `Class_Initialize` probably belongs inside of the `Activate` method now.**

The `Deactivate` method is called when the real object, not the Context object, is destroyed. The real object is destroyed under two conditions:

- ❏ The object has been involved in a transaction that has now been completed
- ❏ A client has released the last outstanding reference to the Context object, and the real object was either non-transactional or was not used after being created.

The `CanBePooled` method is called just after `Deactivate` is called by MTS. The function returns a Boolean value. If the value returned is True, future versions of MTS might re-use the object for subsequent creation requests by other clients. The idea is that pooling created objects is much quicker than the time it takes to create them using the COM runtime. Unfortunately, MTS 2.0 does not currently implement object pooling.

Finally, let me just point out that the lifetime of the Context Wrapper and object is identical to that of any other COM object, that is, it is destroyed when the last client reference to it is released.

Thread Pooling in MTS

So far in this book we've tried to avoid the subject of threads. However, threads form an essential part of any scalable system, especially in MTS, so let's bite the bullet and give you a brief run down on them.

Put simply, you can think of a thread as a lightweight process. Unlike a process though, threads do not actually own system resources. When you start an application under Windows such as Notepad, the operating system will create a process in which the application executes. This process will have its own address space, will be isolated from other processes, such that if the applications go seriously wrong, the integrity of others in the system is maintained.

Inside of a process you always have at least one **thread**, known as the main thread. A thread is the basic entity to which the operating system allocates CPU time. So, if we have 10 processes, each with a thread that is doing some intensive work, the operating system will give each thread 10% of the overall available CPU time.

A process can contain multiple threads that run concurrently. Each thread shares the system resources owned by the process, such as its virtual address space. This means that threads can execute the application's code, access global memory and other resources such as files, whilst not consuming too much additional resources.

Because threads are 'cheaper' than processes, truly scalable systems will always use a thread per client, rather than a process per client, because the resource saving is greater. Depending upon how the system is partitioned, the system might use multiple processes for different applications, with a thread per client. MTS does this by enabling each package to be configured to run in its own process. Such packages are known as **server packages**. We shall cover packages later, but for now think of a package as a group of related components.

MTS takes care of threads for you by pooling them just like the resource dispenser does with database connections. MTS does this very efficiently for you. When the thread pool is exhausted, components will start to share threads in a round robin fashion. So if we had a thread pool size of 5, the sixth component created would share the first thread, the seventh the second and so on. Again the beauty of MTS is that there is no need to write thread managers within your code. MTS handles the threading for you.

Activities

When a base client creates an object running under MTS, an activity is created to host it. Each base client has its own activity, and each object is associated with *one* activity:

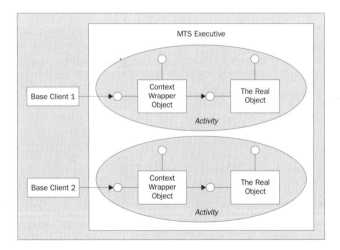

As objects interact inside of MTS, MTS tracks the flow of execution through each activity, preventing any two objects in the same activity from being active at the *same* time. This ensures the integrity of the application's state, by ensuring two components can not run at the same time and interfere with common state. Activities effectively result in a single logical thread of execution through one or more activities, potentially distributed across several machines. By having one logical thread, application development is simplified no end.

A Stateless Programming Model

In Chapter 2 we discussed how an object has three main characteristics: identity, behavior and state. An MTS object has all of these properties, but it is important to understand the lifetime of the object's state may be short if it is involved in a transaction, because MTS is creating and destroying the real object.

When a transaction is committed in MTS by calling `SetComplete`, all of the objects that formed part of the transaction are deactivated and destroyed. So any state that was manipulated and held within the objects during the transaction is lost. The reason for doing this is to free resources consumed by the objects. Because a component could be holding on to precious resources such as database connections, or unneeded resources such as large quantities of data that consumes memory, the deactivation makes a lot of sense, as it potentially makes the overall application more scalable.

Essentially an object does have state in MTS, but it generally only lasts for the duration of one call from a base client into a root object.

> *The component that initially causes a transaction to be started is refereed to as the **root object**. All subsequent objects that share the transaction are called secondary objects. When the root object commits or aborts the transaction, all of the work of the secondary objects will be committed or aborted. However, note that if **any** of the objects abort the transaction, the entire transaction is aborted.*

If a transactional object requires state, the approach is to pass it as additional parameters to each method call. An object can call several of its own private methods, so it would be incorrect to say that state only lasts for one call in all cases. It is possible to have stateful objects in MTS, but considerations as to the scalability of it should probably be a concern.

Sharing Data Between Components in MTS (aka SPAM)

When creating MTS-hosted components, you must generally try and make transactional components stateless, because, as we just discussed, objects within transactions are generally deactivated and destroyed between each call to the root object by the base client. If you want to have a global count variable which could hold how many times a method had been called, or if you wanted to share state between two MTS objects you could use the **Shared Property Manager (SPM)** resource dispenser:

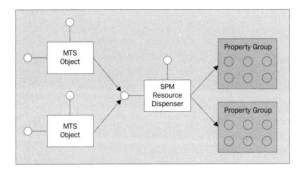

The SPM groups share state into *named* property groups. Each group generally contains one or more named properties that a component can create, manipulate and share with other components.

The MTS on-line help suggests that property groups can be used for things like web page counters. Whilst this is a reasonable suggestion, the counter would have to be read from a database or file when it is initially created, and we would have to persist its value on a regular basis.

MTS Security

MTS makes creating a secure server simple and painless. It provides a friendly user interface for declarative configuration of user rights, and a simple API for programmatic checking of security from within a component.

Security under MTS only works when MTS is running on a Windows NT machine, it does not work under Windows 9x. Security is only available to components that are configured to run in a server package. Library packages can not implement security, as they run in the process space of the base client, which generally means it is too late to call the COM APIs to set security up. We will cover the difference between server and library packages shortly.

A Brief Note about NT Security

I can tell you now that security can be a confusing and reasonably complex subject. I'll give you a brief overview of how it works here but it's really out of the scope of this book.

NT objects such as processes and files can be secured using an **Access Control List (ACL)**. These structures contain a number of **Access Control Entries (ACE)** that describe what a user *can* and *can not* do with an object. A user is uniquely identified using a **Security Identifier (SID)**, so each different type of ACE contains the SIDs and the associated permissions that are either allowed or denied:

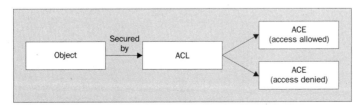

Roles

MTS encapsulates all of these structures by using **roles** and declarative security via the MTS Explorer. A role is essential an ACL with a name. For example, we could create a role called 'Order Processing Users' and assign one or more user accounts to be in that role. A component can then check if the base client using it is a member of that role. So if Phil wanted to secure his order processing system, he could create several roles, and have the component check the roles of a base client performing any operations.

Let's take a break from all this discussion and see MTS in action.

Using MTS

Now that we've covered the basic theory of MTS, let's move onto to how we actually use it. Fortunately, for us, MTS is very simple to use. It only requires the addition of a few lines of code to make our components run in MTS, and Microsoft have provided a handy graphical user interface to help us manage our MTS components.

The Transation Server Explorer

The **Transaction Server Explorer** allows us to administer our MTS components quickly and easily. Under Windows NT the Transaction Server Explorer is a snap-in for the **Microsoft Management Console** (MMC), while in Windows 9x it is a separate executable:

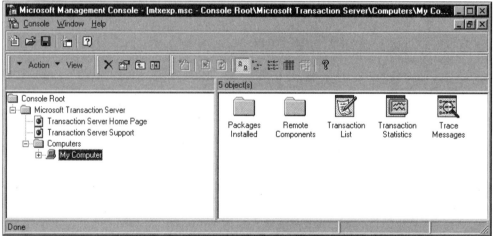

MTS Explorer under Windows NT

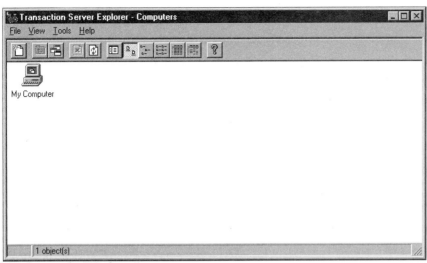

MTS Explorer under Windows 9x

From now on, all the screenshots you will see will be of the Transaction
Server Explorer running on Windows NT. Due to the lack of some key
functionality of MTS on 9x, we'll only cover using MTS in Windows NT

The Transaction Server Explorer is accessed through the Start menu.

If you expand the My Computer node you will be able to access a list of all the Packages Installed in
MTS and you will also have access to some administrative tools that the Explorer provides:

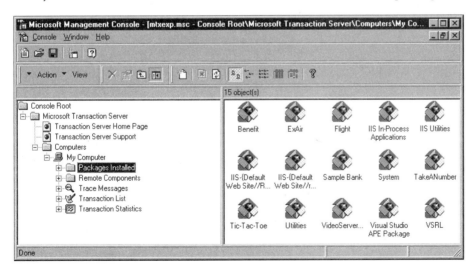

MTS Packages

When components are hosted in MTS they are added to a **package**. A package is one or more components that have been grouped together so that they can be easily set up and managed as a collective group. With packages it is a lot easier to distribute, administer, and use multiple components. You may have a project with multiple classes that will need MTS services. Instead of working with each one on an individual basis, you can create packages that can be distributed to other MTS servers or clients through a single install process.

A package can be configured to host objects in their own process space when set to run as a Server package, or to create components in the process space of the calling base client, when configured as a Library package.

An important feature of both types of packages is that unnecessary component loading and unloading can be prevented, with components being quickly created and destroyed. An MTS package can be configured to stay loaded for a period of time, even when there are no clients using it. This enables MTS to reduce unnecessary loading and unloading of the DLL and EXEs. The default period is 3 minutes.

By right-clicking on a package you can access a package's property pages:

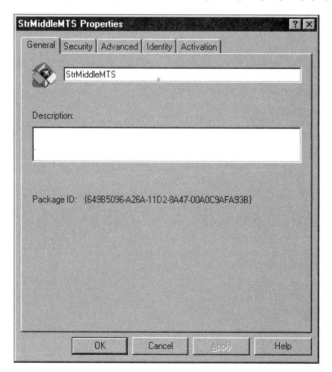

Here you can see a package's
Security, Identity and
whether it is a Server
package or Library Package:

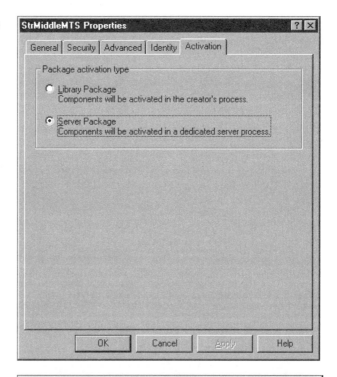

Also note on the Advanced
tab that you can specify the
length of time a package
remains loaded:

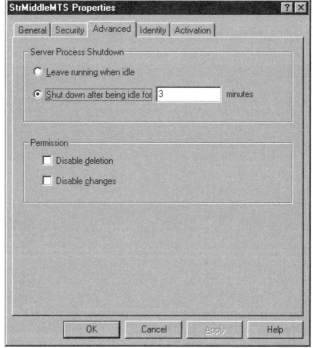

This can be useful to know, especially when developing MTS packages. If a package is active and an error occurs you will need to wait until it is unloaded until you can try it again. Having to wait several minutes in-between each run can be rather irritating and time consuming.

There are two sub-folders for each package: Components and Roles. The Components folder contains the classes/objects that can be instantiated, each represented by a black ball with a green cross:

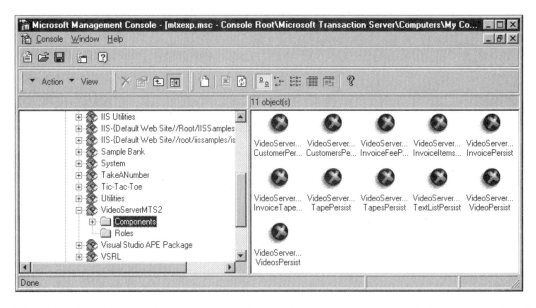

The Roles folder is part of the security mechanism implemented by MTS that we discussed earlier:

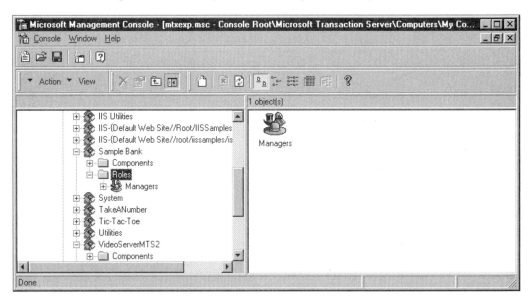

Because Windows 9x doesn't support this security system there are no Roles associated with packages installed in MTS on 9x platforms.

Writing MTS Components with Visual Basic

When you write components for use with MTS, you write them as if they are going to be used by a single user. MTS provides all the infrastructure to deploy your components for use by potentially thousands of clients.

Before we can write some components that we can use in MTS we need to understand few things about how we create MTS objects.

Creating MTS Objects with Visual Basic

Visual Basic provides two ways of creating objects: the `New` keyword and the `CreateObject` method. MTS works differently with each of these ways, and also introduces a third method: `CreateInstance`.

The New Keyword

The `New` keyword, although it acts jut like `CreateObject` when creating an object from another ActiveX server, actually bypasses some COM processing when it creates an instance of a class within the same server.

Using the `New` keyword only creates a **Private** instance of the object – that's why we must use it for creating instances of classes with an Instancing property of 1- Private or 2 – PublicNotCreatable. As it's private MTS won't know anything about it, a context object won't be created and it won't be able to be involved in any transactions. It will simply run as regular code.

The CreateObject Method

The `CreateObject` method is almost the exact opposite of the `New` keyword – it always uses COM to create an instance of class regardless of whether the class is in the same server or not.

If an object in MTS is created using `CreateObject`, MTS will treat it as if it had been created by client, i.e. it will get its own Context object. This means that it won't contain any information about the context of the component that created it and so will be outside of the current transaction.

The CreateInstance Method

The `CreateInstance` method of the Context object is the best way to create objects within MTS. `CreateInstance` works just like `CreateObject` except that it performs a bit more work behind the scenes.

When a new object is created with `CreateInstance`, MTS copies the context information of the creating object to the new object's Context object. This means the new object will inherit the same security and transactional environment from its creator.

Making Objects Support Transactions

Visual Basic 6 makes it very easy for us to specify that our objects are to be used in MTS. Each public class now has a MTSTransactionMode property that MTS uses to determine how the object handles transactions:

These settings are associated with the coclass definition for a component in the type library as 'custom' attributes. When you add your component to an MTS package, MTS will see these attributes and import them, so when you use the MTS Explorer, the setting will initially reflect the setting selected by the programmer.

NotAnMTSObject

Specifies that the object will not be involved with MTS. This is the default option.

NoTransactions

The class will not support transactions. An object context will still be created, but it will not participate in any transactions. This value is useful for when you are just using MTS as a central repository for a component class. With this value, there will not be a transaction as part of the class.

RequiresTransactions

This value mandates that the object must run within a transaction. When a new instance of the object is created, if the client has a transaction already running then the object's context will inherit the existing transaction. If that client does not have a transaction associated with it, MTS will automatically create a new transaction for the object.

UsesTransactions

This choice indicates that should a transaction be available when the object is created then it will use the existing transaction. If no transaction exists then it will also run but without any transactional support.

RequiresNewTransaction

This indicates that the object will execute within its own transaction. When a new object is created with this setting, a new transaction is created regardless of whether the client already has a transaction.

Transaction Attribute Considerations

If you have a component that contained two methods, one that required a transaction, and one that didn't, how could you configure this in MTS? The short answer is you can't. I strongly suggest that if you ever find yourself in this position, you factor your components' functionality into two interfaces, each interface implemented by a different component. One component can then be marked as requiring a transaction and implement interface A, and the other can be marked as doesn't require a transaction and can implement interface B.

Now that we've seen the basics behind creating MTS compatible components with Visual Basic, let's go ahead and write some ourselves.

A Simple MTS Project

To demonstrate how to use MTS components in Visual Basic we shall expand on our DCOM project from the previous chapter by adding an additional tier that manipulates the `CompleteName` string. Unlike, the previous examples we shall go through the code twice. The first time we will build the code without MTS support and check if it works and then we will go back and enable it for MTS.

The Middle-Tier Components

All our components will do is reverse the forename and surname separately and then pass the string onto our server.

1. Create a new **ActiveX DLL** project. Change the name of the project to `StrMiddleTier` and the class to `CStringManager`. Since we are not including a user interface, we can specify **Unattended Execution** which ensures that any normal run-time functions, such as messages that normally result in user interaction, are written to an event log:

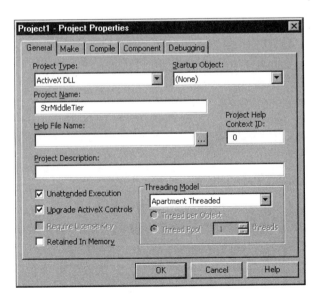

You will notice that once we have set the Unattended Execution option on, the Retained In Memory option becomes available. This option allows you to have your component loaded into memory and then not unload throughout its lifetime. There is an upside and downside to this. The upside is that your component doesn't have to take time to load itself into memory, which can improve performance. The downside is that you have an object out there that does not destroy itself when references are set to 0, which can generate errors in some applications. So be careful if you use this option. We shall leave the option off.

2. Add a reference to the ActiveX Server that we created in Chapter 6:

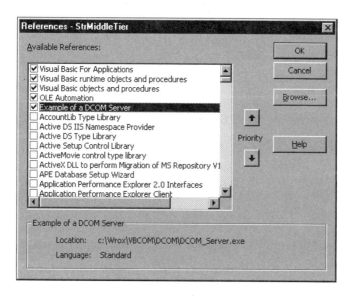

You may want to move the server onto the same machine as the client and these middle-tier components. We will first look at how to get the components running on one machine and then see how to access them remotely using DCOM.

3. Add another Class Module to the project and name it CStringReverser.

The CStringManager object will be used to accept the CompleteName string from the client and then split into the surname and forename. It will then pass each of these strings to the CStringReverser object, which will reverse the character order. Finally, it will rejoin to the two strings and pass them on as one to the server.

4. Add the following code to the CStringReverser code window:

```
Option Explicit

Public Function ReverseString(SubjectStr As String)
```

```
    Dim intLength As Integer
    Dim strResult As String
    Dim intCounter As Integer
    Dim strCharacter As String

    intLength = Len(SubjectStr)

    Do Until intCounter = intLength

        strCharacter = Mid$(SubjectStr, (intLength - intCounter), 1)
        strResult = strResult & strCharacter
        intCounter = intCounter + 1

    Loop

    ReverseString = strResult

End Function
```

5. Now add this code to the `CStringManager` code window:

```
Option Explicit

Public Sub ManipulateString(FullName As String)

    Dim objServer As CDCOM
    Dim objReverser As CStringReverser
    Dim strForename As String
    Dim strSurname As String
    Dim strRevForename As String
    Dim strRevSurname As String
    Dim intSpacePosition As Integer

    intSpacePosition = InStr(FullName, " ")
    strForename = Left$(FullName, intSpacePosition - 1)
    strSurname = Right$(FullName, Len(FullName) - intSpacePosition)

    Set objReverser = New CStringReverser

    strRevForename = objReverser.ReverseString(strForename)
    strRevSurname = objReverser.ReverseString(strSurname)

    Set objServer = New CDCOM

    objServer.Display strRevForename & " " & strRevSurname

    Set objReverser = Nothing
    Set objServer = Nothing

End Sub
```

6. Compile the DLL.

Modifying the Client

We also need to go back to the client code and modify it slightly to use our new DLL.

7. Open the `DCOM_Client` project, and change its name to `MTS_Client`.

8. Change the project references so that it no longer points at our DCOM server but instead points at our new StrMiddleTier DLL:

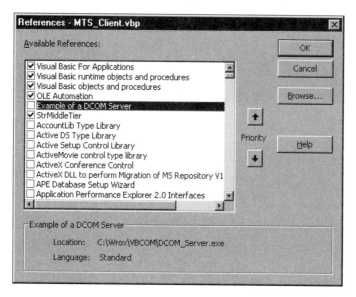

9. Change the code like this:

```
Private Sub cmdSend_Click()

    Dim objReverse As CStringManager

    Set objReverse = CreateObject("StrMiddleTier.CStringManager")

    objReverse.ManipulateString DblTxtBxWiz1.CompleteName

    Set objReverse = Nothing

End Sub
```

10. Now if you run the program, enter a name and hit the **Send** button, the message box you get has the names reversed:

Running the Components in MTS

Now that we have got the components running successfully, we can think about moving them to run under MTS. Before we can install our objects as MTS components, we need to make a few changes.

Changing the Code

1. Open the `StrMiddleTier` project. Change its name to `StrMiddleMTS` to distinguish it from the non-MTS enabled version.

2. In order for our objects to use the `ContextObject` and the `ObjectControl` objects we need to add a reference to the MTS type library. Using the **References** dialog add a reference to the **Microsoft Transaction Server Type Library**:

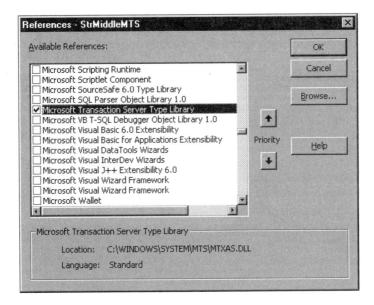

3. Now that our objects have access we need to implement the `ObjectControl` object. First, we need to use the `Implements` keyword to implement the `ObjectControl` interface in our classes:

```
Option Explicit

Implements ObjectControl
```

Once the `Implements ObjectControl` has been added, we also need to add implementation for all the elements of the interface.

4. There are three methods we need to add implementation for: `CanBePooled`, `Activate` and `Deactivate`.

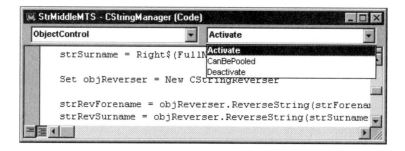

The `CanBePooled` function simply returns a Boolean to indicate whether the object is set up for object pooling. Of course, MTS doesn't yet support this functionality so we'll specify it as `False` for now:

```
Private Function ObjectControl_CanBePooled() As Boolean

  ObjectControl_CanBePooled = False

End Function
```

5. The `Activate` method, on the other hand, can be implemented, and is indeed quite important to our transaction. This method is called by MTS each time our object is about to be used by a new client. We will be using the Context object in our code and so here would be a good time to gain a reference for the Context object. This can be achieved by using a method, supplied by the MTS type library, called `GetObjectContext`. We first need a variable to hold the pointer so declare a modular variable in the **Declarations** section:

```
Option Explicit

Implements ObjectControl

Private mobjContext As ObjectContext
```

Now code the `Activate` method:

```
Private Sub ObjectControl_Activate()

  Set mobjContext = GetObjectContext

End Sub
```

6. Finally, we need to implement the `Deactivate` method. MTS calls this method when the object has finished its task. This would be a good point to release our reference to the Context object:

```
Private Sub ObjectControl_Deactivate()

  Set mobjContext = Nothing

End Sub
```

Now that our object is set up to use the Context object let's do something with it. As you will recall, the Context object has two very important methods: `SetComplete` and `SetAbort`. `SetComplete` indicates that everything went successfully within the object whilst `SetAbort` indicates that something went wrong and the transaction must therefore be rolled back.

7. Using these methods is very simple in our objects - we will simply call `SetComplete` at the end of the Public methods and add error handling to call `SetAbort` if an error occurs. Add the following lines to the `ManipulateString` method:

```
Public Sub ManipulateString(FullName As String)

  Dim objServer As CDCOM
  Dim objReverser As CStringReverser
  Dim strForename As String
  Dim strSurname As String
  Dim strRevForename As String
  Dim strRevSurname As String
  Dim intSpacePosition As Integer

  On Error GoTo MTSErrorHandler

  intSpacePosition = InStr(FullName, " ")
  strForename = Left$(FullName, intSpacePosition - 1)
  strSurname = Right$(FullName, Len(FullName) - intSpacePosition)

  Set objReverser = New CStringReverser

  strRevForename = objReverser.ReverseString(strForename)
  strRevSurname = objReverser.ReverseString(strSurname)

  Set objServer = New CDCOM

  objServer.Display strRevForename & " " & strRevSurname

  Set objReverser = Nothing
  Set objServer = Nothing

  mobjContext.SetComplete

  Exit Sub

MTSErrorHandler:
  mobjContext.SetAbort
  With Err
     .Raise .Number, .Source, .Description
  End With

End Sub
```

8. Since we also want the transaction to be rolled back if an error occurs in the
`CStringReverser` object make the same modifications:

```
Option Explicit

Implements ObjectControl

Private mobjContext As ObjectContext

Public Function ReverseString(SubjectStr As String)

    Dim intLength As Integer
    Dim strResult As String
    Dim intCounter As Integer
    Dim strCharacter As String

    On Error GoTo MTSErrorHandler

    intLength = Len(SubjectStr)

    Do Until intCounter = intLength

        strCharacter = Mid$(SubjectStr, (intLength - intCounter), 1)
        strResult = strResult & strCharacter
        intCounter = intCounter + 1

    Loop

    ReverseString = strResult

    mobjContext.SetComplete

Exit Function

MTSErrorHandler:
    mobjContext.SetAbort
    With Err
      .Raise .Number, .Source, .Description
    End With

End Function

Private Sub ObjectControl_Activate()

    Set mobjContext = GetObjectContext

End Sub

Private Function ObjectControl_CanBePooled() As Boolean

    ObjectControl_CanBePooled = False

End Function

Private Sub ObjectControl_Deactivate()

    Set mobjContext = Nothing

End Sub
```

9. Before we can leave the code there is one more change we need to make. You should remember that all objects in a transaction must be created by other objects on the MTS Server. We can't use the `New` keyword or the `CreateObject` method because they won't link the Context object of the new object back to the context of the creating object. Instead we need to use the `CreateInstance` method on the Context object to create each subsequent object. We therefore need to change the `ManipulateString` method in the `CStringManager` class like so:

```
Set objReverser = mobjContext.CreateInstance("StrMiddleMTS.CStringReverser")
```

10. We have finished modifying the code but we need to indicate to MTS how our objects work with transactions. This is easily done by changing a property setting for each class. Set the `CStringManager` to 4- **RequiresNewTransaction** and the `CStringReverser` to 2 – **RequiresTranasction**.

11. Compile our new `StrMiddleMTS.dll`.

Installing our Components into MTS

Now that we have our DLL all set up to run under MTS, we need to get MTS to recognize its existence. This is done by installing our objects into a package. Installing a component in MTS permanently changes the way that the component is referenced within Windows – or at least until you remove it from within MTS. MTS makes these changes to enable it to intercept the creation of your COM component. This gives MTS complete control over the object creation process, and enables MTS to return an instance of a Context Wrapper object to clients, rather than your object.

We shall first see how to get our objects running under MTS on a local machine and then see how to export them to be used from a remote client.

1. Open the Transaction Server Explorer and browse to the Packages Installed node:

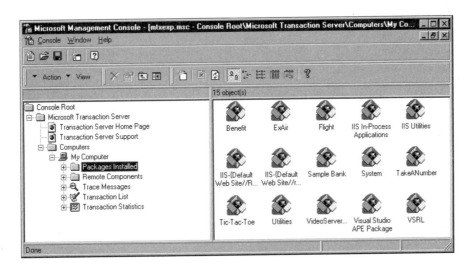

2. We need to add a new package so select Action | New | Package option from the toolbar. MTS will bring up a wizard to guide us through the process of adding a package. The first page asks whether we are creating a new empty package or importing an existing one. Since we haven't placed our DLL into MTS we need to Create an empty package:

3. Next we need to supply a name for our new package. Let's call our package StrMiddleMTS, just like the DLL:

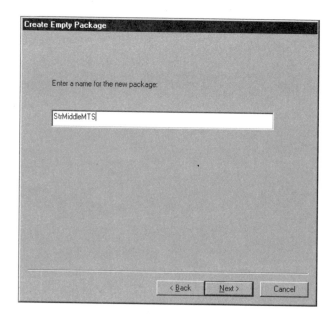

4. Finally, we need to provide MTS with information about the user under which the component will be running (this page doesn't appear under the 9x version). We can either supply a specific user account or use the currently logged-on user. Typically, you'd want to use a specific account but for simplicity we'll just use the Administrator account:

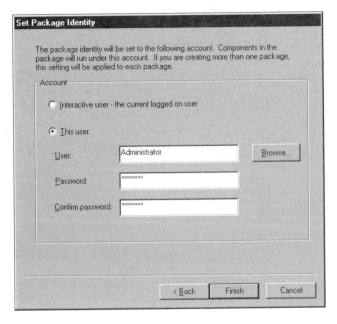

5. Now when we click Finish, MTS will add our new packages to the list of installed packages:

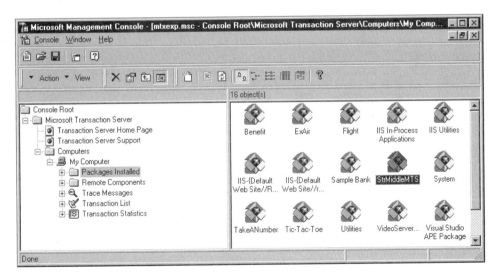

6. So far we've only created an empty package. We need to get our objects from our DLL into the package. This is simpler than even creating the package. It's merely a matter of dragging and dropping. Expand our package until you can see the empty **Components** folder:

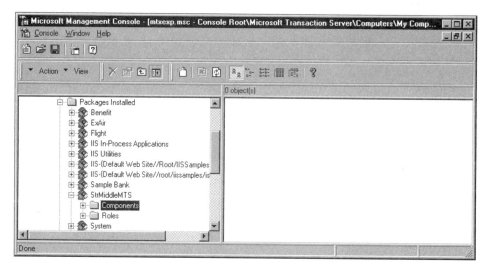

7. Then, using Windows NT Explorer, simply drag and drop the StrMiddleMTS.dll file into the empty **Components** folder. The result will be a listing of all the classes contained in the DLL shown as components of this package:

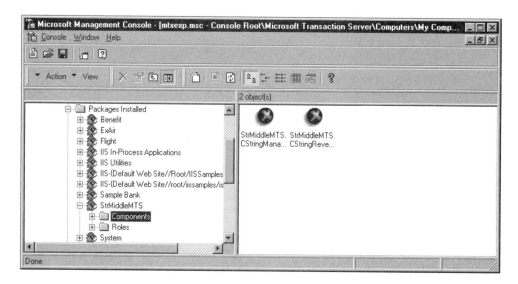

If you then right-click on a component and select Properties you will bring up the property pages for that component. If you then go to the Transaction tab you will see the setting that we specified in the class Properties window:

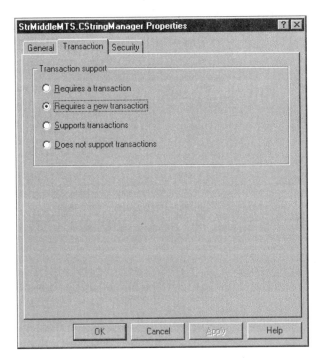

The actual terminology doesn't exactly match those in the Properties window but the mapping is clear enough.

8. That's all we need to do to install our objects into MTS. We will however, have to change the references on our client so that it's using our new DLL:

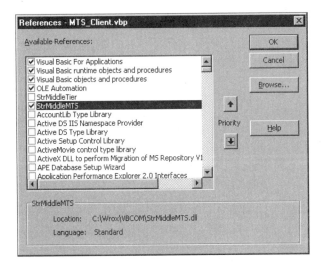

9. Now if you run the program again, after a brief pause while the machine churns away to itself, you will get the same text box result as before but his time our middle-tier objects have been running under MTS. If you run them again then the delay will be a lot less because our MTS package is still running in memory. If you view our components in the Transaction Server Explorer you should see the balls spinning.

Exporting a Package

Running component in MTS on a local machine is all very well but after a while the novelty of watching the spinning balls begins to wear off. What MTS is really designed for is scaling components to be used by multiple clients. We therefore, need an easy method of exporting a package to its clients. Using the MTS Explorer this is easily achieved:

1. Select the package you want to create a client set up for (in our case this is the StrMiddleMTS package) in the MTS Explorer:

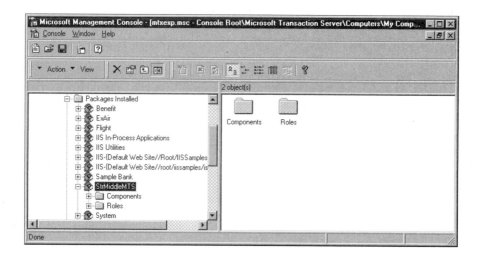

2. Use the Action | <u>E</u>xport option on the tool bar. This will bring up a dialog asking where we want to create the .PAK file. The PAK file can be used to import our package into other installations of MTS:

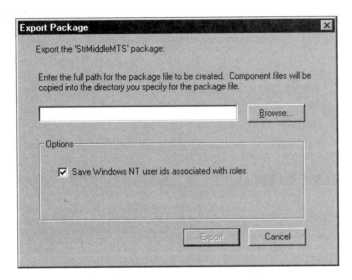

3. Click the Export button and MTS will create the PAK file at the location we specified. MTS will also create a Clients subdirectory beneath this, where you will find the client install program:

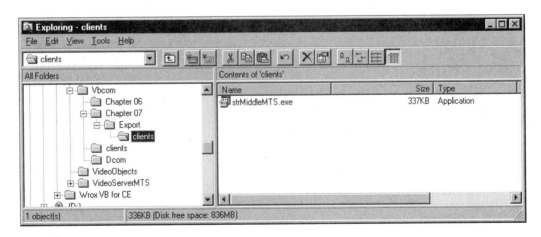

The Windows 9x version cannot generate executables and so you will only be able to create the PAK file.

4. The client install program has everything it needs to install and register your components on a client. All you need to do now is run the executable on the client.

Modifying the Client to Run Remotely

Once you have run the client install on our client machine we need to slightly reconfigure the client to use our components remotely.

1. Open the client project and access the References dialog.

2. Our remote StrMiddleMTS components should now be listed:

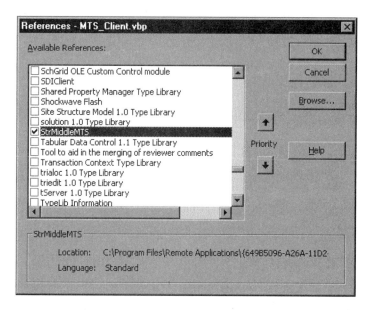

Note that the location is a CLSID in a new `Remote Applications` directory under `Program Files`.

3. We also need to change the `CreateObject` method so that the objects are created remotely:

```
Private Sub cmdSend_Click()

  Dim objReverse As CStringManager

  Set objReverse = CreateObject("StrMiddleMTS.CStringManager", "MTSSERVER")

  objReverse.ManipulateString DblTxtBxWiz1.CompleteName

  Set objReverse = Nothing

End Sub
```

Again, you will need to change `MTSSERVER` *with the name of the machine running MTS.*

4. Now if you run the client you should see the message box appear on the server machine.

Summary

In this chapter we learned how MTS can help make COM components more scalable, functional, and reliable. MTS provides us with database connection pooling, just-in-time activation, thread pooling, and more without us having to write a lot of plumbing code or calling any complex APIs.

We discussed how transactions worked and how they should adhere to the ACID principal of Atomicity, Consistency, Isolation, and Durability.

Last, but not least, we also saw how to build an MTS component and install it into MTS.

Microsoft has made a commitment to MTS. It will be enhanced and extended within the next releases of their operating systems. Microsoft has claimed that at some point, MTS will be integrated into the operating system and MTS will be thought more of as a service than an application. Indeed, when COM+ finally hits the streets you will see elements of MTS in that. If you or your company is building distributed COM applications, I suggest you read on to find out more about this interesting tool, and see if you can save yourself a lot of development effort.

Now, we get to take a step into the future and see how the landscape of Visual Basic and COM will be in the immediate future.

VB COM

8

The Future of COM

Overview

Throughout the book we have talked about the here and now. We have discussed the architecture of COM and how COM came into being, and spent most of the time building COM-based components and realized how they could be leveraged in a distributed computing environment.

Now I plan to break out the crystal ball, cracked as it may be, and try to lead you down the right path to some questions that you may have such as: Will the COM components I create today be obsolete a year from now? How do I take the tools I have learned to use in this book and apply them to a development framework to create full N-tier applications where I may have a mix-and-match environment? What is the next step forward for COM itself?

This chapter will attempt to inform you about technologies such as:

- ❑ Windows DNA
- ❑ COM +
- ❑ Digital Nervous System

So look into the crystal ball, deeply, deeply...

A Precaution

Have you ever taken a trip and got lost? Then when you found someone to help you, they either gave you ambiguous directions ("Head to dem hills right over yonder.") or the person was unaware that their shortcut had been shut down for repairs?

Unfortunately, we will probably run into the same thing. The technologies we will discuss here are new concepts or strategies that Microsoft has bestowed upon the developer. Some have not been implemented fully; others are not even shipping yet. Many things may change, since the computer industry set their clock to Internet-time a couple years ago. I hope though that you will learn new ways of thinking about development by reading this chapter. Let's get started.

Windows DNA

Windows DNA (short for **Windows Distributed interNet Applications**) answered a question Microsoft people were constantly hounded with at conventions, conferences and user groups. The question was, "We know how to create the different parts of an application, but how do we put them all together to create a distributed, N-tier application, Internet/intranet-driven application with Microsoft-based products?" Windows DNA was designed to answer that question.

> **Windows DNA is a guideline on building applications for the Microsoft Windows platform using Microsoft technologies.**

I know that most of you out there are probably saying, "Great, now Microsoft is telling me how to design my applications!" This is not the case. Microsoft is just providing these guidelines for developing applications so that it is easier to develop and maintain your applications. So when I am explaining Windows DNA, I am not saying that Microsoft says you have to do it this way (but I think you will want to after you understand it).

> **An N-tier application is simply an application that is split into 4 or more sections that can be distributed across numerous machines. We shall examine tiers in more detail later.**

Windows DNA Behaviors

Windows DNA applications have certain behaviors that provide an advantage for those adhering to the framework. We will address some of them here.

Connection-Aware

More and more these days we are seeing laptops replacing the common desktop computer. It is now more important than ever to be able to take a computing device out of the office to be used in the field. The proliferation of handheld PCs and palm-size PCs has gained momentum. Therefore, we must be aware that an application may not always be connected to the network.

Take a Sales Force situation as an example. Before our wonderful world of computers, salespeople had to write out (by hand!) the customers that they were going to contact in the field. They would also bring some Invoicing slips to create orders. Then when they got back, they would submit any changes to a clerk who would update a ledger and send the Invoice to the Inventory department who would then send the products to shipping to be sent out to the customer. During all of this, a paper trail was created to track the process.

Nowadays, the customer database is on the network. Invoices can be entered into the customer database via various means, including faxes, email, Web and telephones. The Invoice is filled in by the salesperson, who posts it through the accounting software the company uses, which fires off an email to Inventory to ship out the products. The paper trail is now just ones and zeros on a computer on the network.

With Windows DNA, we make life even easier. When the salesperson grabs their list of customers they can update the customer information on the road, create invoices and update them right on the spot with a simple Internet connection. In our previous scenario, what would happen if the items the customer selected were not in stock? The company might lose that customer's business, whereas if the salesperson was able to see that they did not have that particular item in stock, the salesperson could recommend something else instead. In addition, the process is handed off to the systems back at the office so that there is no lag time, such as when the salesperson would have to come back to the office before submitting an order.

So Windows DNA suggests that you take into consideration that your application may not be connected to the network at all times and should be able to work with or without a network. When there is no network connection (for example when a notebook computer is taken off-site), the disconnected platform becomes both the client and the server machine. When a network connection is established once more, the applications offloads its local messages and transactions to the network.

> **Connection-aware applications adapt to the current connection state and can operate either way.**

Users should be able to use all of an application's functionality whether in the office or on the road.

Rapid Application Development

If a term could be nominated for the most-maligned term, I would nominate this one. **Rapid Application Development (RAD)** although great in theory, has been rough in practice.

> **The term Rapid Application Development is used to describe the creation of applications quickly by a variety of methods; including component reuse; high-level languages (like VB) that focus on solutions rather than technical assembly; and services that enable an application to be developed in a timely matter.**

Windows DNA promotes Rapid Application Development by using COM as its way of handling component interaction and as a mechanism for calling pre-built services and components. We do not have to concern ourselves with how we are going to get our business component to communicate with the database. Rather COM will let us focus on how we want our business component to work and how our database will be designed for speed and robustness. Also, Windows DNA allows us to use services such as Microsoft Transaction Server and Microsoft Message Queue Server (MSMQ) within our applications. In the last chapter, we saw how easy it is to create components that can be hosted in MTS. We can use MTS as a service within a Windows DNA application to provide services for our application.

So Rapid Application Development and Windows DNA are compatible. Windows DNA uses Rapid Application Development to create applications quickly and get them to market faster.

Language-Neutral Components

COM provides language neutrality for components. We can build our Windows DNA components using any language that supports COM-based objects. We can use Visual Basic, Visual C++, or even Microfocus COBOL to create our business components.

> **Windows DNA applications do not tie you into one language over another.**

What you want to build your application with is up to you. Windows DNA allows you to choose the language that is best for the task at hand.

Interoperability

Interoperability allows your Windows DNA application to have interchangeable parts so that it can grow and expand determined by your needs. How many times have you had to change the architecture of your project just because the specification had changed? It happens quite often in projects. "We wrote that a couple years ago but did not think that we would have to write a Web interface for it! Now we are going to have to change our business logic." Heard that one?

Since applications include user interfaces, database access, business components and services, it is important that an application be able to use these interchangeably. Windows DNA promotes this plug and play metaphor. We can write Windows DNA applications where you can use either an Oracle database as your data source or you could switch it out with Microsoft SQL Server and the user would never know the difference.

> **With Windows DNA, you write your applications so that you can provide interfaces without having to worry how the other component provides their functionality.**

Of course, this is not just true of Windows DNA but applies to N-tier architectures in general.

Internet-Aware

Windows DNA applications take advantage of the Internet. For example, if you were building a tax-preparation program, it would be a good idea to let users pull down the latest tax changes from the net or provide Internet sites to which users could go to for tax advice services.

Let's use Microsoft Money as an example. This application not only runs locally on your system, but has links to the Internet that allow you to pull down stock quotes or browse articles about financial matters. The best part is that besides your modem squawking when you connect to the Internet, there is not a noticeable difference between being on the Internet and using the application locally within Microsoft Money.

I want to state that Windows DNA applications are not just related to the Internet, they can also work on an intranet. Windows DNA applications can and will sometimes have no contact with the Internet. Although if your application supports such functionality, it can provide a more robust experience for the user.

Components of a Windows DNA Application

A Windows DNA application consists of a set of application services and three tiers: the Presentation tier, the Business logic tier, and the Data tier. The DNA framework (and indeed any N-tier model) allows a project team to easily break up the work. A team could consist of a front-end developer (who might be using ASP and/or Visual Basic), a business tier developer (creating COM components with Visual Basic) and database administrator for the database.

Presentation Tier

The **Presentation tier**, otherwise known as the User tier, is composed of components and services that provide an interface and navigation to the user. Back in the good old days, we had one particular type of client - the Win32 interface. With its elegant window metaphor and delightful gray background, users toiled for hours within this new visual environment. Then the Internet came around and all of that changed. We now have applications residing within web pages and with the arrival of VB 6 we have the ability to produce DHTML pages and IIS applications containing web classes in our Visual Basic IDE. We even have Windows applications that behave like Web applications such as Microsoft Money:

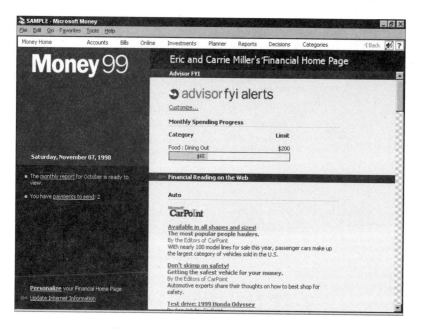

So we cannot automatically start hacking on the Visual Basic form to provide our interface anymore. We need to think about what type of client application we need to create based on what functionality is required.

Microsoft has defined four types of client applications: Internet Enhanced, Internet Reliant, Browser Enhanced, and Browser Neutral.

Internet Enhanced

Internet Enhanced interfaces are the richest clients that you can provide. Internet Enhanced applications typically are Win32 applications that support Internet features such as hyperlinking, use a browser for display of help files and use DHTML to create rich and lively interfaces. Microsoft Visual Basic is an example of an Internet Enhanced application. Although it is a Win32 application, it supports Internet technologies to provide a higher level of functionality.

Internet Enhanced clients should be used when you are sure that the client platform is Win32 driven (or even Windows CE driven!) and you want to provide the richest type of client possible.

Internet Reliant

Internet Reliant applications are those applications that must be connected to the Internet to provide services to the client. An example would be a bank who sends bank customers software that can connect to the bank, check balances, transfer funds, or pull down mortgage and loan rates. These clients must be connected to the Internet to provide these services.

Internet Reliant clients are becoming more popular these days since many products are being "Internetized". Although they are quite similar to the Internet Enhanced client, their biggest drawback is that the performance and functionality of the application is as only good as the connection the client has to the Internet.

Browser Enhanced

Browser Enhanced applications are browser-based applications that take advantage of the browser being used. There should be no surprise that Microsoft hopes that you will use this type of client in most of your browser-based applications. Things such as ActiveX Controls and client VBScript are only supported by the Internet Explorer browser - they won't work with Netscape's Navigator. Microsoft would like it if you were to use Internet Explorer as a piece your development platform where your Web Application takes advantage of what the browser has to offer.

Most Browser Enhanced applications will probably be hosted on an intranet for now. In an intranet environment, you typically dictate which browser is being used. The Browser Enhanced application will take advantage of the browser being used. Increasingly, the two browser giants are adding more and more functionality into their browsers to develop upon. XML (Extensible Markup Language) is now being quite aggressively integrated into the browser and we will probably begin seeing a lot more XML tools provided, not just for Internet and intranet development, but Visual Basic development also.

Browser Neutral

Browser Neutral applications are the typical Web applications that you see today. These applications make sure that whatever browser you are using that you will be able to use the application. A Browser Neutral application works and acts the same whether it is hosted within Internet Explorer or Netscape Navigator. It typically relies on standard HTML to produce the interface.

Applications built this way are good for those Web applications that will be accessed through the Internet such as product registration. Unfortunately, I do not think that the browser giants will ever get along so that we can have standards where we will not have to spend heavy development time trying to make sure that both browsers work with our application.

Win32 Based

Whoa! You thought I said that there were only four types. I have added this type myself. I am not of the belief that since the Internet came around, no one creates a Visual Basic form any more. In fact, most Visual Basic developers that I know are still cranking out Visual Basic forms, not HTML-based pages.

When is it a good idea to use **Win32 Based** clients? You should use them when you have a development team that is not familiar with designing web applications. You may want to use it when you are not sure which browser software is being used but you know what OS they are running (Windows). Additionally, your user environment may not even support Internet access, so the Win32 Based client is a good idea.

The Win32 application is not dead, it is just important to think about the *best* way to provide an interface to your clients when designing an application.

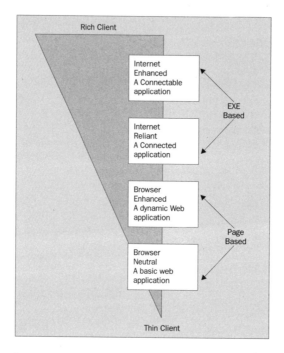

Another thing that you might want to think about is that you may not always be writing to a desktop PC. With the proliferation of handheld PCs, we're likely to see more applications that will be driven by these handheld devices. In addition, your users may have the new Terminal PCs. Therefore it is important not to be desktop PC biased when creating applications. Windows DNA does not dictate that your user will be using a PC. A client may be a desktop PC, a terminal, or a handheld PC running the Windows CE operating system.

Here is a list of popular technologies and tools that can be used to create/host our interfaces for Windows DNA applications:

Technologies:

- ❑ HTML
- ❑ Dynamic HTML
- ❑ StyleSheets
- ❑ Win32 Forms (such as VB Forms)
- ❑ VBScript
- ❑ JavaScript
- ❑ ActiveX Controls

Tools:
- ❑ Internet Explorer
- ❑ Microsoft Frontpage
- ❑ Microsoft Visual Interdev
- ❑ Microsoft Visual Basic

As you can see, Microsoft provides many different tools to develop the Presentation tier for your Windows DNA application. Remember that although you may want to include Internet technology in your application, Windows DNA does not dictate that it is a requirement. Hopefully, you can see that the Windows DNA framework is quite extensible and allows you to pick the best tools and technologies that will fit within your development effort.

The Presentation tier should only contain that which is necessary to provide the interface to a user. This is similar to the client/server architecture using Visual Basic. For several years, Visual Basic programmers have been told to separate their logic from their forms. Within a Visual Basic form module, there should not be any code that provides business logic or data access. These types of functions are usually delegated to an ActiveX DLL or a class module. Why is this so important? What if you had to change something on the form or the form went away and a new form was used instead? You would have to do cutting and pasting and probably rewrite some code. Instead, when you break up the presentation from the logic, you can create a disposable interface that you can just plug the logic into without having to rewrite it.

I have seen quite a few Visual Basic programmers learn logic/presentation partitioning the hard way, so make sure that you think about how you can create the separation between logic and the presentation. We will now focus on the next tier, which is the Business Logic tier.

Business Logic Tier

The Business Logic tier is responsible for encapsulating logic for the application but also as a bridge between the Presentation tier and the Data tier. The Business Logic tier is composed of three services: Web, Component, and Messaging Services.

Web Services

The Web Services are responsible for handling Web requests such as page retrieval and FTP functionality. For example, this tier is where you would host your Active Server Pages. Active Server Pages contain script (typically VBScript or Jscript) and run on the server. These pages, unlike HTML, which is generally used for presentation only, would include code that would calculate sales figures, get data from a database, or send a greeting card email.

In addition, Internet Information Server is a part of Web Services. IIS is Microsoft's web server and provides things such as HTTP, FTP, SMTP and other web-based services needed to run a web application. IIS makes it very easy to host a web application with its ease-of-use features.

Component Services

This is where you come in. In this book, we've spent quite a lot of time discussing how to create COM components. The components we create can do anything from holding **business logic** on how to calculate loan payments to accessing a database. The business tier is the best place for these components. You can create a component that accepts parameters from the presentation tier, sends it to your component on the business tier, which would request the data from the database on the data tier.

Doesn't that sound a lot like client/server? Yes, it does. Windows DNA does not replace client/server. It extends it by including other services that can be made available.

Your component can be directly called by the presentation tier component such as a Win32 app or a Web page. However, remember that we need to make sure that the business logic is separated from the presentation code. So creating COM based components to handle this is quite easy.

The Business tier is where **Microsoft Transaction Server** (MTS) services are located since it provides enhancement for our business logic components.

Message Queue Services

Messaging Services allow messaging to occur. Now you might be thinking of an email message, right? I am talking about a different type of message. For example, what if we had an order form in the Presentation tier, which sent a request to the business object that we created on the Business Logic tier and when it tried to update the database with an order, the database was not available?

> *Remember that we don't need to know if our Presentation tier is in the form of a web page or a Win32 client. Windows DNA dictates that each tier provides its services without relying on another tier. We just know that an order will be handed over to the Business tier to be taken care of.*

Messaging takes care of this. Microsoft has a product called **Microsoft Message Queue Server**, known as MSMQ. MSMQ will take a message and place it into a queue until the database is available again, then it will empty the queued messages it had stored into the database.

This is a great product. How many times have you tried to update a record in your database, only to have it fail because of connectivity/communications issues or maintenance issues? Of course, none of you, because you are perfect! But MSMQ is able to handle these types of situations.

> *If you want to learn more about MSMQ see Professional MTS MSMQ with VB and ASP by Alex Homer and David Sussman, also published by Wrox Press.*

Business components also allow you to extract data from existing systems. Let's say that you are still chugging away on a mainframe computer. The mainframe probably has its own API that allows a client to talk with the data. What you could do is create a business component that encapsulates to mainframe-specific API in a way that makes sense to someone who is developing an interface.

Which makes sense? Calling the mainframe API directly?

```
SET DATA-SET 1343465 FOR CALL
INDICATE DATA FUNCTION
INITIALIZE DATA FUNCTION
INTERPRET 1343465 FOR CALL
MAP HOLDER
HOLDER = CALLBACK DATA FUNCTION
SEND HOLDER
```

Or creating a component where the call looks like?

```
oOrder.GetOrder(1343465)
```

Remember that our components are based upon COM, which enables us to create them so that they are interoperable between each of the tiers. Our Business tier components can be used to provide a bridge between the Presentation and Data tiers.

Data Tier

The data tier is responsible for providing data access. This data does not just have to be data that sits in a database, but can also be data such as email boxes and file systems.

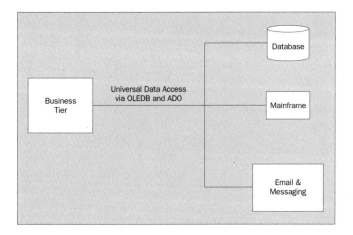

To provide access to all these different types of heterogeneous data stores, Microsoft provides **Universal Data Access** (**UDA**). Universal Data Access is a strategy for ubiquitous data access. This is done through two technologies: **OLE DB** and **ADO**. These two technologies form the pipeline between the Business Logic tier and the Data tier. OLE DB is the successor to the long-time data architecture favorite ODBC. OLE DB is a technology where data access is defined by a specific set of COM interfaces. So for example, a company that has a database store, whether it is an object database or a map store, can create an OLE DB provider that supports the specified COM interfaces, which will allow anyone to access the data store.

So how do you as a Visual Basic developer access these OLE DB providers? The answer is **ActiveX Data Objects** (ADO). ADO provides data access to OLE DB providers just like DAO provides access to Jet database stores. ADO is included in Visual Basic 6.0 and can also be downloaded from Microsoft's web site (`http://www.microsoft.com`).

As you can see, Microsoft has provided a few OLE DB providers for use in our Visual Basic 6.0 projects (including one for Oracle):

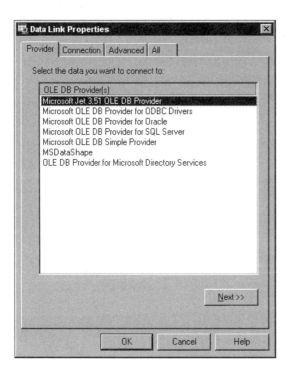

ADO's object model is also quite simple compared to that of DAO or RDO because it is written to a higher level of abstraction. DAO and RDO have many objects to support whereas ADO only uses seven: `Connection`, `Command`, `Parameter`, `Recordset`, `Field`, `Error`, and `Property`. That's all. ADO is very simple to use.

> *I am not going to go over ADO more than this since the good people of Wrox have several good books on the subject such as Instant ADO 2.0 and Beginning Visual Basic 6 Database Programming. They give it more justice than I could ever do here.*

Since we can encapsulate business data transfer with the COM components that are in the Business Logic tier, we can use mainframe databases or any other type of data store as long as there is a provider for it.

Advantages of Windows DNA

Windows DNA provides many advantages for the developer.

❑ Windows DNA provides an architecture for your applications that is scalable, distributable, and robust if you follow its guidelines. Windows DNA is not a silver bullet application or technology - it's more like a specification on how to integrate a collection of technologies with your specific system requirements.

❑ Windows DNA does not dictate a build-it-yourself architecture. Windows DNA allows you to take advantage of services provided by the operating system and by application services such as MSMQ and MTS.

- Windows DNA does not limit you to one language or interface. You can create components with any of the languages provided by Visual Studio. In addition, you can create rich interfaces depending on the requirements of your application.
- Windows DNA is not a replacement for the work you have done; it is just an extension of it.
- Tiers can easily determine tasks for a development team.

Creating Windows DNA Applications Today

So how do you begin creating Windows DNA applications today?

- Start by designing your application into three tiers: Presentation, Business Logic, and Data
- Decide how to create the Presentation tier based on the richness of the client and what provides the broadest client reach
- Write your business logic with COM components (with Visual Basic) and host them within MTS
- Finally, start using OLE DB providers to gain access to all different types of heterogeneous data and use ADO in your development efforts to communicate with these providers

By following these four simple steps, you will be creating Windows DNA applications that will be scalable, distributable, and robust.

COM+: The Next Generation

COM+ is the next evolution of the Component Object Model. COM+ will integrate Microsoft Transaction Server and Microsoft Message Queue with new services and functionality. The next Visual Studio upgrade (version 7 or VS 2000?) will provide support for creating components that take advantage of COM+. Microsoft has assured developers that components that have been written with COM/MTS will work just fine within the new COM+ environment without the need for any code changes.

Only recently has Microsoft been pushing the feature set behind COM+ and at the time of this writing it was not very complete according to the press releases and PowerPoint slides.

COM+ will have an interface using the COM+ Explorer that will reside within the Microsoft Management Console. It will look quite similar to Microsoft Transaction Server Explorer. You will still have the spinning black balls with the green Xs! It will be within the COM+ Explorer that you will be able to manage, maintain, and secure COM+ components.

Now let's take a look at some of the features that are going to be a part of COM+.

Attributes

Attributes predetermine the behavior of a component before compilation or even after compilation. Attributes are not the same as properties. Attributes are essentially statements applied to components that declare their system requirements/interactions. Setting an Attribute within code will look something like:

```
Attributes:
    Datasource = "orders; 'sa', ''"
    Queue = "orders"
    Transaction = "requires new"
```

Looking at the sample code, this component would have an Attribute that would hold the connection string for the component. We would be able to specify a queue, such as that found within MSMQ, to place orders into and we could also require a new transaction for the component we create when deciding its transactional state.

Component Attributes can be changed at any time determined by the security level of the component. For example, a developer may decide that the component should send orders to the "order" queue, but later on the environment has changed and now it should be placing them in the "day_order" queue. An administrator or the developer can change the Attribute without having to replace the code and recompile. An important point here is that some of the current burden on developers may be shifted to the administrator of Windows DNA systems. System administrators will be able to tailor the attributes of components on the network, if developers don't declare Attributes up front in code.

Attributes have been marketed towards the C++ crowd. But you will find that Attributes will work much like the `MTSTransactionMode` for Visual Basic classes. You can set the `MTSTransactionMode` property within your class module, but that setting could be easily overridden by a user with the proper security rights within the COM+ Explorer.

Component Queuing

Component Queuing is an interesting feature. Component Queuing allows you to create components whose behavior is the same whether the component is used in a connected or disconnected environment.

The easiest way to explain is with an example. Let's say that you have an order processing component and you are a salesperson out on the road. While you are out on the road, you are placing orders within your order entry application on your laptop. Now, once you are back in the office, the component will then update the database with the new orders that you have created.

With Component Queuing, your component stores orders within a self-managed queue similar to Microsoft Message Queue. So when an order has been placed on the laptop in a disconnected environment, it stores the orders until it is notified that the user is in a connected state and to update orders to the headquarters' orders database.

Although I have seen this demonstrated at Microsoft events, I have yet to see the code to handle this kind of operation. But I like the idea of making my life easier to create distributed applications.

Dynamic Load Balancing

The term **Dynamic Load Balancing** is used to describe being able to dynamically add resources to support user loads upon a process or machine. An example would be to have a component running on one machine with 10 users. No big deal, right? What happens when the same component now has to handle 100 users at the same time? Now the user is getting frustrated because it is taking a long time for the component to finish its processing. What if another machine with the same component was added to the network to handle the load? Now each component could have 50 users connected to each of them. That is load balancing.

The dynamic part comes in where the second component does not fire up unless needed. If there is only one connection opened in the early morning, is there a need to have the second component loaded? With dynamic load balancing, the second component does not initialize until necessary.

With the COM+ Explorer, an administrator will be able to decide how to distribute loads between components on different machines by simply adding a new server much like we did in the last chapter.

Event Services

COM+ plus will have robust **Event Services**. COM+ events will fall into two categories: publishing and subscription services.

Publishing services will allow events created within your COM+ event to be published so that other components and applications can subscribe to the events in which they can be notified by a certain event. For example, you may have a component in charge of checking on servers on your network. When it finds a problem, an event is triggered and published so that other components may respond to it.

```
Public Function On_FindDownServer ()
    On_FindDownServer = Server.Down("MATVICHUK", 597, "No network connection")
End Function
```

Subscription services will allow you to subscribe to multiple events from within one or more COM+ components. For example, you may have an email component that subscribes to the published COM+ event above. When the event is published, since the email component subscribed to the event, it can act accordingly by sending an email or page the system administrator.

In-Memory Database

The **In-Memory Database** (IMDB) is designed for speed; hence, the database is in-memory and is an in-process access to data. The IMDB will cache data on the *middle* tier. It will be able to take data from the data store and create temporary tables at run-time. The IMDB will be an OLE DB provider so that you can use ADO and OLE DB to connect to it.

Security Roles

The new security built around COM+ will be an extension of how security works within Microsoft Transaction Server. We discussed in the previous chapter how users or groups of users could be placed within a **Role**. Then components could be assigned security privileges by role. We could have a Marketing role that includes marketing users and groups who could only use components which allow that role.

COM+ security will take advantage of the new Windows NT Active Directory. Now you will be able to administrate component security and use the Active Directory to create roles for your COM+ components.

Summary of COM+

All of these new COM+ features may or may not be a part of COM+ when it ships with Windows 2000 (previously named Windows NT 5.0). Nevertheless, Microsoft has said that COM+ will be an integral part of that release and the next release of Visual Studio.

Keep an eye on new information that comes from Microsoft on COM+ since it is more than likely that it will make it easier to develop COM-based components and administer them.

The Digital Nervous System

If you have heard any speech within the last year from Bill Gates, you have probably heard him speak about the **Digital Nervous System**. The Digital Nervous System can be thought of as what your network is or should be. Like the nervous system within a human body, it is always on, responding and reacting to different things going on throughout the body. The Digital Nervous System works like this, using bits and bytes instead of neurons and electrons to respond and react to different stimuli. For instance, what will the application do when the stock price goes down? How is the best way to use marketing funds for a new product? The Digital Nervous System helps to provide the technological edge to handle different business issues.

So what does the Digital Nervous System have to do with Visual Basic COM development? Your COM components will make up part of this Digital Nervous System. Just like the body's nervous system, your components will get information from other parts of the system, respond to events, and provide actions. It is important to realize that what you build is a piece of a bigger puzzle. Do you want a little tip on how to be a better developer? Think outside of the programming box. Think how the component will react with other services on the network and how they can take advantage of those services. For example, why build in email functionality into a component when it could easily connect to a Microsoft Exchange Server on the network?

I can tell when someone new to enterprise development has been placed on the team. You can see them trying to solve problems within their head with coding instead of thinking how the application will relate to other business processes. I have been in meetings where a new consultant would say something like "We could use RDO to talk to your database and write a .DLL to pull all of it together." They just looked at him and said "What?!?" Instead the better approach would have been "Which data sources are available throughout the company, not just databases, but any other repository of data?" This made one of the attendees bring up the fact that a lot of the information was already stored within Microsoft Excel spreadsheets publicly posted that we could use COM to gain access to. There was no need for the .DLL or to use RDO for that matter.

Behaviors of a Digital Nervous System

A Digital Nervous System has behaviors associated with it. We will look at the following five: act faster, react to anything, make more informed decisions, focus on the business and get closer to customers.

Act Faster

A Digital Nervous System makes it easier to act faster when certain events occur. For example, you might have a component that you developed which goes out onto the Internet and queries information based on stock that the company owns. The component may have an indicator when the stock goes below a certain level, the CFO may be paged or emailed so that the CFO can make a decision whether to sell or hold on.

By adhering to the principles of the Digital Nervous System, an organization can be flexible and respond quickly to things effecting its business thanks to technology that responds to business stimuli.

React to Anything

A Digital Nervous System allows you to react to unplanned events in an organization. What if your organization is being audited? This happens quite often to businesses. A lot of time is used up trying to appease the auditors and get them the information they need. With a Digital Nervous System, it is easy to give them access to intranet sites that hold financial information within Microsoft Excel spreadsheets. Email can be sent to accounting employees to make them aware of the situation. Also, data within databases can easily be recalled since most information is in binary form instead of some warehouse storing a lot of paper.

Make More Informed Decisions

Decisions are easier to make when you have all the information available that you need. A behavior of the Digital Nervous system is that it can provide information easily through an intranet or application and can provide all types of sources. For example, what if you were to make a decision on whether or not to roll out a new consumer product? You could look up sales for new products such as the one you are about to distribute to see when is the best time to sell it (Don't sell many lawn mowers in December!). In addition, you might look within the Public Folders of your mail server to find another department head, in case the release of a product might cannibalize sales for another.

It is important that the Digital Nervous System not only provides methods for access to information, but also a way to interpret the information to make informed decisions.

Focus on Business

The Digital Nervous System tries to make organizations focus more on the business than the technology being used. For example, with the proliferation of Web applications, training costs have been able to come down. Using the Back button is the same in every application when everyone is using a browser.

In addition, companies should be thinking of the customer rather than the technology. This can be a hard thing to do, especially for developers. We are constantly thinking about the technology. We should ask ourselves when we develop applications, "How will this effect the user? Are these error messages indecipherable except to the developer? Should I make this a Wizard instead of having the user go through a multi-step process to achieve the functionality they want?" It is important for developers to think of how they can solve business problems instead of how to implement the technology. It sounds familiar, doesn't it?

Get Closer to Customers

The Digital Nervous System can make the relationship between an organization and its customers much closer. For example, you may have a merchant sent from Japan to decide which fabrics to sell back in Japan. With an extranet, you could create a Web application of the new fabric lines so that the trip is unnecessary. Using technology to bring customers closer to the business can provide an advantage over those who create hurdles for their customers to gain access to information about the company.

The Digital Nervous System is the host of the COM components we write. In fact, much of the communication that goes on between parts of the Digital Nervous System is based on COM. COM is the glue that binds all of it together.

Summary

In this chapter, we looked at a new way of designing the architecture of N-Tier applications using Windows DNA. Windows DNA provides a framework for applications using Microsoft tools and technologies. Using Windows DNA as a guide, you can create applications that are scalable, distributable, and robust.

We then peered into the crystal ball to take a look at COM+, the successor to COM. Although not fully completed, I provided you with a glimpse into the future and showed some of the features that will be available to the COM+ developer.

Finally, we talked about the Digital Nervous System. The Digital Nervous System is a network that responds and reacts to its environment. We discussed why your components should be aware of what is going on around them and how they can fit into the Digital Nervous System.

So with these in mind, you can begin writing components that will be able to take advantage of COM+ to build Windows DNA applications that will be a part of the Digital Nervous System.

This is the end of the last chapter, but before I go, I would like to say just a few more words.

VB COM

Not the End, But Merely the Beginning

Congratulations! You are about to reach the end of my little opus. I hope that you have enjoyed the journey, even if it was a little arduous at some points. However, you shouldn't think that you've reached the summit yet. Rather, this book is just the first step of your journey into COM.

All this book is really intended to do is to open your eyes to the wider world of COM. You should no longer feel afraid and that it is better left to our friends in the C++ domain. COM has been around for a while and is going to be around for quite a while to come. It is fortunate that we, as Visual Basic programmers, have been able to survive for so long without knowing too much about COM but times have changed. Visual Basic has now matured, such that serious enterprise development is now quite possible, and future releases should only facilitate this trend. A strong understanding of COM is essential for producing effective, reusable and scaleable components in an enterprise setting. We can no longer afford to stick our heads in the sand and pretend that we can let Visual Basic do all the hard COM work for us. If we ignore the implications of COM we will never benefit from the advantages, such as language and location independence, that COM confers on our components.

In this book, I have attempted to redress the balance by introducing COM to Visual Basic programmers who may not have even heard of COM before. The sooner that we, as a community, begin to realize the implications of the COM decisions that VB is making on our behalf, the sooner we can begin to use Visual Basic as a serious enterprise development tool.

We started off with a brief introduction to what COM is all about and how it has evolved. From there, we dived headlong into a discussion on the underlying architecture. This introduced us to one of the key concepts in COM, that of the interface.

We then moved into more familiar territory of ActiveX DLLs and EXEs. We saw how we can use these components to define our own interfaces and how and when it is best to use either. From there, it was a short hop into ActiveX controls and how they interact with their container using COM.

Then we began to push the envelope a little by exploring how to operate and distribute our components on different machines using DCOM. We also discovered how to provide easy, scalable multi-user support by installing our components into MTS.

Finally, we had brief foray into what the future for COM and component development might hold.

As it says on the cover this book is an 'introduction' to COM, and as such I hope to have given you a taster for what COM and component development is all about. This book has been designed to lay the foundations for the rest of your journey into component application development. Your next step maybe to continue on with the *Wrox VB COM Series* which is specifically designed to take VB programmers from the very basics of COM right up to the enterprise level. Don't think that the knowledge you have gained here is of limited scope. You'll find that COM comes up again and again, so your next step may instead be to broaden your horizons and look into something like object-oriented programming. I also recommend that you simply start experimenting. You can learn so much more through practical experience than you can ever really learn from a book.

Whatever path you may choose next, I wish you bon voyage!

VB COM

COM & The System Registry

It should be clear by now that the System Registry plays a very important part in the proper functioning of COM. Furthermore, since the system and application configurations, the user preferences and the security database (under NT) are all stored in the registry, the registry is vital to the health and well being of the system as a whole.

In this appendix, we'll introduce the registry editor, and we'll cover how to use it in order to examine and modify many of the vital entries related to COM object operations.

The registry editor may be used to:

❑ View registry entries
❑ Add, delete and modify registry entries
❑ Backup the registry

We can use this tool, as a viewer, to take a look at how the COM runtime buries away the essential information.

The registry editor is not the best tool for simply viewing COM entries and so we'll also look at another tool provided by Microsoft, that you will have seen throughout the book: OLEView.

OLEView may be used to:

❑ Browse, in a structured way, all of the Component Object Model (COM) classes installed on your machine.
❑ See the registry entries for each class in an easy-to-read format.
❑ Configure any COM class on your system. This includes Distributed COM activation and security settings.

- ❑ Configure system-wide COM settings, including enabling or disabling DCOM.
- ❑ Test any COM class, simply by double-clicking its name. The list of interfaces that class supports will be displayed. Double-clicking an interface entry allows you to invoke a viewer that will "exercise" that interface.
- ❑ Activate COM classes locally or remotely. This is great for testing DCOM setups.
- ❑ View type library contents. Use this to figure out what methods, properties, and events an ActiveX Control supports!

The Registry

The registry is little more than a database. It stores data in a hierarchically structured tree. Each node in the tree is called a **key**. Each key can contain both **subkeys** and data entries called **values**.

The Registry Editor

Find the registry editor on your system and run it. In Windows 9x, it's called `Regedit.exe`. When it loads you will see an Explorer style interface. There are six subtrees that are displayed in the left pane, each of which has associated keys and information:

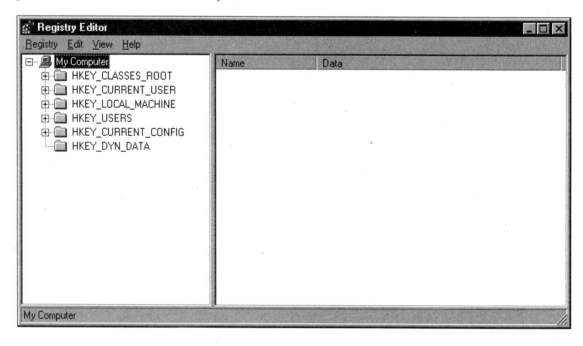

In Windows NT 4.0, it is called `Regedt32.exe`. On running it, you'll find that only five subtrees are displayed and this time, each subtree has its own window:

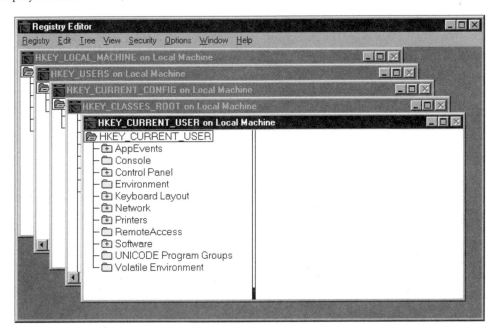

Windows NT does also have `Regedit.exe`. *Each program just allows you to do slightly different things and the differences are not relevant to our discussion here.*

Backing up the Registry

Before you go playing about with the registry it's always a good idea to create a backup copy, just in case anything goes wrong.

This is easily done by using the Export Registry File... entry on the File menu. This allows you to save a copy of the registry:

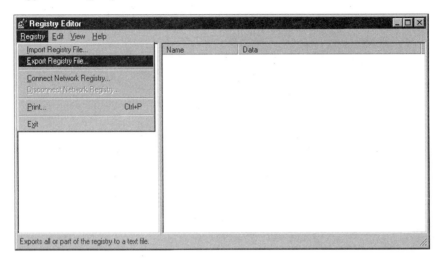

Enter COM, Stage Right

The subtree that we, and COM, are interested in is the HKEY_CLASSES_ROOT subtree. When we expand this subtree, we'll typically find a very large list of keys. One interesting key is the CLSID key. Try expanding this one:

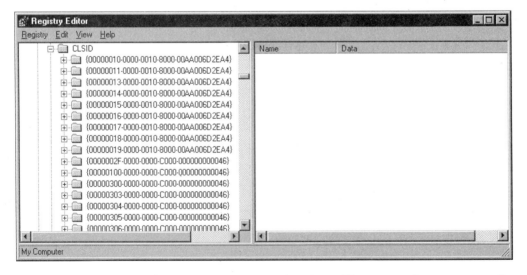

You'll be greeted with a large list of CLSIDs, remember them? These, as we know, are actually 'names' or 'keys' for classes of COM objects. If you expand any one of them, you'll see that they have additional subkeys (attributes) which describe the class further. The attributes you see listed here are dependent upon the type of component.

DLLs

DLLs have a key called `InprocServer32`. This key indicates to the COM runtime that the CLSID represents an in-process server or DLL. The named values under this subkey typically include a `(Default)` and a `ThreadingModel`:

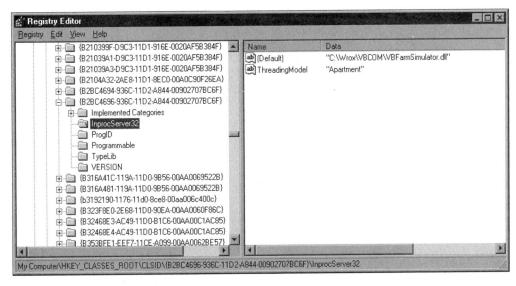

The COM runtime looks into the `(Default)` value to find out where the DLL is located. The `ThreadingModel` value gives COM an indication, unsurprisingly, of what sort of threading model the server will support.

EXEs

For COM objects that are local server based, you'll find a `LocalServer32` key that will provide the COM runtime with a path to find the server EXE:

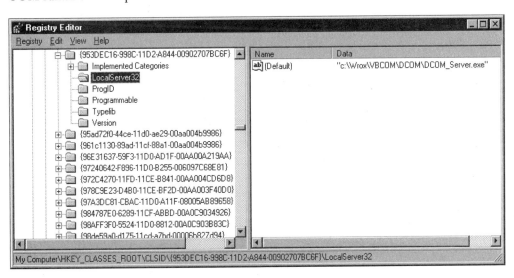

You'll also see a lot of other keys, which are covered in the table below.

Controls

Controls also have an `InprocServer32` key, because they are also in-process servers, which provides COM with the location of the OCX file. However, they also have a `Control` key that marks the server as an ActiveX control:

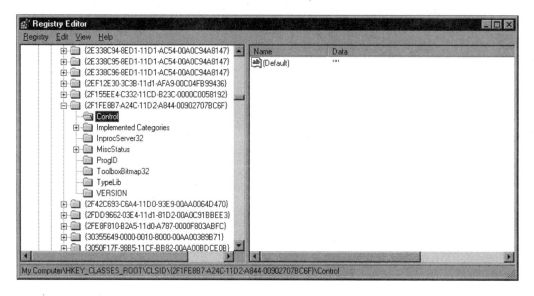

The COM Attributes in Full

The following table summarizes some of the many keys that you'll find under `\HKEY_CLASSES_ROOT\CLSID\{-----}`

Key Name	Applies To	Comment
InprocServer	16/32-bit servers	Path to 16/32-bit DLL on same machine. Implements an in-process server.
InprocServer32	32-bit servers	Path to 32-bit DLL on same machine. Implements an in-process server.
InprocHandler32	32-bit servers	An object handler is nothing more than a piece of code that implements the interfaces expected by a container when an object is in its loaded state (i.e. it isn't running yet). In other words, it's a glue object that provides the interfaces but doesn't necessarily provide the full functionality.

Key Name	Applies To	Comment
LocalServer32	32-bit servers	Path to 32-bit EXE on same machine. Implements a local server running in a separate process.
Insertable	32-bit servers	Indicates that the 32-bit server can be used by existing 16-bit applications.
ProgId		A programmatic identifier. The default value of the key is a human readable string uniquely (but not universally) identifying a class that can appear in an Insert Object dialog box.
Verb	OLE objects	Verbs are specific actions the object can execute that are meaningful to the end user. A container (client app) looks at this key in the registry to find out what verbs the object supports, in order to present them to the user, typically in a pop-up menu.
Control		If the key is present, the object is a control.
Typelib		Type library ID for the object.
MainUserType		The constant name referring to the currently installed version of the server.
AuxUserType		Auxiliary names, for example, a short name for the class, a real-world name for the application when necessary to present to the user, etc.
DefaultIcon		Contains icon information for iconic representations of the object. It includes the full path to module (DLL or EXE) where the icon resides and the index of the icon within the executable.

This list is certainly not exhaustive, and any particular pair of COM objects can establish their own private use of keys associated with the CLSID. What we attempt to cover here are the most common ones that we may encounter in our ActiveX programming activities. This explains how COM can know so much about a class given a CLSID. The ProgId entry above, for example, is an interesting entry - it gives a human readable string for locating a CLSID. If you go up a level to HKEY_CLASSES_ROOT you can scroll through this subtree and find a string relating to your class. Under this key you will find a Clsid subkey which you can copy to the clipboard and search the registry for.

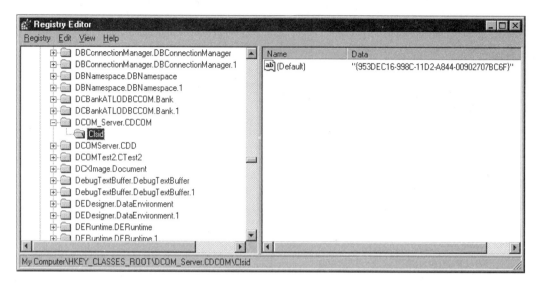

This makes it unnecessary to use and remember CLSIDs in most programming activities.

Type Libraries

One final key that I want to look at is `TypeLib`. It is also found under `HKEY_CLASSES_ROOT` and if you expand this node then you will again find a large list of GUIDs:

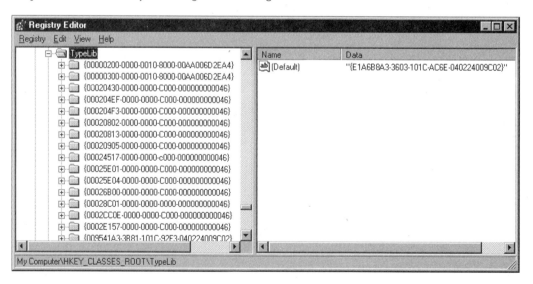

This is what Visual Basic uses to provide the list of components in the References dialog:

Object Browsing Made Easier: OLEView

After working with the registry editor for a while during COM programming and debugging, you'll wish you had a more intelligent tool available. The problem with the registry editor is that it isn't specific to COM, and relies on you as the intelligent filter to get to the information you need.

Microsoft has released an excellent tool that practically makes the registry editor obsolete as a viewer. The tool is called the Object Viewer, in the form of `Oleview.exe`. This tool combs the entire registry, looking up all the OLE objects and controls, stores and sorts all the relevant object information entries, and then presents the compiled information in an easy-to-use format that can be browsed.

> `Oleview.exe` *is now a standard item including with distributions of Visual Studio 6. However, you can still download the latest version of it Microsoft's website.*

Sounds too good to be true? You can try Object Viewer for yourself. Once started, Object Viewer displays all its collected information on two panes:

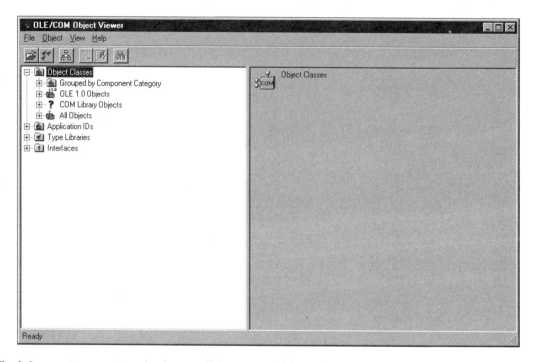

The left pane is a tree view displaying all the various COM objects, AppIDs, Type Libraries and Interfaces that are installed on the system. The right pane displays information about the registry settings, and additional settings, associated with the item selected in the right pane:

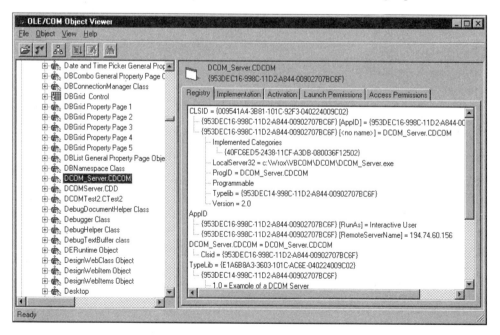

The left pane also provides a certain degree of component grouping allowing you to more easily locate types of components. However, for your ActiveX DLLs and EXEs you are more likely to use the All Objects node:

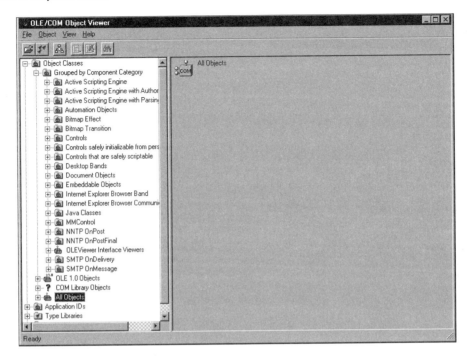

Instantiating Objects using OLEView

One of the most useful functions provided by OLEView is its ability to instantiate an instance of any COM object. This provides a quick and easy method of checking that your component can be instantiated properly and is especially useful for testing remote DCOM components.

Creating an instance is very easy to do. Simply select the object you wish to create an instance of in the left pane and then either double-click the entry or expand the node. If you do this you will find a list of all the interfaces the object supports:

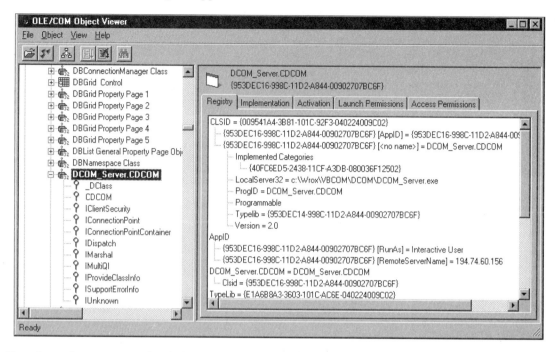

To release the instance right-click on the object entry and select Release Instance the node should then retract. Simply contracting the node with the - box will not release the object instance.

If you want to test a DCOM component by instantiating the object on another machine then you need to right-click on the object and select Create Instance On... This will bring up a dialog asking for the name or IP address of the machine on which you want to create an instance:

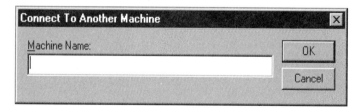

Viewing Type Libraries

Another useful feature of OLEView is that allows you to easily view the type library for any given component. There are several ways that you can do this:

❑ Expand the Type Libraries node in the left pane and scroll through all type libraries registered on the system

❑ Find the COM object for the type library you are interested in and from the pop-up menu, you get by right-clicking, select View Type Information...

❑ Hit the View TypeLib button on the tool bar or select View TypeLib... from the File menu. Either of this will bring up the Open dialog and allow you to browse your hard disk for the type library file.

Any of these methods will open a new window, the ITypeLib Viewer, which allows you to browse the interfaces and coclasses your object supports:

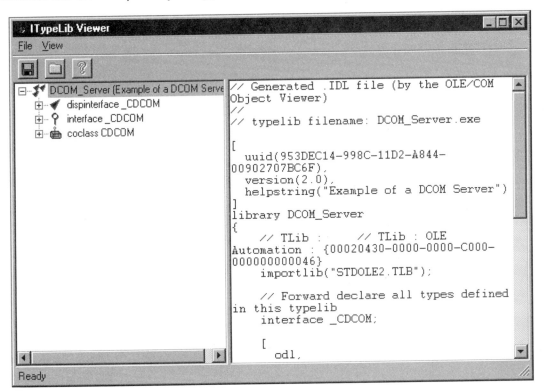

Unfortunately, OLEView is just that, a viewer. If you want to adjust and tweak object registry setting directly, you'll still need to use the registry editor. Therefore, you will frequently find instances of Visual Studio, Object Viewer, and the registry editor all opened on the typical COM developer's desktop (and the manager asks why COM developers need at least 64MB of memory, and a 21-inch monitor!).

VB COM

Index

VB COM

Beginning Visual Basic 6 Objects

Author: Peter Wright
ISBN: 186100172x
Price: $39.99 C$55.95 £36.99

Who is this book for?

This book is aimed at programmers who have some knowledge of programming with Visual Basic and want to learn how to do object-oriented development. You should be familiar with controls and their properties, methods and events, but no previous knowledge of classes or ActiveX is assumed.

What does this book cover?

Teaches object-oriented programming from scratch
Loads of practical Try It Out examples to explain every concept
All code explained simply and fully
End of chapter questions with full solutions
How to create and use classes in object-oriented development
How to develop object hierarchies
In depth explanation of ActiveX controls and components, and how they relate to object-oriented programming
Introduction to COM and object components
How to achieve object persistance
Teaches the fundamentals of object-oriented design and why every developer should know them
Wraps it all up in an object-oriented final project
Practical introduction to object-oriented design methods using UML and Visual Modeler

Beginning Visual Basic 6 Database Programming

Author: John Connell
ISBN: 1861001061
Price: $39.99 C$55.99 £36.99

Who is this book for?

This book is for everyone who wants to learn more about working with VB 6 and databases. Whether you've just learned to program with Visual Basic or you're after a briefing on the latest developments in VB ADO database programming, this book is for you.

To get the most out of this book you should be running VB Professional edition or higher, although most of the examples can be run on the standard edition.

What does this book cover?

The principles of database design and construction
Building functional VB user interfaces for database access
Using the full range of VB database access facilities, from the basics with DAO through to advanced ADO
Programming with ADO for fast Universal Data Access
Introduces SQL
Beginning programming Internet applications using ADO and ASP
Data Mining
Advanced ADO techniques in VB6

Visual Basic 6 Business Objects

Author: Rockford Lhotka
ISBN: 186100107x
Price: $59.99 C$89.95 £55.49

Rockford Lhotka on VB6 Business Objects

This book is about the design of business software with Visual Basic 6.0, following my object-oriented philosophy and incorporating DCOM and MTS. I demonstrate my component-based, scalable logical architecture that allows business code to be reused. My architecture allows different UIs and back-end databases to be added as circumstances dictate, with minimum disruption to your core business code. Over the course of the book, we'll create and implement a fully-worked example to demonstrate my architecture in a solid object model. Along the way, I'll cover the specific techniques that make this whole concept work efficiently in the Visual Basic environment. In addition, I'll demonstrate how my general architectural techniques can apply equally well to all development - whether it be for single-tier, multi-tier or Internet-based applications.

This book is aimed at experienced Windows application developers. It assumes you know how to program with Visual Basic, but takes the time to cover version 6.0 innovations and issues. I also provide coverage of the server technologies DCOM, MTS, IIS, DHTML, and ASP.

What does this book cover?

Defining and using business objects
Designing business objects using Visual Basic
Creating component-based applications in Visual Basic 6
How business objects can make UI design more flexible
Using scalable database access - ADO and OLE DB
How to use DCOM to full advantage in a client-server connection
Adding transaction support with MTS and SQL Server
Packaging up code for client distribution
Building the 'VideoStore' example to illustrate my theory in action

Visual Basic 6 WIN32 API Tutorial

Authors: Jason Bock
ISBN: 1861002432
Price: $39.99 C$59.95 £36.99

Jason Bock on VB6 WIN32 API Tutorial

With this book, I'll teach you how you to master the Win32 API or Application Programming Interface and use this knowledge to enhance your VB applications. API allows you to take control of the inner functionality of Windows to truly exploit its potential. I'll start by going through the basics of API, how to declare API calls and when to use them. Wherever possible, I'll also demonstrate API calls in action using code examples. I'll walk you through each Win32 DLL, and I'll describe in detail each call I use so you can understand exactly how they work. I'll also cover some calls that do not come from these core DLLs. Once I've taught you the basics we'll use API to manipulate multimedia functions and graphics, customize common dialog boxes, and leverage file shell operations.

This book is designed to give someone who has had previous experience working with Visual Basic all the information they need to explore the Windows programming environment. It assumes you are familiar with Visual Basic but have no prior experience with API programming.

What does this book cover?

How to declare API calls
How to avoid the common pitfalls of working with API calls
File operations using API
Graphics and Multimedia API calls
How to find undocumented calls
Windows callbacks and finding the address of a function
Subclassing and intercepting Windows messages
The functionality contained within the three core Win32 DLLs
An Encryption program to demonstrate many of the API calls in practice

Wrox writes books for you. Any suggestions, or ideas about how you want information given in your ideal book will be studied by our team. Your comments are always valued at Wrox.

Free phone in USA 800-USE-WROX
Fax (312) 893 8001

UK Tel. (0121) 687 4100   Fax   (0121) 687 4101

VB COM

Name _____

Address _____

_____

_____

City_____ State/Region _____

Country_____ Postcode/Zip _____

E-mail _____

Occupation _____

How did you hear about this book? _____

☐ Book review (name) _____

☐ Advertisement (name) _____

☐ Recommendation _____

☐ Catalog _____

☐ Other _____

Where did you buy this book? _____

☐ Bookstore (name)_____ City _____

☐ Computer Store (name) _____

☐ Mail Order_____

☐ Other_____

What influenced you in the purchase of this book?

☐ Cover Design

☐ Contents

☐ Other (please specify) _____

How did you rate the overall contents of this book?

☐ Excellent   ☐ Good

☐ Average   ☐ Poor

What did you find most useful about this book? _____

What did you find least useful about this book? _____

Please add any additional comments. _____

What other subjects will you buy a computer book on soon? _____

What is the best computer book you have used this year?

_____

Note: This information will only be used to keep you update about new Wrox Press titles and will not be used for any othe purpose or passed to any other third party.

wrox

NB. If you post the bounce back card below in the UK, please send it to:
Wrox Press Ltd., Arden House, 1102 Warwick Road, Acocks Green,
Birmingham. B27 6BH. UK.

——— *Computer Book Publishers* ———

BUSINESS REPLY MAIL
FIRST CLASS MAIL   PERMIT#64   CHICAGO, IL

POSTAGE WILL BE PAID BY ADDRESSEE

WROX PRESS
29 S. LASALLE ST.
SUITE 520
CHICAGO IL 60603-USA